JOHN
THE JEWISH GOSPEL

CARROLL ROBERSON

WestBow
PRESS®
A DIVISION OF THOMAS NELSON
& ZONDERVAN

WestBow Press books may be ordered through booksellers or by contacting:

WestBow Press
A Division of Thomas Nelson & Zondervan
1663 Liberty Drive
Bloomington, IN 47403
www.westbowpress.com
1 (866) 928-1240

ISBN: 978-1-5127-6816-9 (sc)
ISBN: 978-1-5127-6817-6 (hc)
ISBN: 978-1-5127-6815-2 (e)

Library of Congress Control Number: 2016920646

Print information available on the last page.

WestBow Press rev. date: 12/30/2016

CONTENTS

PREFACE

When we research the gospel of John and dig deeper in order to better understand the history, the author, and the intent of the book, the truths seem to be endless. There is so much more than what appears on the surface. I recall going to a production of Handel's *Messiah*. I went because my dear wife wanted to go and I thought that it would be something that I could tolerate for a couple of hours. Well, the first hour I appreciated the musicians and singers, even though I really didn't care for Baroque-style singing. The second hour I began to appreciate the incredible work of a genius named George Frederic Handel who, in 1741, composed the oratorio in just three weeks. By the end of the production, I was reading through all of the Bible verses that Handel connected together to present the story of the Messiah. It was then that I realized that if there had been no holy scriptures at that time, Handel would have had nothing to build from. The scriptures gave him the inspiration to write the words as well as the music. The more we study the gospel of John the more we realize that it's not just about the style, the structure, the author, or the date it was written, it's all about Christ, the Son of the living God!

The aged apostle John, the son of Zebedee, or the Hebrew *Yochonan Ben Zavdai*, had been called by Jesus at an early age, maybe when he was twenty three or twenty four years of age, to be one of His closest disciples. It is believed that John was an early disciple of John the Baptist who started following Jesus (**John 1:35-37**). Jesus later specifically called John away from the fishing business to be His disciple (**Matthew 4:21**). The young John walked with Jesus along the dusty roads of Israel, heard His beautiful sermons, saw His breathtaking miracles, and was one of the most intimate disciples with the Master. John was there at the raising of the daughter of *Yair* (**Mark 5:37**), at the mount of transfiguration (**Luke 9:28**), and when Jesus prayed in the garden of Gethsemane (**Mark 14:33**). John leaned on the bosom of the Son of God (**John 13:23**) and John is the one that Jesus left in charge of caring for His mother (**John 19:26-27**). He is referred to as "the disciple whom Jesus loved" (**John 13:23, 19:26, 20:2, 21:7, 21:20**). John was also among the first to suffer loss for the Gospel when his brother, James, was the first apostle to be martyred (**Acts 12:2**).

According to Eusebius and Jerome, John is believed to have written his gospel account between the years of 90-102 AD while he was living in Ephesus. Jerome also states that John wrote his gospel on one of the hillsides in Ephesus. All of the other disciples had long since passed away and there were only a few of Jesus' earthly relatives still alive, which, according to Hegesippus, included two grandsons of Jude. One of the primary reasons for John writing his gospel was to counter the heresy that was started by Cerinthus and other heretics, such as the Edionites, who were leading many astray by denying the divinity of Jesus. There is no doubt that, by this time, John had been able to read Matthew, Mark, and Luke's accounts and he felt inspired by the Holy Spirit to write about some events that were not recorded in the other narratives. As we will see, John's gospel is unique to the other gospels and is one of the greatest books in the entire Bible.

I had the privilege to be on the Isle of Patmos a few years back. One of the history books there said that John lived to be 99 and died in the year 104 AD. This fits with the historical date of John's birth being around 5-6 AD. However, it is recorded by Jerome that the apostle John died sixty-eight years after the passion of our Lord. We believe that Jesus died and rose again in the year 32 AD, so this would place John's death in the year 100 AD. While we cannot be one hundred percent sure about the date of his death, we do know that God had a special plan for John: to be the author of the fourth gospel, the epistles of John, and the mysterious book of the Revelation of Jesus the Christ. Jerome also recorded that the aged apostle had to be carried into the church at Ephesus where John spoke his last words for the congregation: "Little children, love one another!"

INTRODUCTION

I have always believed the Bible to be the inspired Word of God, even from my early childhood days. At the age of twenty-eight, the Lord's Spirit drew me to salvation. It was at that point that He began a new life for me and completely changed my interests. I found myself drawn to the sacred scriptures, even though I didn't understand very much at the time. Within about two years, I felt the calling to surrender to full-time ministry work and, from that day until now, I have been immersed in the Word of God. As I transitioned from pastoral work into evangelism in 1987, I felt the Spirit of God leading me into a deeper walk in the scriptures. Little did I know what a comprehensive, spiritual journey was ahead of me. While realizing that traditional church services were needful and provided a place for us to learn more of the Bible and have fellowship with other believers I also realized that the western world's interpretation of Christianity was far removed from where our faith originated: the land of Israel. This troubled me deeply, but I didn't know what to do about it. I was studying different commentaries on the Bible and, even though I found a lot of wonderful truths, there was still a question that was troubling me. How were the scriptures heard and lived out by the first Jewish followers of Jesus?

After hosting my first study group to the land of Israel, I realized what I had been missing. I felt as though I knew so little about the real Jesus and I uttered a prayer that was heard and that has been answered by our gracious Lord:

> *Lord, would you teach me your Word? And would you guide me to have wisdom and understanding? And then, Lord, would you give me the opportunities to share those God-given truths with your people?*

I was led to start studying the Hebrew language of Jesus and I took several courses from teachers who taught at the Hebrew University in Jerusalem. The scriptures then began to connect with one another and my hunger and thirst began to be satisfied. I observed that all English translations of the Bible, even the most accurate with the best intentions, had hindered me from knowing the real way to study. Even though the translations are needful for evangelism and have helped all of us to hear the gospel of Christ, there is so much more to know about our Hebrew Lord by understanding his words and teaching within the framework of first century Jewish language and culture.

The good Lord has been gracious enough to entrust me with taking dozens of other trips to Israel. While leading others has been the focus, each new pilgrimage has added a new chapter to a life-changing journey for me as well. Sometimes I would find myself walking along the shore of Galilee and bathing in the mystery of how a somewhat, simple man from the hills of Mississippi could be leading others to Israel. I knew the Lord was doing something in my life that wasn't just for me. He was shaping and teaching me so I could help others, Because our pilgrimages to Israel began to focus more and more on the life of Jesus, I turned a good deal of my studies toward the four gospels of Matthew, Mark, Luke, and John. When one examines the four gospels from the original Jewish perspective, you are also directed to countless Old Testament passages, as well as the first-century writings of the apostles in the New Testament. All of scripture connects to the gospels and the life of Jesus.

It's common knowledge among most serious Bible students that Matthew, Mark, and Luke, make up what is called the *synoptic* (Latin - *synpoticus,* Greek - *synoptikos*) gospels because all three present the life of Jesus in a similar way and retell many of the same events. The fourth gospel, the gospel of John, is unique in style and tells us about many events that are not written in the *synoptic* accounts. My library has several wonderful commentaries on the gospel of John, but it has troubled me for years that they all try to teach the words and works of Jesus from the Greek (gentile) perspective. While this is understandable, since John's gospel is in the Koine Greek, the *lingua franca* (common language of trade) of the day, they seem to ignore the Jewish background of the gospel. We do not know if John wrote his original writings in Greek or Hebrew, but this fourth gospel was compiled and preserved for us in the Greek language. Did the Jewish Messiah speak in Greek? I don't think so but, if He did, there is no proof of it. However, there is a lot of evidence that Jesus spoke in the Hebrew language in the Jewish synagogues and the Aramaic language to many of the peasants in Galilee.

So John, being a Jew, is communicating the Jewish Messiah to a Greek-speaking audience. But for us to properly interpret the gospel of John, we need to go back to the setting of when the events took place. For example: how does it help me to understand the words and works of Jesus by dissecting a Greek, Latin, or even an English word?

Someone may say, *"You are being too technical, and you don't have to know that to love Jesus!"* Of course we do not have to know these things to love our Lord, or to go to heaven, but for those who desire a deeper understanding of who our Lord really is, and what He really said, I do think it is important enough to spend the time to write this commentary. If the Lord does not return in my lifetime, maybe someone will read this book in later years and come to a deeper walk with Jesus their Savior, or maybe even invite Jesus to come into their hearts to be their personal Savior!

It is documented in church history that Prochorus, one of the seven deacons in the book of **Acts 6:5**, was one of the seventy disciples that was sent out by Jesus in **Luke 10**. It is believed that he copied down the gospel of John for the Greek-speaking communities, as he was also the scribe who copied down the book of the Revelation from John while they were exiled on the island of Patmos. While some people may have a problem with this information, we need to make it clear that John communicated to Prochorus from a Jewish understanding while Prochorus probably used the closest Greek words available to translate John's teachings. One of the evidences that there may have been another person writing is the phrase "the disciple whom Jesus loved." It was not the Jewish custom to exalt one's self while writing, and John was much too humble of a disciple to refer to himself in that manner. But in either case, the gospel of John was still a work of the Holy Spirit *through* John. (**John 20:24**)

It amazes me that, while some of the scholars are wonderful and very intellectual, they could miss this all-important truth. Many want to act pious and say things to me like: "I believe that every word of God is inspired and inerrant, and you are casting doubt on the Bible!" I believe the *true* Word of God is inspired and inerrant, but not all inspired Words of God are translatable under the same inspiration. The embodied truth of God's Word is infallible, not the *translations*! The Greek, the Latin, and the English do not match the Hebrew thought perfectly and this caused scholars like the 4th century Jerome and the Masoretes of the 7th-10th century to go back to the Hebrew meanings of the scriptures instead of the Greek. For example: the Greek Septuagint *(from the Latin septuaginta, or seventy)* was written in the 3rd century BC by seventy-two Jewish scholars, but was commissioned by the Greek King of Egypt, Ptolemy II. It was needful for the Hellenized, Alexandrian Jews who lived in Egypt and other parts of the Eastern Mediterranean world, but it cannot be superior to the original Hebrew Old Testament scriptures. We can praise God for the godly men who suffered and died to translate the sacred scriptures into the English language, but our Lord did not speak English and the English language cannot be superior to the Hebrew language of God. So, again, the focus needs to be on the truth and the Person that the scriptures are setting forth, not in a particular translation. (**John 1:1**)

When the Christian faith left Israel, the scriptures were seen as an anti-Jewish document and the temple being destroyed by the Romans in 70 AD was thought to be the end of the Jewish faith. The Jews were ordered to leave Israel in 135 AD by the Roman emperor, Hadrian. Bible historians and theologians took that to mean that God was through with Israel. They were saying that the Gentiles had taken Israel's place. In their minds, since the gospel of John was written in Greek, this must be the proper way to interpret it. The Greek language that had been brought into Israel and the world through the pagan Alexander the Great (356-323BC) was so loved and so widely used that the story of Jesus began to be interpreted through Hellenized eyes. But, again, the apostle John was not a Hellenist. He was a Jew!

While it is true that the gospel of Matthew is the most Jewish of all the gospels (believed to have been first written in Hebrew in 37 AD), the gospel of John is not anti-Jewish. It is Jewish in thought hidden behind the common language of the Roman Empire. So the purpose of writing this commentary is not to just repeat what many wonderful scholars have already stated, but to try and give you some different and unique thoughts that have been hidden for centuries. While our words are but a faint whisper compared to the inspired scriptures, I pray that the Holy Spirit will take my simple explanations and help His people.

Before I leave this Greek-Hebrew argument, I want to give you a case in-point so you will not think that I am just making all of this up in my own thoughts. John translated many Hebrew words back into the Greek because he was speaking to a Greek audience. Here are some examples: Sea of Galilee – *Sea of Tiberias* (**John 6:1, 21:1**); Cephas – *Peter* (**John 1:42**); Messiah – *Christ* (**John 1:41**); Rabbi – *Teacher* (**John 1:38**); Siloam – *Sent* (**John 9:7**); Rabboni – *Teacher* (**John 20:16**). At other times John translates the Greek back into Hebrew like in **John 19:17**, and **19:13**. This changing of Hebrew to Greek and Greek to Hebrew proves that the original thought was different than the translation.

Another good example is the Greek word for *Jews* in John's gospel: *Ioudaios* (pronounced *ee-oo-day-yos*). This Greek word cannot fully define what the context is saying. The Greek word, *Ioudaios,* is a general term for all *Jews* in this gospel, but it does not convey the sub-group of Jews within the Jewish community to whom John is writing and referring. In many places, such as **John 8:22**, *Ioudaios* is referring to the religious leaders in Jerusalem in a *negative* sense. Then the same Greek word refers to the *Jews* in a *positive* sense in places like **John 4:22**. This is because there was only one Greek word to describe the term *Jews*.

Everyone who lived outside of Israel, considered all *Jews* to be just *Jews*.

The term *Jew* goes back to the Hebrew word *Yehudi* and refers to the people originally from the tribe of Judah. It also can refer to the *Jews* who lived in Judea, but not exclusively to that one area. Coins have been found from the Maccabean period (around 100 BC) and as far back as the Persian period (538-323 BC) that have the Hebrew word *Yehudi* written on them. Through the Greek translation, *Ioudaios,* to the Latin, *Iudaeus,* to the Old French, *Giu,* and to the Old English, *Iew,* it became translated as *Jew.*

That one word, *Jews,* that is translated into the Greek translation used in John's gospel has caused much anti-Semitism in the world and has even hidden the Jewish message from countless believers who truly love Jesus. I believe this has been a work of the Israel-hating adversary to blind God's people from seeing the Jewish perspective of the gospels. To gentile thinkers, John's gospel may seem anti-Jewish on the surface but it is only anti-Jewish when referring to the corrupt, unbelieving religious leaders in Judea at the time of Christ, not to *Jews* as a whole.

THE UNIQUENESS OF
JOHN'S GOSPEL

We find Jesus (or *Yeshua*, as the Hebrews called him) sounding different in John's gospel. He is more *theological* and less rabbinical. We don't find the *parables* in John that we do in the other gospel accounts. The kingdom of God is described in a way that it can be better understood outside the realm of Judaism. As I have already mentioned, the writer is thinking in Aramaic and Hebrew, but he is writing in Greek.

In John's gospel we see more of a contrast between the Jews who followed Jesus in Galilee and the corrupt Jewish establishment in Judea that consisted primarily of the scribes, Pharisees, and Sadducees. One reason for this may be that, by the end of the first century, there was a major division between the religious Jews and the believing Gentiles. With this in mind, it seems intentional that John places more emphasis on the Judean ministry of the Messiah than he does on the Galilean ministry. We would not have record of a great deal of Jesus' earthly ministry in Jerusalem if it were not for John's inspiration. Thus, the gospel of John stands alone. As John is writing during the latter part of the first century, he is giving his readers a unique piece of thought and theology to stir their minds.

Eternal life is a central theme in John's gospel. Here, we find that Jesus is not only offering eternal life in the future, but also eternal life beginning immediately upon receiving Him by faith. A life that is filled with Christ is a new life, a transformed life, and enjoys life free from the fear of death here and now. Eternal life is much more than just something to hope for when we leave this world. We can begin to experience the peace and joy that Jesus imparts to His children. When a redeemed individual passes from this physical life, they go from life to life, not life to death.

In his gospel, John gives us seven unique sign miracles that authenticate the Messiahship of Jesus of Nazareth:

1. *Water into wine*   **John 2:1-11**
2. *Healing the nobleman's son in Cana* **John 4:43-54**
3. *Healing at the pool of Bethesda*   **John 5:1-15**
4. *Feeding the multitude*   **John 6:1-15**
5. *Healing of the man born blind*   **John 9:1-12**
6. *The resurrection of Lazarus*   **John 11:1-44**
7. *The resurrection of Jesus*   **John 20**

I would like to mention that, among the miracles in John's account, there seems to be a strange composite to the *eating* and *drinking* metaphors. It's strange to me that the first miracle of Jesus is turning the *water into wine* in Cana (**John 2**). Jesus deliberately went through Samaria, which was unthinkable to religious Jews in that day, to offer an outcast woman *living water* (**John 4:10**). Then we find the miracle of the *loaves and fishes* that were given to the multitude in **John 6** and Jesus explaining the deeper meaning of the *physical feeding* later in that chapter in **John 6:54**. He went on to say that we must internalize our Lord by faith and He uses the metaphors of *eating* and *drinking* of His blood in order to have everlasting life. In **John 7:37–38**, while at the Feast of Tabernacles in Jerusalem, Jesus again offers *living water* to all who are spiritually *thirsty*. Jesus tells His disciples that, if they abide in Him, they will bring forth much *fruit* (**John 15:2**). This takes us back to the creation story in **Genesis 1:11–12** where *fruit* trees are created with a seed within themselves in order to provide man physical health for centuries to come. The Messiah would provide spiritual food for His people that would last forever. Before the gospel of John closes, we find Jesus performing another miracle by providing *fish* for the disciples on the shore of Galilee (**John 21**). We then have the conversation where Jesus tells Peter to *feed* His sheep. So John seems to be building a story within the main story: that true followers of the Messiah will have Jesus living inside of them *(like eating bread, fish, fruit, and drinking water and wine)* and in turn, if they love Him, they will give His life-changing message to other people. Salvation is not just for His people alone. It is so crucially urgent that they are to share with those who are *hungry* and *thirsty* for something this world cannot provide.

As it has been rightly stated many times over the years, there are seven major "I am" sayings of Jesus in the gospel of John that prove His divinity. I would like to also give you the Hebrew-English transliteration of each one of these all–important sayings:

Anee lechem ha cha yeem
I am the bread of life.
John 6:35

Anee or ha olam
I am the light of the world.
John 8:12

Anee ha shah ar
I am the door.
John 10:9

Anee ha roei ha tov
I am the good shepherd.
John 10:11

Anee ha te chee ya
veh ha cha yeem
I am the resurrection
and the life.
John 10:25

Anee ha derech ha emet
veh ha cha yeem
I am the way, the
truth, and the life.
John 14:6

Anee ha gefen ha amee teet
I am the true vine.
John 15:1

CHAPTER ONE

John 1:1-2 – *In the beginning was the Word, and the Word was with God, and the Word was God. The same was in the beginning with God.*

There is little or no ambiguity in describing who the Messiah of Israel really is! John wants us to realize that Jesus of Nazareth, the carpenter, was also the Lord of Glory! The wording is specific and easy to follow, but what does it mean? Though the thought is deeply rooted in the Semitic culture, it was drafted into a language that had universal appeal. But the language is not limited to any particular culture, time or place. The strange thought of describing Jesus as the Creator Himself would appeal to all classes of people, Jews, Christians, and pagans. The humble seekers of God would bow down to Him while the intellectual philosophers might stumble over the truth, though they would still find the thought to be intriguing indeed.

When John describes who the Messiah is, he takes us

back to the very beginning of creation (*bereshit* in Hebrew thought). There is a strong correlation between **John 1:1** and many other verses in the scriptures. Here are a few of them:

Genesis 1:1 - *In the beginning God created the heaven and the earth.*

Proverbs 8:22-23 - *The Lord possessed me in the beginning of his way, before his works of old. I was set up from everlasting, from the beginning, or ever the earth was.*

John 17:5 - *And now, O Father, glorify thou me with thine own self with the glory which I had with thee before the world was.*

I John 1:1 - *That which was from the beginning, which we have heard, which we have seen with our eyes, which we have looked upon, and our hands have handled, of the Word of life;*

Revelation 3:14 - *And unto the angel of the church of the Laodiceans write; These things saith the Amen, the faithful and true witness, the beginning of the creation of God;*

Jesus is described as the *Word,* or the Greek *Logos.* While *Logos* is a good translation in the Greek, it cannot convey the deep, mysterious meaning of the Hebrew concept of the *Word.* In Greek thought, the *Logos* is abstract and implies a philosophical interpretation. The Hebrew *Davar* is more concrete and I believe this is the original thought that John had in mind. *Davar* (or the Aramaic, *Memra*) comes to be intimately associated with a Person who spoke the world into existence. Because of the zeal for the Greek language among many of the early church fathers, like Augustine, they failed to see the connection between Jesus and **Genesis 1** during the first three centuries of Christianity. But *the Word* is not a philosophy or a body of teachings. It is the person of Christ! This sets Jesus apart from any other person who has ever walked this planet in human history. When we want to know what God thinks or what God would do, we read about Jesus in the gospels. In the gospel of John, we learn that God's thoughts became a Person. In the life of Jesus, we can see God's power, His love, His compassion, His justice, and His forgiveness.

In Hebrew thought, one cannot separate the *speech* and the Person. In the first chapter of the Bible, we find eight times where it says, "And God said." This phrase is found hundreds of times throughout the Old Testament. We know the Word that was spoken was Jesus! He is the speech, or *the Word* of God. God's *Word* was sent forth and Jesus was sent forth into the world. Another biblical example of this Hebrew thought is written in Isaiah:

> *For as the rain cometh down, and the snow from heaven, and returneth not thither, but watereth the earth, and maketh it bring forth and bud, that it may give seed to the sower, and bread to the eater: So shall my <u>word be that goeth forth out of my</u>*

mouth: it shall not return unto me void, but it shall
accomplish that which I please, and it shall prosper
in the thing whereto I sent it.
—Isaiah 55:10-11

John says, "the Word was with God," which tells us that
Jesus is separate from the Father, and yet they are one and the
same. John records these words of Jesus later in his gospel:

I and my Father are one.
—John 10:30

…he that hath seen me hath seen the Father:
—John 14:9

So John's gospel starts off by emphasizing the Triune
Godhead, which the 2nd century Latin scholar, Tertullian,
would later call the *Trinity*. There is only one God Almighty,
but He operates in three persons: the Father, the Son, and
the Holy Spirit. Jesus was and is the *Eternal* Son of God
and the Second Person of the Trinity that was sent into
the world.

The *Jehovah's Witnesses* teach that Jesus was the son of
"a god" while the *Islam* teaches that Jesus was not divine.
To *Muslims* He was just a prophet who is subservient to
Muhammad. Hindus believe in many gods. *Buddhists* believe
there is no god and that man is his own god. The biblical
truth that Jesus is God also divides *Judaism* from *Christianity*
and this may be one of the primary reasons why John starts
his gospel off in this way. He is disclosing God's plan that

has been operating since the beginning of time and space itself. The Lord Jesus the Christ invented history, while you and I never had a history until we were born into this world. I often think of how I would have loved to have lived during the time when Jesus walked the hills of Galilee, but that was almost 2,000 years before I was even born. But, when Jesus came into the world, He came from eternity into time and changed the course of history. He *transcends* all of history and can be as personal to us today as He was to those first followers in the first century.

THE RELATION OF JESUS WITH THE UNIVERSE

> **John 1:3-5** - *All things were made by him; and without him was not any thing made that was made. In him was life; and the life was the light of men. And the light shineth in darkness; and the darkness comprehended it not.*

Christ brought *life* to mankind because He is *life*. The word *life* is used in John's gospel over 40 times. I do not want to belabor the point I am trying to make about the Greek translation versus the Hebrew thought, but I would like to give you another example. The Greek word for *life* is *zoe* and it simply means *life*. The Hebrew word for *life* is *chay* (pronounced *khah-ee*) meaning *alive, fresh, and strong*. The Hebrew is much more vibrant and definitive. Again, Hebrew was the original language of the Old Testament as well as the language of Jesus. Jesus came into the world

5

where mankind was spiritually dead. He came to give them life and *life more abundantly* (**John 10:10**). Jesus created *life* in the beginning, *life* for plants, animals, and in His image He created man and gave Him *life*. When we place our faith in Him, we receive *eternal life* and then, when we leave this earth, we go back to Him. It's only when we have His life do we understand our purpose in this world and find peace and joy in service to His kingdom. I'm reminded of what John would later say in his epistle:

> *He that hath the Son hath life; and he that hath*
> *not the Son of God hath not life.*
>
> **—I John 5:12**

John is again taking us back to the creation story: "And God said, Let there be light: and there was light" (**Genesis 1:3**). Many of the ancient Jewish scholars stated that the *light* in **Genesis 1:3** was talking about the light of the Messiah because the sun and the moon were not created until four days later in **Genesis 1:16**. The age of the Messiah had finally come and Jesus of Nazareth would be a *light* to His people Israel and to the Gentiles as the Prophets wrote about. The theme of *light* and *darkness* had been used in Jewish writings for centuries and was even found written within the Dead Sea Scrolls. It's interesting to me also that this comparison of *light vs. darkness* runs throughout the entire Bible, and especially John's gospel. **(John 1:4, 5, 7, 8, 9; 3:19; 3:20; 3:21; 5:35; 8:12; 9:5; 11:9; 11:10; 12:35; 12:36; 12:46)**

In comparison once again, the Greek word for *light* is

phos and it means *to shine, make manifest*. The Hebrew word for *light* is *owr* and it means *illumination, lightning, happiness, bright, clear, morning sun*. Which thought do you think John had in mind? Under the inspiration of the Holy Spirit, the apostle John is saying that Jesus, the Word of God, was the *divine illumination* of God! The world was a very dark place when Jesus came but, like the morning sun bursting through the darkness of night, the Savior shined His *light*. Every morning when the sun shines upon the earth, I think about the *light* of my Lord.

The darkness of the world could not stop the *light* of the Son of God. He would burst through with His glorious *light* at His birth, in His revolutionary earthly ministry, and through His victorious death and resurrection.

THE RELATION OF JESUS WITH JOHN THE BAPTIST

> **John 1:6-9** - *There was a man sent from God, whose name was John. The same came for a witness, to bear witness of the Light, that all men through him might believe. He was not that Light, but was sent to bear witness of that Light. That was the true Light, which lighteth every man that cometh into the world.*

Try to imagine a religious Jew or a religious, Hellenized Jew reading about a man being sent from God whose name was *Yochonan* where the Hebrew meaning is, "God is gracious." John made it clear repeatedly that he was not the Light, but God sent him to be the forerunner of the Light. Notice the words, "that all men might believe," and "lighteth every man that cometh into the world." God desired for *all** to believe, and the light of Christ shines upon *every* person in their life at some given moment.

The doctrine of Calvinism is not based on a thorough interpretation of the scriptures but, rather, on a man-made systematic theology that originated centuries later. This view holds the position that God has elected some for destruction. Sadly, his heresy is taught in many colleges and churches throughout the world.

We will look more in detail at the ministry of John the Baptist a little later in this chapter. There were three primary reasons why John the Baptist is mentioned in the gospels:

- *He was prophesied.* (**Isaiah 40:3**; **Malachi 3:1**)
- *He was sent from God.*
- *He was to bear witness to the Light.*

THE RELATION OF JESUS WITH THE WORLD

John 1:10-13 - *He was in the world, and the world was made by him, and the world knew him not. He came unto his own, and his own received him not. But as many as received him, to them gave he power to become the sons of God, even to them that believe on his name: Which were born, not of* *blood, nor of the will of the flesh, nor of the will of man, but of God.*

In the other gospel accounts, Jesus is referred to as the *King* who offers people the kingdom of heaven. In John's gospel, Jesus is the *Creator* who comes into the world and He is either rejected or *received*. Those who *receive Him* will be given a new spiritual birth. What a statement John makes here: "He was in the world and the world was made by him, and the world knew him not." This presses home the thought of the previous verses, that Jesus is the *Word of God*, the *Light*, and He is the *Creator* who made the world. This thought changes the way a person should read the gospel of John. It sets the stage for the rest of the book.

"He came unto his own, and his own received him not." The wording here in the English translation from the Greek has caused much anti-Semitism in the world. Many still believe that this verse emphasizes that Jesus came to the *Jews* and all of the *Jews* rejected Him. But John is not presenting Jesus the Messiah as a Galilean, but as *Judean*. What this verse is saying is that Jesus was rejected by a sub-group of people in Israel: mainly the religious leaders in Judea. The New Testament and history proves this is the true interpretation. While many did reject Christ, the first followers were Jewish and most of the people who were saved on the day of Pentecost were Jewish.

John goes on to say that many did *receive* Jesus and they were given the power to become God's children. They were not automatically born into God's family simply because they were Jewish. They, like all humanity, had to *receive* Jesus into their life. There is a great application for all of us here. No matter how religious we are, or how good of a family we were born into, we must have a spiritual birth to be in God's family. Salvation is not something that someone talks us into or just a decision that we make by joining a church and getting water-baptized. Salvation is a work of God whereby a person surrenders to the Lordship of Christ and believes with all of their heart that Jesus is God in the flesh. This leads us to the powerful next verse.

THE RELATION OF JESUS WITH HIS PEOPLE

> **John 1:14 –** *And the Word was made flesh, and dwelt among us, (and we beheld his glory, the glory as of the only begotten of the Father,) full of grace and truth.*

This would have to be one of the most important verses in the word of God! The introduction of the gospel of John does not offend religious Jews, but this verse is one they really have a problem with. The fact that the God of Moses, the God of Abraham, the God of Jacob, and the God of Isaac would become human flesh is beyond their comprehension. God becoming human is just unacceptable in their eyes. Jesus is more than a man, He is more than a super-man, and He is more than just divine. *Jesus is God in the flesh*! We should never get to the point that we lose the wonder of this truth.

When John says the Word was made flesh and "dwelt among us," we find a very interesting Old Testament comparison. Here the Greek word for *dwelt* is *skenoo* and it means *to tent or encamp* which <u>does</u> accurately convey the Hebrew thought. The Hebrew word for *dwelt,* or *to dwell,* is *shakan.* It is used when God promises *to dwell* with His people in the tabernacle (**Exodus 29:45**). When the God of Moses told him to build a tabernacle, He had a reason:

> *And the Lord spake unto Moses in the wilderness of Sinai, in the tabernacle of the congregation.*
> **—Numbers 1:1**

The Almighty would speak to Moses in the tabernacle! God desires fellowship with His people. He is not content on just looking down from heaven at them. He wants to engage in a relationship with us. So in the New Testament we find here that *Yeshua* the Messiah is the Tabernacle of God and He has pitched His tent among us. He became the dwelling place of God where He was filled with the *Shekinah,* the glory of God. So here we have the presence of God in the tabernacle of old and the incarnation of God in the person of Jesus. Wow!

When John walked with the very Son of God, he saw His inner glory shining through the fabric of His *tent,* that is His flesh. This takes us to an even deeper truth when we realize that God desires to dwell inside His people. Our body is referred to as a *tabernacle* that will one day fold as we will fly into the arms of our Lord. Read these blessed words:

> For we know that if our earthly house of this tabernacle were dissolved, we have a building of God, an house not made with hands, eternal in the heavens.
> **—2 Corinthians 5: 1**

> We are confident, I say, and willing rather to be absent from the body, and to be present with the Lord.
> **—2 Corinthians 5: 8**

In this earth-shaking verse of **John 1:14**, we also find that John saw His *glory* and it was "the glory of the only begotten of the Father." Here the Greek word for *glory, or doxa*, does not carry the meaning of the Hebrew. The Hebrew word *kabowd* means *weight, splendor, or copiousness*. Think of *weight* in a good sense, combined with the *abundant splendor* that was inside of Jesus, the Word of God!

The very end of this verse holds an equally intriguing thought: "full of grace and truth." In Jesus was the *full* measure, not just a partial measure, of *grace and truth*. He was the ultimate expression of *grace*. We see this during His earthly ministry in His forgiving of others and the giving of Himself to the world. Jesus is *grace*! He is also the ultimate expression of what is *truth* and the revelation of what is real! There is absolute truth in the universe and Jesus revealed that *truth*. Jesus is *truth*!

THE WITNESS OF JOHN THE BAPTIST

> **John 1: 15–18** - *John bare witness of him, and cried, saying, This was he of whom I spake, He that cometh after me is preferred before me: for he was before me. And of his fulness have all we received, and grace for grace. For the law was given by Moses, but grace and truth came by Jesus Christ. No man hath seen God at any time, the only begotten Son, which is in the bosom of the Father, he hath declared him.*

The main reason why the apostle John makes mention again of the ministry of John the Baptist is because, before he became a disciple of Christ, he was a disciple of John the Baptist. John the Baptist knew what his job was and he was a *witness* with passion. That passion was carried over into the hearts of those first disciples of Jesus. John the Baptist *cried* out when he bore witness of Jesus. Try to imagine a preacher some two thousand years ago, in the desert, about twenty miles east of Jerusalem, at the lowest point on planet earth, just north of the Dead Sea, on the banks of the Jordan River, *crying* out a message that would cut to the deepest needs of the human heart. The One who was going to be baptized by John the Baptist was the Word of God incarnate. The people needed to know that Jesus was not just another person, but that He was the long-awaited *Mashiach* of Israel. We can see everything leading up in a crescendo because, in this first chapter of John's gospel, we have been given the imageries of: *life and light - grace and truth - the Word becoming flesh – dwelt among us.* John the Baptist was sent to prepare the way for this revolutionary figure. He and all those who would follow Jesus would receive blessing after blessing, or *grace for grace.*

It sounds a little confusing, but John is saying that Jesus, who is coming "*after* me," was "*before* me" in time. John the Baptist realized that it was all from God's *grace* that he had been sent to bear witness of the Messiah. He knew that his place would be short-lived. He was not given a full revelation of the church-age, but his message would prepare the way for the Messiah.

"For the law was given by Moses, but grace and truth came by Jesus Christ." The mistranslation of this verse has caused a lot of debate and confusion over the years. The little word *but* (which is not in the original translation) was added by the King James translators in 1611 AD. This makes it sound like the *law of Moses* is in contrast and is opposite from the *grace and truth* that Jesus brought into the world. What John is actually saying is that the *law* that God gave to Moses was realized and embodied in the Person of Jesus Christ.

A dominant emphasis of contrast between the *law* and the *gospel* grew over the course of church history, particularly during the Reformation period of the 15th and 16th century. This led to false teachings like *Amillenialism* (No future restoration of Israel and no coming kingdom) and *Replacement Theology* (God's promises to Israel now belong to the church). But the *law* was a foreshadowing of the coming Messiah. It is not to be understood as something made null and void or no longer applicable. Jesus came to fulfill the *law*. He came to show us the proper interpretation of the *Law* of Moses without all of the added interpretations *(fences around the Torah)* that the religious leaders were teaching in His day. Think of all of the beautiful types and shadows throughout the Books of Moses that pointed to the coming Messiah. Jesus was the law lived out in His perfect life and He fulfilled the *sacrificial system* of the *law* when He died on the cross. However, many of the principles and lessons of the Old Testament still apply to us today. While we are not in bondage to try and live up to the Mosaic *Law* since Jesus our Savior did that for us, once we receive Christ into our life, the *law* is written on our hearts. The Holy Spirit starts to live out the *law* in our lives each day. He helps us to keep in mind what God told Jeremiah centuries before Jesus came.

> *Behold, the days come, saith the LORD, that I will make a new covenant with the house of Israel, and with the house of Judah: Not according to the covenant that I made with their fathers in the day that I took them by the hand to bring them out of the land of Egypt; which my covenant they brake, although I was an husband unto them, saith the LORD: But this shall be the covenant that I will make with the house of Israel; After those days, saith the LORD, I will put my law in their inward parts, and write it in their hearts; and will be their God, and they shall be my people. And they shall*

*teach no more every man his neighbour, and every
man his brother, saying, Know the LORD: for they
shall all know me, from the least of them unto the
greatest of them, saith the LORD: for I will forgive
their iniquity, and I will remember their sin no more.*
—**Jeremiah 31: 31-34**

So a better translation of **John 1:17** would be: *For the law
was given by Moses and grace <u>and</u> truth came by Jesus Christ.*

"No man hath seen God at any time: the only begotten Son,
which is in the bosom of the Father, he hath declared him." The
revelation of Jesus the Messiah was superior to that of
any other dispensation. Men of God, like Moses and the
Prophets, witnessed certain manifestations of God, but no
one has seen the full essence of God or has *fully* known
Him. This was a continuing thought in the apostle John's
mind. Ponder these other verses:

John 5:37 - *And the Father himself, which hath
sent me, hath borne witness of me. Ye have neither
heard his voice at any time, nor seen his shape.*

John 6:46 - *Not that any man hath seen the Father,
save he which is of God, he hath seen the Father.*

I John 4:12- *No man hath seen God at any time.*

"…the only begotten Son, which is in the bosom of the Father, he
hath declared him." The real meaning of "the only begotten
Son" is that Jesus was equal with God. He is the Second

Person of the Triune Godhead and therefore had full knowledge of God. He came forth from the Eternal God, who is a Spirit, (**John 4:24; Hebrews 9:14**), to be a Man!

"*...which is in the bosom of the Father.*" This idea comes from ancient middle-eastern culture and describes when someone had an intimate relationship with another person who knew their deepest character and innermost thoughts. This image sheds a deeper light on the picture at the last supper when John the apostle is leaning on the *bosom* of Jesus. This shows us how close John was to our Lord and was showing Peter that John had a closer relationship to Jesus than he did!

> *Now there was leaning on Jesus' bosom one of his disciples, whom he loved.*
>
> —**John 13: 23**

Jesus has fully *declared* the Almighty God! When we read about Jesus in the gospels, we are reading about God! When we see the miracles of Jesus, we are seeing the miracles of God! When we feel the compassion of Jesus, we are feeling the compassion of God! When Jesus tells us how to live, we are hearing the very words of God!

> *God, who at sundry times and in divers manners spake in time past unto the fathers by the prophets, Hath in these last days spoken unto us by His Son, whom he hath appointed heir of all things, by whom also he made the worlds.*
>
> —**Hebrews 1:1-2**

THE PHARISEES AND JOHN THE BAPTIST

> **John 1: 19–28** - *And this is the record of John, when the Jews sent priests and Levites from Jerusalem to ask him, Who art thou? And he confessed, and denied not; but confessed, I am not the Christ. And they asked him, What then? Art thou Elias? And he saith, I am not. Art thou that prophet? And he answered, No. Then said they unto him, Who art thou? that we may give an answer to them that sent us. What sayest thou of thyself? He said, I am the voice of one crying in the wilderness, Make straight the way of the Lord, as said the prophet Esaias. And they which were sent were of the Pharisees. And they asked him, and said unto him, Why baptizest thou then, if thou be not that Christ, nor Elias, neither that prophet? John answered them, saying, I baptize with water: but there standeth one among you, whom ye know not; He it is, who coming after me is preferred before me, whose shoe's latchet I am not worthy to unloose. These things were done in Bethabara beyond Jordan, where John was baptizing.*

We know that by **Luke 3:1** that John the Baptist had begun his ministry in the wilderness in the year 28 AD, or the "fifteenth year of the reign of Tiberius Caesar." In this passage, we need to keep in mind that the term *Jews* is not referring to *all* of the Jews, but to a sub-group within Israel: mainly the religious leaders in Jerusalem or the Judean establishment. The Pharisees were officially given power over the religious affairs in Jerusalem by a woman named *Alexandra* who was the widow of a *Hasmonean* king. She ruled over Israel for nine years between the years 76-67 BC. She would later have a daughter named *Mariamne* who would become one of the wives of the wicked Herod the Great. The Pharisees held a faction within the Sanhedrin in Jerusalem, the rest were made up of Sadducees.

The Pharisees could not understand why this water ceremony down in the middle of nowhere was causing such a stir among the people. What authority did this wild man have to draw such a crowd? This whole idea of the religious establishment *not knowing* who John the Baptist was or who Jesus was is woven throughout John's gospel.

I find it interesting that Israel of old had wandered in the wilderness for forty years and now God is calling Israel back to the place where their forefathers crossed over into the Promised Land: the Jordan River. John the Baptist was in line to be a priest at the temple because his father, Zachariah, was a priest. However, John was sent to show the corruptness of the priests. His diet and his clothing were in direct opposition to the Sadducees and Pharisees. He did not need the approval of the priests in Jerusalem. He had been sent by God! Notice the people who John the Baptist says that he is not:

- *He is not the Messiah*
- *He is not Elijah*
- *He is not "that prophet"* **(Deut. 18:15)**

John the Baptist was only a *voice in the wilderness,* but what a powerful voice he was. His *voice* was so powerful that people from everywhere were lined up on the banks of the Jordan to be baptized by John as a symbol of repentance. Water baptism was a Jewish way to be identified with someone or with some religious act. *(Notice, in* **Luke 12:50**, *Jesus uses the word baptism to be identified with His pending death.)* As important as water baptism was, it was never intended to become a doctrine of salvation like some churches would later proclaim. This was the result of not understanding the *Jewishness* of the ministry of Jesus. John is immersing people *in water,* but the most important baptism is the immersion *in the Holy Spirit* by Jesus the Son of God.

"...whose shoe's latchet I am not worthy to unloose." John the Baptist is saying that he was not even worthy to be perform the act of a slave to the One who was about to come. The feet of the Messiah were so holy because they were the actual feet of God. John the apostle would later witness the glorified Christ and describe His feet, which had once trod this sinful earth wrapped in sandals, as "fine brass, being burned in a furnace." **(Rev. 1:15)**

"These things were done in Bethabara beyond, Jordan." *Bethabara* is a Hebrew word that means *house of the ford, place of crossing.* Some translations called it *Bethany beyond Jordan.* This is confusing because there are two places called *Bethany:* one being the place where John baptized and the other being the home of Mary, Martha, and Lazarus. There are differences of opinion on the exact location of this *Bethany,* or *Bethabara.* According to ancient maps (especially

20

the 6th century *Madaba Map*) this location was just north of the Dead Sea. The territory would have been called *Perea* in Jesus' time. Most likely, the place where Jesus was baptized is in present-day Jordan and today it is called, in the Arabic language, *Al-Maghtas*.

THE BAPTISM OF JESUS

> **John 1:29-34** - *The next day John seeth Jesus coming unto him, and saith, Behold the Lamb of God, which taketh away the sin of the world. This is he of whom I said, After me cometh a man which is preferred before me: for he was before me. And I knew him not: but that he should be made manifest to Israel, therefore am I come baptizing with water. And John bare record, saying, I saw the Spirit descending from heaven like a dove, and it abode upon him. And I knew him not: but he that sent me to baptize with water, the same said unto me, Upon whom thou shalt see the Spirit descending, and remaining on him, the same is he which baptizeth with the Holy Ghost. And I saw, and bare record that this is the Son of God.*

The phrases "the next day" in **vs.29**, "the next day" in **vs.35**, "the day following" in **vs.43**, and "the third day" in **John 2:1** seem to be another way that John the apostle is drawing his readers back to the creation story in **Genesis 1**. As we will see, the scene that is about to unfold in the baptism of Jesus is somewhat a *parallel* to the scene when God created everything in the beginning. John's gospel gives a different account of the baptism of Jesus than the synoptic gospels. He gives special attention to the importance of the Holy Spirit and the significance of Jesus being the Lamb of God.

"Behold the Lamb of God." So far, in this first chapter, Jesus has been called God, the *Word*, the *Light*, the *Messiah*, the *Son of God*, and the *One who baptizes with the Spirit*. Here, He is called the *Lamb of God*. I find this to be absolutely amazing! Think of all of the thousands and thousands of lambs that had been offered up as a covering for the sins of Israel over the centuries of time. Now, God was about to offer up His own Lamb, Jesus, who would *take away the sin of the world*. This idea of Jesus being called the *Lamb of God* takes us back to the story of the *Passover* in **Exodus 12** & **Numbers 9**. The death angel would pass over every house where the blood of the lamb was placed on the doorposts. In fulfillment of the Old Testament *Passover*, all who have the blood of Jesus on their lives would not face the judgment that is to come. Hallelujah!

"...but that he should be made manifest to Israel." The water baptism of John the Baptist was not only meant to identify people with repentance, but it was also to be the beginning of *manifesting* the long-awaited Messiah to Israel. This marks a major transition in the gospel of John. Even though this all was taking place down in the desert on the banks of the Jordan River, there would be people from everywhere who would come to know who Jesus was. This phenomenon

would continue throughout the centuries of time until the present day.

"I saw the Spirit descending from heaven like a dove, and it abode upon him." The *dove* is a symbol of the Holy Spirit and this is the very first time that the Spirit is mentioned in John's gospel. I am reminded of Noah and the ark, in **Genesis 8**, where Noah sent out a *dove* and it finally came to rest on dry ground. The *dove* became a symbol of safety, hope, and peace. Here the *dove* comes to rest upon the Son of God, who would be our safety, hope, and peace, forever! The *dove* was also a symbol of sacrifice, as we find shortly after the birth of Jesus, in **Luke 2:24**. I believe there is also another hidden meaning here connecting with when "the Spirit of God moved (or *rachaph*) on the face of the waters," in **Genesis 1:2**. The Spirit *brooded* over the waters to bring about a new creation and all who would place their faith in the Son of God would be made new creatures through the Spirit of God.

When I consider the baptism of Jesus, I think of seven *major* events concerning Jesus the Messiah that we find in the gospels. Each one of these events is monumental and crucial to having a deeper understanding of just who the person of Jesus really is:

- *Creation* – **John 1:1-2,10**
- *Incarnation* – **John 1:14**
- *Baptism* – **John 1:32-33**
- *Transfiguration* – **Luke 9:28-36**
- *Crucifixion* – **John 19:16-30**

- *Resurrection –*   **John 20-21**
- *Ascension –*   **Luke 24:50-51**

Even though our finite minds cannot fully understand it, Jesus the Messiah would be the *perfect* sacrifice. All of the sins from Adam throughout the centuries of time would be placed on this one Man. Here we can see this beautiful *shepherd-sheep* dichotomy of Jesus being the *Lamb of God* who would also be called *The Good Shepherd* in **John 10:11**. This would not be the only time in the gospel of John where something would rest upon the person of Jesus. Later on in this chapter, we find Jesus telling Nathanael that "angels would be ascending and descending on the Son of Man." (**John 1:51**)

"Upon whom thou shalt see the Spirit descending, and remaining on him, the same is he that baptizeth with the Holy Ghost." In the Old Testament, the Spirit of God would come and go upon the Prophets of old. They would have to say "The Lord hath said." But we find a major turning point in the eternal pages of the sacred scriptures. The Holy Spirit would light upon the man Christ Jesus, but the Holy Spirit would not leave Him and He would say, "Verily, verily, I say unto you." Here again, we have the focus changing from water baptism to the baptism of the Holy Spirit. Let's look at two phases of water baptism. There were six major reasons for *water immersion* in Jesus' time:

1. *Proselyte baptism – Gentile converting to the Jewish faith*
2. *Ritual baptism – Before entering a place of worship*

3. *To take the Nazarite vow –* **Numbers 6**
4. *Committing one's self to follow a Rabbi*
5. *Consecration to ministry*
6. *To be identified with someone or some movement*

Jesus did not take the Nazarite vow but He certainly was a Nazarite in a much deeper way by coming from Nazareth and being called *The Branch.* (**Isa.4:2; Isa.11:1; Jer. 23:5-6; Zech.3:8-9; 6:12-13**) John the Baptist was to live an ascetic life in the wilderness, while Jesus was to be a Man of the people and be in their midst. So the reasons for Jesus being *water immersed* were the fact that He was *consecrating* Himself to His earthly ministry and He wanted to be *identified* with His people.

Before we leave this beautiful baptismal scene of John the Baptist and Jesus, I would like to mention several other reasons why I believe the *Holy Spirit* came upon Jesus in the Jordan River:

- *To vindicate the ministry of John the Baptist*
- *To confirm to John the identity of Jesus*
- *Because Joshua, who was a type of Messiah, led their forefathers across the Jordan River into the Promised Land*
- *To anoint the <u>Man</u> Jesus for His earthly ministry*
- *To show the Father was pleased with His Son*
- *To give a symbol of new creation to all believers*
- *To manifest the Messiah to Israel*

THE PUBLIC MINISTRY OF JESUS

> **John 1: 35-42 -** *Again the next day after John stood, and two of his disciples; And looking upon Jesus as he walked, he saith, Behold the Lamb of God! And the two disciples heard him speak, and they followed Jesus. Then Jesus turned, and saw them following, and saith unto them, What seek ye? They said unto him, Rabbi, (which is to say, being interpreted, Master,) where dwellest thou? He saith unto them, Come and see. They came and saw where he dwelt, and abode with him that day: for it was about the tenth hour. One of the two which heard John speak, and followed him, was Andrew, Simon Peter's brother. He first findeth his own brother Simon, and saith unto him, We have found the Messias, which is, being interpreted, the Christ. And he brought him to Jesus. And when Jesus beheld him, he said, Thou art Simon the son of Jona: thou shalt be called Cephas, which is by interpretation, A stone.*

The two disciples of John who started following Jesus were Andrew and, as many scholars believe, the beloved disciple John, who is writing this book. John the Baptist knew his job was to point others to Jesus and here he lets his disciples know again by proclaiming "Behold the Lamb of God."

"What seek ye?" Jesus knew what they were thinking but He wanted to here it from them. When they asked, "where

dwellest thou," Jesus said unto them "Come and see." This invitation of Jesus reminds me of another time when Jesus said to His disciples, after the resurrection, "Come and dine." (**John 21:12**) They came and saw where Jesus was lodging and spent the rest of the day with him. While we cannot be certain, there are some Hebrew scholars that believe this took place on the *Sabbath* day because it mentions that it was only two hours before night, or "the tenth hour." I have often tried to imagine what a life-changing day this was for those two disciples - walking with the One that John the Baptist had just baptized, being able to hear His voice, and knowing that they had been chosen by God to experience this moment in time. They would never get over this day and we are still reading about it two thousand years later.

"He first findeth his own brother." If there had been no Andrew, there would have been no Peter. This was a true picture of love for a brother: wanting him to know who Jesus was. Andrew is overshadowed by Peter in the gospels, and rightfully so, since Peter was given the keys of the kingdom. But we should be reminded of how important Andrew was to the spreading of Christianity in the first century. The Greek Orthodox Church calls him *Protokletos*, or *The First Called*. History says that Andrew preached in the regions of Scythia and Thrace and died sometime during the middle part of the first century as a martyr for the cause of Christ. Legend says that he died on an X-shaped cross because he said that he was not worthy to die like Jesus.

"We have found the Messias, which is, being interpreted, the Christ." The wording for *Messiah* being *Messias* comes from the transliteration from the Greek to the Latin and the Latin to English. The Hebrew word is *Mashiach* and means *anointed. Anointed* in Greek is *Christos* and transliterated in English as *the Christ.* But what a powerful message Andrew brought to his brother. "Peter, we have found the long-awaited Messiah of Israel!" The treasure Andrew *found,* he shared first with his brother.

"Thou art Simon the son of Jona: thou shalt be called Cephas, which is by interpretation, A stone." Simon's name would be changed to the Hebrew/Aramaic *Cephas,* or *Kepha,* both meaning *the rock.* Simon Peter would become the leader of the apostles and Jesus would give him the *keys of the kingdom.* (**Matt.16:19**) Peter would use those keys to open the door to many Jews on the day of Pentecost in **Acts 2** and to open the door officially to the Gentiles in **Acts 10**. So much controversy has risen over the centuries between the Catholic Church and the Protestant Church about the role of Peter in the church. But the key is that, in a word study of **Matthew 16:18**, Peter is the *petros,* or *the little rock,* while Jesus is the *Petra, the big rock.* As important as Peter's role would be, the church would not be built upon a man. The church would be built on the truth of Jesus being the Son of God! Peter himself would later clarify:

> *Wherefore also it is contained in the scripture, Behold, I lay in Sion a chief corner stone, elect, precious: and he that believeth on him shall not be*

confounded. Unto you therefore which believe he is precious: but unto them which be disobedient, the stone which the builders disallowed, the same is made the head of the corner, And a stone of stumbling, and a rock of offence, even to them which stumble at the word, being disobedient: whereunto also they were appointed.

—I Peter 2:6-8.

John continues:

John 1:43-46 - *The day following Jesus would go forth into Galilee, and findeth Philip, and saith unto him, Follow me. Now Philip was of Bethsaida, the city of Andrew and Peter. Philip findeth Nathanael, and saith unto him, We have found him, of whom Moses in the law, and the prophets, did write, Jesus of Nazareth, the son of Joseph. And Nathanael said unto him, Can there any good thing come out of Nazareth? Philip saith unto him, Come and see.*

So we see clearly that three of the disciples of our Lord were from the town of Bethsaida: *Philip, Andrew, and Peter.* Scholars believe that Peter and Andrew probably later moved just a few miles up the shoreline to Capernaum because they were fishermen and needed access to the loading docks there. *Bethsaida* was originally a village when the disciples lived there, but was expanded to a city by Herod Philip in 30AD and renamed *Bethsaida Julias*. It was located on the northeastern shore of the Sea of Galilee. The ruins today are a few miles from the water because of the geographical changes that have occurred over the centuries due to major earthquakes that caused a shift in the course of the Jordan River. Guides and archaeologists have various opinions about this place but soil samples reveal that the water of the lake came close to *Bethsaida* in Jesus' time.

"*Philip findeth Nathanael.*" *Nathanael* in Hebrew is *Netan'el* and means *God has given*. What Philip told Nathanael is absolutely astounding:

> *We have found him, of whom Moses in the law, and the prophets, did write, Jesus of Nazareth, the son of Joseph.*

What a statement this was! Jesus, the carpenter's son from Nazareth, is the one that Moses wrote about and the one the prophets foretold who would come into the world. I can just imagine what was going through their minds. Wasn't the Messiah supposed to come in great power and great glory and bring peace on the earth? How could someone so humble who lives in an obscure village possibly be the Messiah of Israel? Their misunderstanding was primarily due to the fact that their religious leaders had taught them about only one coming of the Messiah. They did not know about the servant Messiah who would come as a sacrifice the first time and as a King the second time. As we go through this gospel, we will clearly see that the religious leaders did not know the scriptures very well. They had been following the traditions of the Jews more than the scriptures. It's interesting to me that Jesus used this same Old Testament pattern that Philip used when describing who He was to the two men on the road to Emmaus:

> *And beginning at Moses and all the prophets, he*
> *expounded unto them in all the scriptures the things*
> *concerning himself.*
> —**Luke 24:27**

"Can any good thing come out of Nazareth?" Scholars have thought for centuries that Nathanael said this because Nazareth was only a village of probably around 150 people in those days. But another reason may be that there was a religious faction of unbelieving Pharisees from Jerusalem who taught in Nazareth at that time. The religious leaders in Judea looked down on the Galileans, so this may be the reason why Nathanael had a bad opinion of Nazareth.

> **John 1:47-51** - *Jesus saw Nathanael coming to*
> *him, and saith of him, Behold an Israelite indeed,*
> *in whom is no guile! Nathanael saith unto him,*
> *Whence knowest thou me? Jesus answered and*
> *said unto him, Before that Philip called thee, when*
> *thou wast under the fig tree, I saw thee. Nathanael*
> *answered and saith unto him, Rabbi, thou art the*
> *Son of God; thou art the King of Israel. Jesus*
> *answered and said unto him, Because I said unto*
> *thee, I saw thee under the fig tree, believest thou?*

> *thou shalt see greater things than these. And he saith*
> *unto him, Verily, verily, I say unto you, Hereafter*
> *ye shall see heaven open, and the angels of God*
> *ascending and descending upon the Son of man.*

Nathanael has been very overshadowed by some of the more popular disciples. He was a pure Israelite: not just a natural born Jew, but someone who was a spiritual Jew who was looking for the Messiah. He was pure in heart. His simplicity and openness caused Jesus to say, "In whom is no guile." There was no hypocrisy in Nathanael and he was the kind of man that Jesus wanted among His closest followers.

"Before that Philip called thee, when thou wast under the fig tree, I saw thee." The fig tree was considered to be a place where people could meditate about the God of Israel and God would reveal His deep mysteries to them there. **I Kings 4:25, Micah 4:4.** Jesus knew Nathanael had been sitting under a fig tree and, as we will see, He even knew what he was thinking about. When Nathanael heard these words coming from Jesus of Nazareth, he called him three different titles: *Rabbi, Son of God,* and *King of Israel.*

"...the angels of God ascending and descending upon the Son of man." Evidently, Nathanael had either been reading or thinking about the life of Jacob, one of the patriarchs of Israel, while under the fig tree. Think on these verses found in **Genesis 28:10-17:**

> *And Jacob went out from Beersheba, and went*
> *toward Haran. And he lighted upon a certain place,*

and tarried there all night, because the sun was set; and he took of the stones of that place, and put them for his pillows, and lay down in that place to sleep. And he dreamed, and behold a ladder set up on the earth, and the top of it reached to heaven: and behold the angels of God ascending and descending on it. And, behold, the Lord stood above it, and said, I am the Lord God of Abraham thy father, and the God of Isaac: the land whereon thou liest, to thee will I give it, and to thy seed; And thy seed shall be as the dust of the earth, and thou shalt spread abroad to the west, and to the east, and to the north, and to the south: and in thee and in thy seed shall all the families of the earth be blessed. And, behold, I am with thee, and will keep thee in all places whither thou goest, and will bring thee again into this land; for I will not leave thee, until I have done that which I have spoken to thee of. And Jacob awaked out of his sleep, and he said, Surely the Lord is in this place; and I knew it not. And he was afraid, and said, How dreadful is this place! this is none other but the house of God, and this is the gate of heaven.

Because Jesus knew what Nathanael was studying, He revealed to him that *Jacob's ladder* was only a type of what he was about to see. Jesus came down from heaven to earth, and the angels of God would follow him all through His earthly ministry, from His glorious birth to the empty tomb. Angels would then escort Him back to the Father from the Mt. of Olives after the forty days that He would spend with His disciples. Because Nathanael was pure in heart, God would allow him to witness supernatural events in the life of Jesus. Jesus of Nazareth, the Messiah, would be the fulfillment of Jacob's dream. How would Jacob's descendants bless the nations? Through faith in the Messiah! Jews and Gentiles alike, who trusted in Jesus the Messiah, would partake of the covenant that God made with Jacob. Hallelujah!

John 1 is a powerful and progressive chapter regarding the manifestations of the person of Jesus! Let's reflect for just a moment:

John 1:1, 14	**John 1:34**	**John 1:45**
The Word	*The Son of God*	*The son of Joseph*
John 1:7–8	**John 1:36–37**	**John 1:45**
The Light	*Jesus*	*The One Moses and the prophets wrote about*
John 1:18	**John 1:38, 49**	
The Son	*Rabbi*	
		John 1:49
John 1:23	**John 1:41**	*The King of Israel*
The Lord	*Messias, the Christ*	
		John 1:51
John 1:29	**John 1:45**	*The Son of man*
The Lamb of God	*Jesus of Nazareth*	

CHAPTER TWO

John 2:1-12 - *And the third day there was a marriage in Cana of Galilee; and the mother of Jesus was there: And both Jesus was called, and his disciples, to the marriage. And when they wanted wine, the mother of Jesus saith unto him, They have no wine. Jesus saith unto her, Woman, what have I to do with thee? mine hour is not yet come. His mother saith unto the servants, Whatsoever he saith unto you, do it. And there were set there six waterpots of stone, after the manner of the purifying of the Jews, containing two or three firkins apiece. Jesus saith unto them, Fill the waterpots with water. And they filled them up to the brim. And he saith unto them, Draw out now, and bear unto the governor of the feast. And they bare it. When the ruler of the feast had tasted the water that was made wine, and knew not whence it was: (but the servants which drew the water knew;) the governor* *of the feast called the bridegroom, And saith unto him, Every man at the beginning doth set forth good wine; and when men have well drunk, then that which is worse: but thou hast kept the good wine until now. This beginning of miracles did Jesus in Cana of Galilee, and manifested forth his glory; and his disciples believed on him. After this he went down to Capernaum, he, and his mother, and his brethren, and his disciples: and they continued there not many days.*

"And the third day." In the creation account of **Genesis 1:9–13**, it is written that only on the *third day* of creation did God say not once, but twice "and God saw that it was good." So the Jews thought that the *third day (Tuesday* on our calendar) was the perfect day to have a wedding.

"…there was a marriage in Cana of Galilee." This place has been identified as *Khirbet Qana* and is located about eighteen miles southwest of the Sea of Galilee. It is mentioned as one of the towns where Josephus had his headquarters in the first century. *Kfar Qana*, the place where Israeli guides take you today, is also considered to be a possibility, but was a much later find. I find it very interesting that the very first miracle of our Lord happened in the hometown of Nathanael (**John 21:2**), the person who experienced that life-changing conversation with Jesus, back in **John 1:45–51**.

"…the mother of Jesus was there: And both Jesus was called, and his disciples, to the marriage." The family of Jesus was from Nazareth, which was only a few miles away from Cana, and

the disciples of Jesus were evidently friends with the family of the couple that was about to be married. We must keep in mind that both communities of Nazareth and Cana were small and relatively close together, so the people would have been well acquainted with each other. The fact that Jesus was even there, and the fact that this is the place of His first miracle, shows His approval upon earthly marriage. Jesus, being the great *Bridegroom*, certainly understood how important it was for the Cana bridegroom to make a good impression on everyone who was at the wedding feast. A wedding feast in Jesus' time would last about seven days and was the most festive event in everyday Jewish life. We will see the wedding motif seen in other passages in John's gospel as well.

"They have no wine." It was the bridegroom's responsibility to provide wine for the wedding and there were probably more guests attending than he had anticipated. To run out of wine was a tremendous embarrassment to the bridegroom. Wine, or the Hebrew *yayin,* was a symbol of joy and was part of the Jewish culture in Jesus' time, as we find in places like **Matthew 11:19, Mark.2:22,** and **Acts 2:13–15.**

"Woman, what have I to do with thee? Mine hour is not yet come." The word *hour* is used in John's gospel over twenty times. Sometimes it is referring to a major happening in the life of the Messiah's ministry, like in **John 12:23.** Hebrew scholars believe that the reason Jesus used what seemingly was a harsh reply to His mother was to let her know that the *hour* had not arrived for the messianic kingdom that would occur when He comes the second time. Jesus even used the

customary address of *Woman* again when He was on the cross, in **John 19:26**. Jesus talked about drinking wine with His disciples in the future kingdom in **Matt.26:29**:

> *But I say unto you, I will not drink henceforth of this fruit of the vine, until that day when I drink it new with you in my Father's kingdom.*

I understand that teaching that Jesus turned the water into fermented wine is offensive to some because many think that even touching fermented wine is a sin. But it is not the wine that is a sin. It is the drunkenness that is a sin. It is not a sin to eat, but it is a sin to be a glutton. It is not a sin to have sexual relations with one's own wife or husband, but it is a sin to commit fornication or adultery. Just because alcoholism is a social problem in our day, we shouldn't try to read that into the customs of 2,000 years ago during the early first century. Wine in Jesus' time was not like wine in our day, it was normally a mixture of two-thirds water and one-third wine. It was commonly believed in Jesus' time that there would be an excess of wine during the future kingdom. Here is one biblical example:

> *And in this mountain shall the LORD of hosts make unto all people a feast of fat things, a feast of wines on the lees, (results of fermentation) of fat things full of marrow, of wines on the lees well refined.*
>
> **—Isaiah 25:6.**

"...six waterpots of stone, after the manner of the purifying of the Jews, containing two or three firkins apiece." The water that had been used for Jewish ritual purposes would find its fulfillment in the blood of Christ. This miracle of turning the water into wine was a foreshadowing of the blood that Jesus would shed when He died on the cross. The water pots were made out of *stone,* which kept the water clean and free from contamination. If you wanted to run with the typology you could compare them to the sinless Messiah who would be the fulfillment. In modern-day measurements, these water pots contained between twenty and thirty gallons each. So the first miracle of Jesus resulted in between 120-180 gallons of wine. Wow!

"And they filled them up to the brim." This was an intention of Jesus, to bring bountiful joy to the marriage feast. Not just half full, or three-fourths full, but *up to the brim.* I am reminded of **John 6:12** when Jesus fed the multitude on the shore of Galilee, they *were all filled.*

"Draw out now, and bear unto the governor of the feast." Jesus told the servants to give the wine to the governor of the feast who was guest that had been chosen to manage the affairs of the feast. The fact that the governor called the bridegroom so casually in **verse 9** implies that he was also a guest at the feast.

"...but thou has kept the good wine until now." The governor was saying in simple terms that normally, after men were a little intoxicated, they gave them the worst wine. But the rich tasting, well-aged wine had been saved for the last. Jesus turned water into *aged* wine: 1) without grapes, 2)

without sunshine, and 3) without process of time. When He created the earth, He created it to look thousands of years old. When He created Adam, he was already a grown man. So what could this first miracle possibly mean? It meant that Jesus of Nazareth was none other than the Creator Himself in human form.

"This beginning of miracles did Jesus in Cana of Galilee, and manifested forth his glory; and his disciples believed on him." Not only did Jesus perform this miracle for the sake of the bridegroom, but also for His own disciples. Think of what might have been going on in the minds of the disciples. This Rabbi that we started following is much more than just a Rabbi, He is the true Messiah of Israel! Even though their faith would be up and down (just like you and me), miracle after miracle, Jesus would prove to them who He was and it started in Cana of Galilee. He *manifested forth his glory.* This meant that the *kavod* or *heavy weight* of God's glory was in Jesus of Nazareth. His glory came forth!

"After this he went down to Capernaum, he, and his mother, and his brethren, and his disciples: and they continued there not many days." Capernaum is about eighteen miles away from Cana, so they could have easily traveled that distance in one day. Notice that Jesus' earthly father, Joseph, was not listed here. Most Hebrew scholars believe that Joseph died sometime while Jesus was growing up in Nazareth. But the mother of Jesus, His brothers, and possibly His sisters (**Mark 6:3**) went with Him to Capernaum. The reason they did not stay very long in Capernaum was because the Jewish Passover was nigh. This tells us that Jesus turned the

water into wine either the very last of March or the very first of April.

JESUS AND THE MONEY CHANGERS

> **John 2:13-17** - *And the Jews' passover was at hand, and Jesus went up to Jerusalem, And found in the temple those that sold oxen and sheep and doves, and the changers of money sitting: And when he had made a scourge of small cords, he drove them all out of the temple, and the sheep, and the oxen; and poured out the changers' money, and overthrew the tables; And said unto them that sold doves, Take these things hence; make not my Father's house an house of merchandise. And his disciples remembered that it was written, The zeal of thine house hath eaten me up.*

This is the very first Passover that Jesus attended in Jerusalem. It was a long eighty-mile journey down the Jordan Valley to Jericho. From there, they made the climb through the Judean mountains into Jerusalem. So Jesus would have walked from Galilee, which is 650 ft. below sea level, to Jericho, which is about 1200 ft. below sea level, to Jerusalem, which is over 2500 ft. *above* sea level. This is why the gospel accounts tell us that Jesus *went up to Jerusalem.*

"And found in the temple those that sold oxen and sheep and doves, and the changers of money sitting: And when he had made a scourge of small cords, he drove them all out of the temple, and

41

the sheep, and the oxen; and poured out the changers' money, and overthrew the tables." What made Jesus so angry?

- *They were in the temple area and not in their normal marketplace on the streets below.*
- *They had raised the price of the sacrificial animals during the feast of Passover.*
- *They were making money on exchanging the foreign money into Tyrian shekels, which was used in the temple.*

Try to imagine the grief that Jesus must have felt when He was making the scourge. He didn't want to do it, but the scene was so disgusting that, in His righteous indignation, He had to act. Those sacrificial sheep were a type of the Lamb of God that would soon die on the cross. The religious rulers who were involved were making profit on something that was supposed to be holy and sacred.

"Take these things hence; make not my Father's house an house of merchandise." Jesus is saying that they had made the house of worship unholy by turning it into a profit-making industry. It was supposed to be the *Father's house*, not *their* house. This also helps to explain why Jesus said in **Matt.23:38**: "Behold, your house is left unto you desolate." It's also wonderful to know that in the Messianic kingdom that all vessels will be holy and there will be no more merchants or traffickers in Jerusalem as prophesied in **Zechariah 14:21**:

> *Yea, every pot in Jerusalem and in Judah shall be holiness unto the LORD of hosts: and all they that*

sacrifice shall come and take of them, and seethe therein: and in that day there shall be no more the Canaanite (Means merchant or trafficker) *in the house of the* LORD *of hosts.*

"And his disciples remembered that it was written, The zeal of thine house hath eaten me up." The other gospel accounts connect **Isaiah 56:7** to this dramatic scene, where it says *"My house shall be called by all nations the house of prayer,"* thus placing the emphasis on Israel's mistreatment of the Gentiles. But John's gospel is the only one of the gospel accounts that connects it all to **Psalm 69:9**: "For the zeal of thine house hath eaten me up." The passion and commitment that Jesus had to reforming Israel had been demonstrated and the disciples remembered this verse from the **Psalms**. This was a revelation of the Spirit of God, bringing that Old Testament verse to their minds about the Messiah. Wow!

> **John 2:18–22 -** *Then answered the Jews and said unto him, What sign shewest thou unto us, seeing that thou doest these things? Jesus answered and said unto them, Destroy this temple, and in three days I will raise it up. Then said the Jews, Forty and six years was this temple in building, and wilt thou rear it up in three days? But he spake of the temple of his body. When therefore he was risen from the dead, his disciples remembered that he had said this*

unto them; and they believed the scripture, and the word which Jesus had said.

"What sign shewest thou unto us." When asked for a sign, Jesus alludes to His resurrection. He does it by giving them a cryptic expression: *Destroy this temple, and in three days I will raise it up.* Of course the religious leaders thought Jesus was talking about the physical temple in Jerusalem that had been in the building process for *forty and six years.* We believe that the miracle of turning the water into wine and the Passover in **John 2** occurred in the year 29 or 30 AD, which would place the beginning of the construction of Herod's Temple in about 17 BC.

"But he spake of the temple of his body. When therefore he was risen from the dead, his disciples remembered that he had said this unto them." Jesus was the Living Temple of the Lord that was filled with the glory of God. This also helps us to connect the prelude in **John 1:1–14** even better. After the resurrection of Jesus, the disciples remembered what Jesus had said. They saw His physical temple die on a tree, and then they saw Him raise it up on the third day.

"…many believed in his name, when they saw the miracles which he did. But Jesus did not commit himself unto them, because he knew all men, And needed not that any should testify of man: for he knew what was in man." We are not given the details of these miracles, but we can assume that they were miracles of healing the crippled and blind, like most of the other miracles Jesus performed in Galilee. But Jesus did not need man to testify about who He was at this time. Jesus knew

what they were thinking and He knew the time was not right for Him to be offered up. The Master's mission was not to start a revolution or to bring glory to Himself. His real mission could not be understood until after the resurrection.

Nevertheless, we can see here, in the first visit of Jesus to Jerusalem, the beginning of a movement that would eventually grow into throngs of people at the Triumphal Entry and ultimately result in thousands of Jewish believers in the book of Acts. This movement would continue to include believing Gentiles and has been extended down to us today!

CHAPTER THREE

John 3:1-8 – *There was a man of the Pharisees, named Nicodemus, a ruler of the Jews: The same came to Jesus by night, and said unto him, Rabbi, we know that thou art a teacher come from God: for no man can do these miracles that thou doest, except God be with him. Jesus answered and said unto him, Verily, verily, I say unto thee, Except a man be born again, he cannot see the kingdom of God. Nicodemus saith unto him, How can a man be born when he is old? can he enter the second time into his mother's womb, and be born? Jesus answered, Verily, verily, I say unto thee, Except a man be born of water and of the Spirit, he cannot enter into the kingdom of God. That which is born of the flesh is flesh; and that which is born of the Spirit is spirit. Marvel not that I said unto thee, Ye must be born again. The wind bloweth where it listeth, and thou hearest the sound thereof, but canst not tell whence*

> *it cometh, and whither it goeth: so is every one that*
> *is born of the Spirit.*

"There was a man of the Pharisees, named Nicodemus, a ruler of the Jews." This man is identified in Jewish history as *Nakdimon ben Gurion*, who was among the three wealthiest people living in Jerusalem. Because he was so wealthy, it was said "when he left the House of Study expensive carpets were unrolled before his feet." He was considered to be a Sage of the Sanhedrin who was looking for the Messiah to come. The words that he would hear from the Messiah would forever change his life. This is why **John 3** is considered to be one of the greatest chapters in the entire Bible.

"The same came to Jesus by night, and said unto him, Rabbi, we know that thou art a teacher come from God: for no man can do these miracles that thou doest, except God be with him." Nicodemus was seeking truth, and there was something about Jesus that convinced him that He was *from God*. On this April evening, probably on one of the flat roofs in Jerusalem, the Passover moon was a visitor to this conversation between a top Jewish ruler and the miracle-worker from Galilee. Jesus knew what was in his heart and Jesus knew that Nicodemus was seeking the Messiah. Remember, the people that are recorded in the gospels were people who made an eternal impact in the first century for the kingdom of God. The stories are not just there accidently. Nicodemus desired to see the Roman authorities defeated and the Kingdom of God to come and

set Israel free. He was thinking in his heart: *Could it be that this man, Jesus, could be the one who will set us free?* But what Jesus was about to say was telling of a different kind of kingdom than what Nicodemus had in mind.

"Jesus answered and said unto him, Verily, verily, I say unto thee, Except a man be born again, he cannot see the kingdom of God." Jesus knew where the interests of Nicodemus lay, but he also knew that the real need in his heart was spiritual, even though he was a religious ruler. The phrase *born again* has been so misunderstood over the centuries in the church, especially in the western world mindset. I've heard many great sermons about this subject and a lot of truth was given without giving the context. This phrase was a rabbinic concept that was already in use and was spoken on several important occasions in a man's life:

- When he started manhood at the age of thirteen – *born again*
- When he was married – *born again*
- When he became a rabbi at the age of thirty – *born again*
- When he became a member of the Sanhedrin – *born again*
- When Gentiles were converted to the God of Israel – *born again*

It was written in the Talmud, "One who has become a proselyte is like a child newly born." (Yevamot 48b) The Jews considered a Gentile convert to have actually died and then come back to life again. This explains why Nicodemus answered Jesus the way that he did, referring to being in the mother's womb. So Jesus was taking a very familiar concept, *born again,* and using it to bring Nicodemus under conviction.

"Nicodemus saith unto him, How can a man be born when he is old? can he enter the second time into his mother's womb, and be born?" Nicodemus was saying, *How can I convert to Judaism? I am already Jewish.* But Jesus is going to tell him that being Jewish is not enough! This is why Jesus answered by using the contrast between the physical and spiritual birth.

"Jesus answered, Verily, verily, I say unto thee, Except a man be born of water and of the Spirit, he cannot enter into the kingdom of God. That which is born of the flesh is flesh; and that which is born of the Spirit is spirit. Marvel not that I said unto thee, Ye must be born again." A Jew gives birth to another Jew, but the Spirit gives birth to the spiritual man. There have been many churches that have attempted to use this passage to prove that one must be water baptized to in order to be saved. But, because they did not understand the Jewish culture in Jesus' time, they interpreted the verse from a western worldview. Being *born of water* is talking about the *physical birth* as Jesus explained in the next verse, "That which is born of the flesh is flesh." Verses five and six are parallel. So Jesus is giving Nicodemus this contrast between the *physical birth* and the *spiritual birth.* Nicodemus thought that being a natural born Jew would automatically allow him entrance into God's kingdom and that Gentiles were the ones who had to be converted to Judaism in order to be a part of God's kingdom. What a radical statement Jesus made to one of the most influential rulers in Jerusalem.

"The wind bloweth where it listeth, and thou hearest the sound thereof, but canst not tell whence it cometh, and whither it goeth: so is every one that is born of the Spirit." This happens to be one of my personal favorite verses in the Bible. Every time I feel the wind blow it reminds me of what Jesus said to Nicodemus. Imagine a brisk, windy, springtime night in Jerusalem with the breeze blowing the hair off the shoulders of Jesus. Jesus was saying to Nicodemus that you cannot tell where the wind is coming from, but you can feel it and you can hear it. *All you know, Nicodemus, is that the wind is surely blowing. The spiritual birth is a mysterious thing, Nicodemus. It cannot be reached by intellectualism or outward ceremonialism.* There is a beautiful word play in the Hebrew language here. The word for *wind* is *ruach,"*which is the very same word for *spirit. Observe the wind Nicodemus, and realize that you need a spiritual rebirth to be in God's kingdom.*

> **John 3:9-13** - *Nicodemus answered and said unto him, How can these things be? Jesus answered and said unto him, Art thou a master of Israel, and knowest not these things? Verily, verily, I say unto thee, We speak that we do know, and testify that we have seen; and ye receive not our witness. If I have told you earthly things, and ye believe not, how shall ye believe, if I tell you of heavenly things? And no man hath ascended up to heaven, but he that came down from heaven, even the Son of man which is in heaven.*

Jesus is saying to Nicodemus: *You are a religious Sage in Israel and you do not know about this spiritual birth? If you do not believe me when I explain the basic spiritual needs of the human heart, then you certainly will not understand when I tell you about the deeper things.* Jesus the Messiah is the authority on heavenly things because no on else has ever seen or experienced heaven as He has. People like Moses, Enoch and Elijah had entered into heavenly precincts but no one had ever experienced the Divine Realm in full measure like Jesus the Messiah. Jesus uses incredible language when he told Nicodemus that He was the Divine Son of man that descended from heaven. And His descent from heaven presupposes that He must also *ascend* back to heaven. Try to imagine what was going through the mind of Nicodemus when Jesus started revealing to him those *heavenly things.*

> **John 3:14-15** – *And as Moses lifted up the serpent in the wilderness, even so must the Son of man be lifted up: That whosoever believeth in him should not perish, but have eternal life.*

The title *Son of man* that Jesus uses to describe Himself has to be connected to the apocalyptic *Son of man* in **Daniel 7:13-14**. Before the *Son of man* in **Daniel** can descend to the earth and set up His dominion on the earth, He first must be the incarnate *Son of man* in **John** in order to die for the sins of His people and ascend back to heaven.

We need to keep in mind how much Nicodemus reverenced the Torah Here the preacher from Nazareth is saying that the events recorded in the Torah were types and shadows and that He was the *Son of man* that would fulfill what Moses wrote about. There are two meanings of this passage: one is very basic and one is very mysterious. The first meaning is of course referring to the crucifixion. The venom of the sin has poisoned humanity, but anyone can be healed through looking up to Jesus on the cross, as the people looked up to the brazen serpent in Moses' time. But there is a more mysterious meaning here. Let's look at the verse Jesus is quoting from, in **Numbers 21:8**:

> *And the LORD said unto Moses, Make thee a fiery serpent, and set it upon a pole: and it shall come to pass, that every one that is bitten, when he looketh upon it, shall live.*

The Hebrew word for *pole* is *nec* (pronounced *nace*). It means *a flag, sail, token, or banner.* It is also the one of the words that is used in Hebrew for *miracle.* It is believed by many Hebrew scholars that Moses just cast the brazen serpent into the air and it stayed there miraculously. It wasn't on a *pole* like we normally would think. It was a miracle! What a miracle the *cross* really was! God became a Man in order to be capable of dying! God is an Eternal Spirit and He cannot die! How can He die for *all* of the sins of mankind? This necessitated a virgin birth and a sinless life to be the perfect sacrifice! Furthermore, the *ascension* of the Messiah, which Jesus has just mentioned, would be the crucified and risen Lord, being *lifted up* into the clouds and going back to heaven!

These are the so-called heavenly things that Jesus referred to and *how* a person could be *born again*. Jesus is taking the religious Nicodemus to multiple levels of truth, truths that he had never heard in his life. Repeat this with me:

> **John 3:16-21 –** *For God so loved the world, that he gave his only begotten Son, that whosoever believeth in him should not perish, but have everlasting life. For God sent not his Son into the world to condemn the world; but that the world through him might be saved. He that believeth on him is not condemned: but he that believeth not is condemned already, because he hath not believed in the name of the only begotten Son of God. And this is the condemnation, that light is come into the world, and men loved darkness rather than light, because their deeds were evil. For every one that doeth evil hateth the light, neither cometh to the light, lest his deeds should be reproved. But he that doeth truth cometh to the light, that his deeds may be made manifest, that they are wrought in God.*

Nicodemus would not have understood this powerful statement like we would today. Here is a religious Jew, a ruler of Israel who thought that only the Jews were destined for God's kingdom and that the Gentiles would have to convert to Judaism to have any part in it. But here the Messiah, who is here referred to as *God's Son*, signifying the second person of the triune Godhead, is telling Nicodemus that God not only loves Israel, but He loves the entire world! *Whosoever* believes in Him will have eternal life!

I ended up getting into an argument years ago with a gentleman who attended a particular church that taught that no one could be saved by just believing in the truths of **John 3:16**. In his view, when a person sought salvation, he or she had to join the local church, be water-baptized, and keep themselves saved by the way they lived and were obedient to the Lord. I will not go into everything I told him, but I can tell you that he never bothered me again. My dear friends, there is enough truth in **John 3:16** to save the whole world! This is one of the most treasured verses in the Bible. Of course we need to become a part of a local congregation, follow our Lord in baptism, and strive to live a holy life. But none of those things can save anyone! It's God sending His Son into the world and the Son finishing the work that He was sent to do that provides eternal life! I pray, dear reader, that you have placed your sincere trust in *who* Jesus is and *what* He has done for you! If not, please take time out this very moment and surrender to the Savior!

"For God sent not his Son into the world to condemn the world; but that the world through him might be saved." We should never read **John 3:16** without reading **John 3:17**. The God of the Bible is love. When He sent His Son Jesus into the world, He did not send Him to condemn people, but to save them. Now, getting back to the Jewish context, here Jesus is talking to Nicodemus, who was a *judge* of the Sanhedrin. He was used to pronouncing judgment on others according the strict Law of Moses. The Messiah's

way of judgment would be totally different. Read this description of the judgment of Israel's Messiah according to **Isaiah 11:3:**

> *And shall make him of quick understanding in the fear of the LORD: and he shall not judge after the sight of his eyes, neither reprove after the hearing of his ears:*

The Lord would *see* the sins of the people, and *hear* their cursing and unbelief, but He would show them forgiveness if they would embrace Him. This is what we see when we read the gospels. Jesus is not condemning the open sinners, but He is saving them. What a revelation this must have been to Nicodemus! Many would be judged to everlasting hell, but only because of their rejection of Jesus. His mercy is everlasting and if anyone will confess their sins and turn to Him by faith, He will save them.

There is something so powerful about **John 3:17** that moves me to joyful tears every time I read it. Read it and read it again! We can learn a great lesson from this verse as well. When we try to witness to others, we must not have an attitude of judging them. We must see them through the eyes of Jesus and know that they are precious to Him. There has been a lot of damage done to God's kingdom over the centuries by misguided people who went around judging others which, in turn, caused them to run further away from Christianity. I recall a crusade where I was preaching years ago. One night I preached on **John 3:16** and after the service an old, feeble preacher came by and said, "Son, you did a good job tonight, but why didn't you tell the people about **John 3:17**?" When the old preacher quoted the verse, I felt so convicted about my message that it moved me to repentant tears. Since then, I have tried to never leave it out. Thank you Lord for reminding me through one of your servants!

"...*but he that believeth not is condemned already, because he hath not believed in the name of the only begotten Son of God.*" This is a truth that so many in our world today do not understand. If a person will not believe in Jesus as the Son of God, they are already under judgment. God has already placed His judgment on the world no matter how moral or immoral a person may be or how religious or non-religious they may be. The way people are measured in the eyes of a holy God is through their belief or their unbelief in Christ. Think of the great extremes that God went to, by sending His only begotten Son into the world to die on a cross in order to save a lost world. Everlasting life is in Jesus the Son of God. While those who come to Him have the assurance of eternal life, those who refuse to come to Him have the Word of God that they are under condemnation.

"*And this is the condemnation, that light is come into the world, and men loved darkness rather than light, because their deeds were evil.*" This takes us back to **John 1:7-9**, where Jesus is called the *Light*. This evil world is still a very dark place and the reason why people do not read the Bible is because their evil deeds are exposed by it. The reason why people do not come to Christ is not because He does not desire for them to be saved, but because they love the *darkness rather than light*.

I recall a true story about a missionary who traveled to the remote parts of Africa years ago in order to share Christ with the village people there. They rejected the message of Jesus and refused to give up their voodoo and witchcraft. He got back on the plane and realized why God has to allow people to go hell. It's not because He doesn't love them, it's because they do not love Him! Man's heart is so filled with iniquity that he loves the ways of evil more than the ways of God. If God's Israel of old, God's chosen people, would turn away for the God of Abraham in order to serve false gods, how much more will the pagan world turn away from God.

"But he that doeth truth cometh to the light, that his deeds may be made manifest, that they are wrought in God." When did Nicodemus come to Jesus? At night! He had a heart for God, and during the darkness of the night, he was introduced to the true Light. According to **John 7:50-51** and **John 19:39-40**, Nicodemus became a changed man. Try to imagine what was going through his mind when he and Joseph of Arimathea were holding the dead, nail-scarred body of Jesus. The message that Jesus gave Nicodemus about the lifted-up Son of man and how God had not sent His Son into the world to condemn the world became so real and so alive in his heart. This religious ruler with whom Jesus had this conversation in **John 3** would be the one who would anoint the body of Jesus in **John 19**! Through talking with Jesus the Messiah, this Jewish man in Jerusalem became a true child of Abraham! Hallelujah!

JESUS' EARLY JUDEAN MINISTRY

John 3:22-30 - *After these things came Jesus and his disciples into the land of Judaea; and there he tarried with them, and baptized. And John also was baptizing in Aenon near to Salim, because there was much water there: and they came, and were baptized. For John was not yet cast into prison. Then there arose a question between some of John's disciples and the Jews about purifying. And they came unto John, and said unto him, Rabbi, he that was with thee beyond Jordan, to whom thou barest witness, behold, the same baptizeth, and all men come to him. John answered and said, A man can receive nothing, except it be given him from heaven. Ye yourselves bear me witness, that I said, I am not the Christ, but that I am sent before him. He that hath the bride is the bridegroom: but the friend of the bridegroom, which standeth and heareth him, rejoiceth greatly because of the bridegroom's voice: this my joy therefore is fulfilled. He must increase, but I must decrease.*

Jesus would not proclaim the Kingdom of heaven until after John the Baptist was cast into prison. However, after the feast of Passover had ended, Jesus stayed in Judea and His disciples started immersing people like John did. Jesus seems almost passive in the fact that He did not baptize according to **John 4:2**. At the same time, John the Baptist was still immersing people down at the Jordan. The place

Aenon near to Salim has been identified, on the 6th century Madaba map, as being in the same area as *Bethabara*, just north of the Dead Sea. (**John 1:28**)

"Then there arose a question between some of John's disciples and the Jews about purifying. And they came unto John, and said unto him, Rabbi, he that was with thee beyond Jordan, to whom thou barest witness, behold, the same baptizeth, and all men come to him." There were enough people being immersed by the disciples of Jesus to cause alarm among some of the disciples of John the Baptist. We must remember that this was a time of transition when John's ministry would give way to the public ministry of Yeshua the Messiah in the Galilee. So it's understandable why there was a temporary confusion about who was the real *Rabbi*! But listen to the testimony of John the Baptist:

> **John 3:27–36** - *John answered and said, A man can receive nothing, except it be given him from heaven. Ye yourselves bear me witness, that I said, I am not the Christ, but that I am sent before him. He that hath the bride is the bridegroom: but the friend of the bridegroom, which standeth and heareth him, rejoiceth greatly because of the bridegroom's voice: this my joy therefore is fulfilled. He must increase, but I must decrease. He that cometh from above is above all: he that is of the earth is earthly, and speaketh of the earth: he that cometh from heaven is above all. And what he hath seen and heard, that he testifieth; and no man receiveth his*

testimony. He that hath received his testimony hath set to his seal that God is true. For he whom God hath sent speaketh the words of God: for God giveth not the Spirit by measure unto him. The Father loveth the Son, and hath given all things into his hand. He that believeth on the Son hath everlasting life: and he that believeth not the Son shall not see life; but the wrath of God abideth on him.

Instead of being disturbed or disappointed, John the Baptist was eager to step aside and he had the feeling that his ministry as the forerunner of the Messiah had been a success. He repeats: *I am not the Christ!* The motif of John the Baptist being the *friend of the bridegroom* can also connect us back to the first miracle of Jesus at Cana (**John 2:9**) and the governor at the feast who was the friend of the bridegroom there. He is one that tasted the water turned into wine *first* and John the Baptist was the *first* to publicly witness the Spirit of God anointing Israel's Messiah!

"He must increase, but I must decrease." John the Baptist knew that his ministry was short lived and it brought *joy* to him in knowing that people had started following Jesus. This was his job: to point people to the Messiah. What a lesson for all who are preachers of the gospel. Our job is not to build big ministries or to create a following, but to always point men, women, boys, and girls to Jesus the Son of God! What a humble and powerful servant John the Baptist really was. May we apply this to our own lives.

"He that cometh from above is above all: he that is of the earth

is earthy, and speaketh of the earth: he that cometh from heaven is above all." It's amazingly interesting tom e to see that the words of John the Baptist echo a very similar statement that Jesus made to Nicodemus in **vs.12–13**.

"...for God giveth not the Spirit by measure unto him." All great prophets and saints of old had been given a *measure* of the Spirit of God, but in Jesus would "dwell all the fulness of the Godhead bodily." **Col.2:9**. This connects us back to **John 1:33** when John saw the Spirit of God *remaining* on Jesus in the Jordan River.

"The Father loveth the Son, and hath given all things into his hand. He that believeth on the Son hath everlasting life: and he that believeth not the Son shall not see life; but the wrath of God abideth on him." This final testimony of John the Baptist also has a strikingly similarity to what Jesus told Nicodemus in **vs.16–18**. John is proving his point by stating the *Sonship of the God of Israel*. Listen to these Old Testament passages and then think about what Jesus told Nicodemus and the words of John the Baptist.

> *Who hath ascended up into heaven, or descended? Who hath gathered the wind in his fists? Who hath bound the waters in a garment: who hath established all the ends of the earth? What is his name, and what is his son's name, if thou canst tell?*
> **—Proverbs 30:4**

> *For unto us a child is born, unto us a son is given.*
> **—Isaiah 9:6**

CHAPTER FOUR

JESUS LEAVES JUDEA

John 4:1-4 - *When therefore the Lord knew how the Pharisees had heard that Jesus made and baptized more disciples than John, (Though Jesus himself baptized not, but his disciples,) He left Judaea, and departed again into Galilee. And he must needs go through Samaria.*

The scriptures do not tell us how long Jesus and His disciples stayed in Judea. Once again, the distance between Jerusalem and Galilee was around eighty miles. Because of the emphasis of the *Judean* ministry of Jesus, the apostle John seems to be very concerned about mentioning the different Jewish feasts that were taking place in Jerusalem and that Jesus was there. Did Jesus and His disciples stay fifty days after the *Passover* until the feast of *Shavuot* (Pentecost)? If the miracle at the *Pool of Bethesda* in **chapter 5** happened during the feast of *Pentecost*, which some scholars believe, then they went back to Galilee and came back to Jerusalem in a very short period of time. We just simply do not know, but my guess would be that they stayed in Judea until the feast of *Pentecost*, which was the norm of that day. We find it mentioned in **John 5:1**, "After this there was a feast of the Jews," but we do not know which feast it was. In **John 6:4**, we find that the spring "passover was nigh." Then we find the *Jewish feast of tabernacles* in **John 7:2**, which was in the fall! So the fast pace of the geographical locations and the different feasts that are mentione are a little confusing if we try to follow Jesus' ministry chronologically. But if Jesus stayed in Judea until the feast of *Pentecost*, this would put Him leaving Judea and coming through Samaria sometime in the early part of June.

"*(Though Jesus himself baptized not, but his disciples,)*" As already mentioned, Jesus did not immerse people in water, but His disciples did. The religious Pharisees were disturbed of the growing enthusiasm of the followers of Jesus. John wants us to know that Jesus was not well received among the religious rulers in Judea, so now He departs and "*must needs go through Samaria.*" We have all heard how this was not the route that Jews took when going back to Galilee. They normally traveled a few days out of the way and went down to Jericho then up the Jordan valley to Galilee in order to stay away from the Samaritans.

The Samaritans were hated because of several reasons that go back to when a man named *Shechem* defiled *Dinah*, the daughter of Leah, in **Genesis 34:1-2**. Also, following the Assyrian invasion in 722BC, when most of the Israelites were taken into captivity, Assyria re-populated Samaria with foreigners from other countries they had conquered. As a result, upon Israel's return, they began to marry these foreigners, so the Samaritans were half Jew and half Gentile. Another reason why the Jews hated the Samaritans was because they hindered the rebuilding of the temple in Jerusalem during the 6ᵗʰ century BC. (**Ezra 4:1-10**) In response, the Samaritans built a temple on *Mt. Gerizim* after the marriage between the son of *Eliashib*, the high priest, and the daughter of the Samaritan leader, *Sanballat*, in **Nehemiah 13:28**. This temple was in direct opposition to the temple in Jerusalem. The name *Samaria*, from the Hebrew *Shomron*, means *keepers of the law*. The Samaritans thought that they were the true keepers of the law. There are a few Hebrew scholars who believe that the Samaritans were actually Israelites and that Jesus was going through Samaria to one of the lost sheep of the house of Israel. We cannot be sure, but it certainly is possible. But we shall find that the reasons *why* Jesus deliberately went through Samaria have a much deeper meaning than what lies on the surface.

JESUS AND THE SAMARITAN WOMAN

John 4:5-6 – *Then cometh he to a city of Samaria, which is called Sychar, near to the parcel of ground that Jacob gave to his son Joseph. Now Jacob's well was there. Jesus therefore, being wearied with his journey, sat thus on the well: and it was about the sixth hour.*

Immediately we are drawn to a very important place where the patriarch Jacob bought a piece of land and gave it to Joseph. Because of the significance, I want to mention a few Old Testament verses:

> *And Jacob came to Shalem, a city of Shechem, which is in the land of Canaan, when he came from Padanaram; and pitched his tent before the city. And he bought a parcel of a field, where he had spread his tent, at the hand of the children of Hamor, Shechem's father, for an hundred pieces of money. And he erected there an altar, and called it EleloheIsrael.*
>
> **—Genesis 33:18–20**

> *And Joseph took an oath of the children of Israel, saying, God will surely visit you, and ye shall carry up my bones from hence.*
>
> **—Genesis 50:25**

> *And the bones of Joseph, which the children of Israel brought up out of Egypt, buried they in Shechem, in a parcel of ground which Jacob bought of the sons of Hamor the father of Shechem for an hundred pieces of silver: and it became the inheritance of the children of Joseph.*
>
> **—Joshua 24:32**

By faith Joseph, when he died, made mention of the departing of the children of Israel; and gave commandment concerning his bones.

—Hebrews 11:22

So here we find a connection to the Abrahamic covenant made also with Jacob, through whom God would bless the nations. Israel's long awaited Messiah, Jesus of Nazareth, is in the place where there is a silent witness of the *bones of Joseph*, near to the place where Jacob dug a well and even drank of the water. What was called "no-man's land" to the Jews was a very important place to the heart of Jesus. This has to be one of the most powerful chapters in the earthly ministry of Jesus!

"Jesus therefore, being wearied with his journey, sat thus on the well: and it was about the sixth hour." What a picture we find here of the two natures of the Messiah! He is about to reveal to a woman of Samaria that He is the God of Jacob and yet He is a Man sitting on Jacob's well. He is tired from walking about thirty miles from Jerusalem. Please don't miss these powerful moments in the life of Jesus when both of His natures are clearly seen. It was about twelve o'clock noon, which was the hottest time of the day.

John 4:7-14 – *There cometh a woman of Samaria to draw water: Jesus saith unto her, Give me to drink. (For his disciples were gone away unto the city to buy meat.) Then saith the woman of Samaria unto him, How is it that thou, being a Jew, askest* *drink of me, which am a woman of Samaria? for the Jews have no dealings with the Samaritans. Jesus answered and said unto her, If thou knewest the gift of God, and who it is that saith to thee, Give me to drink; thou wouldest have asked of him, and he would have given thee living water. The woman saith unto him, Sir, thou hast nothing to draw with, and the well is deep: from whence then hast thou that living water? Art thou greater than our father Jacob, which gave us the well, and drank thereof himself, and his children, and his cattle? Jesus answered and said unto her, Whosoever drinketh of this water shall thirst again: But whosoever drinketh of the water that I shall give him shall never thirst; but the water that I shall give him shall be in him a well of water springing up into everlasting life.*

The fact that this nameless woman of Samaria came to draw water in the middle of the day tells us that she probably didn't want to be there either in the early morning or late evening when other women normally came to draw water. However, there could be a correlation of the *sixth hour* with the time that Rachel brought her sheep to be watered in the middle of the day, at *high day,* in **Genesis 29:6-9**. But more important, is that God had ordained the time and Jesus knew the exact moment that the woman would come to draw water.

"Give me to drink." What humility we see here in Jesus! He is asking a woman of Samaria for a *drink of water?* Jesus

knew that this act of humility would be able to start a conversation that would forever change this woman's life.

"(For his disciples were gone away unto the city to buy meat.)" The Jews believed that even the food of Gentiles was unclean. By staying at the well in order to talk with this strange woman, Jesus was not only crossing all Jewish customary lines of His day, but he was also breaking down the paradigms that were in the minds of His disciples.

"How is it that thou, being a Jew, askest drink of me, which am a woman of Samaria?" This woman recognized Jesus as being a Jew because of His traditional Jewish clothing and His accent. It is believed that their conversation was spoken in Hebrew because the Samaritans also spoke a Hebrew dialect that was similar to the Old Testament, *Paleo-Hebrew.*

"Jesus answered and said unto her, If thou knewest the gift of God, and who it is that saith to thee, Give me to drink; thou wouldest have asked of him, and he would have given thee living water." Jesus is simply saying: *If you only knew who you were talking to, you would ask Him for living water, or mayim chayim.* At this moment, the woman didn't know *who* she was talking to, she thought He was just a weary Jewish traveler passing through. If I may leave the context for just a moment and say: If people today only knew *who* Jesus really is, they would *ask* Him for *salvation* and He would graciously give them eternal life!

"The woman saith unto him, Sir, thou hast nothing to draw with, and the well is deep: from whence then hast thou that living water?" Not only did Jesus humble himself to be thirsty and ask for a drink of water from this woman, Jesus didn't

even have a bucket to draw with. It helps us to understand that, in Bible times, when a person was going on a journey, they did not carry clay or wooden water pots that are seen in religious pictures. But they would carry a *leather* bucket that was probably made out of goatskins that could be folded or rolled up when not filled with water. Evidently, the disciples of Jesus had the *leather* bucket and Jesus was left at the well without any vessel to draw with. The woman probably had a *leather* bucket as well because it would be much easier on the top of her head or unbreakable when she carried the water.

"...*the well is deep: from whence then hast thou that living water?*" I had the wonderful and rare privilege of going to Jacob's well in Samaria on one of our Israel trips. What an awesome experience it was! The kind Christian man who guards the Greek Orthodox Church that was built over Jacob's well, told us that the well is 120 ft. *deep*. He poured a cup of water down the well so we could hear how long it took before the water hit the bottom. The woman was of course thinking only of the *physical water* like Nicodemus was only thinking of the *physical birth*. The Samaritan woman could not understand how Jesus could get this *living water* out of such a *deep* well.

"*Art thou greater than our father Jacob, which gave us the well, and drank thereof himself, and his children, and his cattle?*" Little did the woman know that she was talking to the God of Abraham, Isaac, and Jacob! Yes, He was *greater than their father Jacob*! What a question! Especially when you think about Jesus being the fulfillment of Jacob's ladder that He alluded to back in **John 1:51** to Nathanael.

"Jesus answered and said unto her, Whosoever drinketh of this water shall thirst again: But whosoever drinketh of the water that I shall give him shall never thirst; but the water that I shall give him shall be in him a well of water springing up into everlasting life." There was a real, spiritual thirst inside of this woman. How marvelous it is to see how Jesus took a simple need of drinking physical water and used it as a metaphor for internalizing the Holy Spirit of God! And notice that Jesus uses the word *whosoever* again. Jesus is letting this woman know that she is not excluded from the invitation. Jesus used the word *whosoever* while talking to the religious ruler Nicodemus in **John 3:15-16** to show him that eternal life was not just limited to the Jewish people and here He uses the word again to show even further that He meant what He said. *Whosoever* means even the hated Samaritans! Wow!

> **John 4:15-19** – *The woman saith unto him, Sir, give me this water, that I thirst not, neither come hither to draw. Jesus saith unto her, Go, call thy husband, and come hither. The woman answered and said, I have no husband. Jesus said unto her, Thou hast well said, I have no husband: For thou hast had five husbands; and he whom thou now hast is not thy husband: in that saidst thou truly. The woman saith unto him, Sir, I perceive that thou art a prophet.*

70

"Jesus saith unto her, go, call thy husband, and come hither."
When the woman told Jesus to give her the *living water*,
Jesus told her to call her husband. This Jesus did, not to
condemn her, but to let her know that He knew everything
about her. It has been assumed all these years that this
woman of Samaria was a very immoral woman. She may
have been but, to be honest, we do not know. If she was so
terribly bad then, how did she have such a good influence
within the community in **John 4:29-30**? Could it be
possible that this depressed, emotionally alienated poor
woman could have been a victim of five divorces? Maybe
it was because of her inability to have children, or because
some of her husbands had died. It was not normal in that
day for woman to initiate divorce, but it was common for
men to divorce their wives for trivial reasons. Maybe the
man she was living with was not her boyfriend; maybe it
was someone who could help provide for her, possibly a
distant relative. Whatever the case may be, there is one
thing for sure: Jesus was not nailing this woman to the cross
of His moral standards. He was talking with her in order
to let her know that He was all-knowing. He came to give
her *living water* and a new life with purpose and meaning.

*"The woman saith unto him, Sir, I perceive that thou art a
prophet."* In the mind of this woman, Jesus goes from being
just a *Jew,* to *Sir,* and now she calls Him a *prophet.* She sees
that Jesus knows all about her life and He must be a *prophet.*
I think this woman is beginning to feel safe with Jesus don't
you? I believe the look in His eyes was a look of mercy

and compassion. Because the Samaritans were such strong believers in the Torah, this verse comes to mind:

> The LORD thy God will raise up unto thee a Prophet from the midst of thee, of thy brethren, like unto me; unto him ye shall hearken.
>
> —**Deut.18:15**

> Our fathers worshipped in this mountain; and ye say, that in Jerusalem is the place where men ought to worship. Jesus saith unto her, Woman, believe me, the hour cometh, when ye shall neither in this mountain, nor yet at Jerusalem, worship the Father. Ye worship ye know not what: we know what we worship: for salvation is of the Jews. But the hour cometh, and now is, when the true worshippers shall worship the Father in spirit and in truth: for the Father seeketh such to worship him. God is a Spirit: and they that worship him must worship him in spirit and in truth.
>
> —**John 4:20-24**

The conversation so drastically shifts to the subject of comparing the place where the Samaritans worshipped, *Mt. Gerizim* in Samaria, and the place where the Jews worshiped, *Mt. Zion* in Jerusalem. Jesus quickly shifts the focus to the new order of worship that Jesus was bringing about, *true worship*. Jesus clearly was breaking the Samaritan/Judean divide by telling this woman that it's not about Jerusalem; it's not about Shechem; it's all about believing in Him!

"...for salvation is of the Jews." This is one of the most striking statements that Jesus ever made. The gospels portray the religious establishment in Jerusalem as unbelievers for the most part. The gospels also give us a world of verses about the Jews in Jerusalem rejecting Jesus as their Messiah. So what could Jesus mean when He says, "for salvation is of the Jews?" Regarding the argument between the Samaritans and the Jews, Jesus takes the side of the Jews. God's covenant was with Israel and the Savior of the world would come through the tribe of Judah and through the house of David. Just because there was a sub-group in Israel that did not believe in Jesus as the Messiah, did not change the everlasting covenant that God gave to Abraham. I am reminded of this powerful prophecy:

> *The sceptre shall not depart from Judah, nor a lawgiver from between his feet, until Shiloh come; and unto him shall the gathering of the people be.*
> **—Genesis 49:10**

The time had finally arrived for *Shiloh,* another description of the Messiah, to come! This Samaritan woman is going to be an example that He has come to gather the people together. God's kingdom would not be filled with prejudice, hatred, and condemnation of other races and other people.

"God is a spirit: and they that worship him must worship him in spirit and in truth." Connecting this with the story of

Nicodemus, in order for someone to worship God in spirit and in truth, they must be born of the Spirit. (**John 3:8**) The Samaritan woman believed in the written Torah of the Hebrew scripture and now she had been chosen to be face to face with the living Word, Yeshua the Messiah! It's not about the place. It's all about the heart! After the woman hears about worship she says something very interesting.

> **John 4:25-26** – *The woman saith unto him, I know that Messias cometh, which is called Christ: when he is come, he will tell us all things. Jesus saith unto her, I that speak unto thee am he.*

This woman believed in the coming Messiah! There was something in her heart that was pure! There was a real faith waiting to come alive in this woman! Maybe she thought that bringing up the truth about the coming Messiah would end the conversation. The only person who could say anything after that statement would be the Messiah himself, and He did!

"Jesus saith unto her, I that speak unto thee am he." Don't you find it strange that Jesus suppresses His identity among His own people in Jerusalem and Galilee but, here in Samaria, He reveals himself! He declares *I am the Messiah*! This is one of the "I am" statements of Jesus that is overlooked. How highly favored this Samaritan woman was to come to Jacob's well just at the right time! How highly favored she was to be introduced to the Messiah of Israel face to face!

She saw His face, she heard His voice, she felt His love, and she would never be the same!

> **John 4:27-34** - *And upon this came his disciples, and marvelled that he talked with the woman: yet no man said, What seekest thou? or, Why talkest thou with her? The woman then left her waterpot, and went her way into the city, and saith to the men, Come, see a man, which told me all things that ever I did: is not this the Christ? Then they went out of the city, and came unto him. In the mean while his disciples prayed him, saying, Master, eat. But he said unto them, I have meat to eat that ye know not of. Therefore said the disciples one to another, Hath any man brought him ought to eat? Jesus saith unto them, My meat is to do the will of him that sent me, and to finish his work.*

The disciples returned and could not believe that Jesus was talking to not just a woman, but to a Samaritan woman. By this time, they had already heard and seen enough to know better than to ask Him any questions. They brought Jesus something to eat, but He said to them, "I have meat to eat that ye know not of... My meat is to do the will of him that sent me, and to finish his work." Jesus uses the metaphors of *water* and *food*, to talk about *salvation* and *the will of God*. Jesus had already rebuked Satan by saying, "Man shall not live by bread alone," in **Matt. 4:1-4**. It was the Father's will for Jesus the Son of God to meet this Samaritan woman in the middle of the day.

"The woman left her waterpot, and went her way into the city, and saith to the men, Come, see a man, which told me all things ever I did: is not this the Christ?" The woman had told Jesus earlier that He didn't have a bucket. Now she forgets all about her bucket because she has tasted of the *living water* from Jesus! She has to run and tell somebody!

"…which told me all things ever I did." The English wording here is a little misleading. She would not have gone back to the city and talked about all of her sexual immorality, as we assume she did. It's better understood to say: *this man knows all about my life.* The entire life of the woman was known by Jesus. Sometimes our own presuppositions get in the way of properly understanding a passage of scripture. The people came running to Jesus!

> **John 4:35-39** - *Say not ye, There are yet four months, and then cometh harvest? behold, I say unto you, Lift up your eyes, and look on the fields; for they are white already to harvest. And he that reapeth receiveth wages, and gathereth fruit unto life eternal: that both he that soweth and he that reapeth may rejoice together. And herein is that saying true, One soweth, and another reapeth. I sent you to reap that whereon ye bestowed no labour: other men laboured, and ye are entered into their labours.*

Timing this chapter with the month of June fits well into the times of harvest in Israel. The wheat was already topping white and ripe for harvest. But the orchards and the vineyards would be four months later, in September. It is also believed that the Samaritans that would have been running to Jesus would have been dressed in white. So the fields were *white already unto harvest.* The fields that were ripe were the Samaritans, not just the Jews. He was teaching tem to think outside their traditional box. Jesus was telling His disciples to not wait because the Kingdom of God is here! *The harvest truly is plenteous, but the labourers are few.* (**Matt.9:37**)

"*And herein is that saying true, One soweth, and another reapeth. I sent you to reap that whereon ye bestowed no labour: other men labored, and ye are entered into their labours.*" The prophets of old had labored and the disciples were seeing the harvest. Jesus the Messiah had labored while the disciples were gone and they were getting to rejoice in the harvest. A good spiritual application for us here is that we shouldn't desire any credit for what God does. The results that we may see are probably the results of someone else's labors. Some plant, some water, but God gives the increase. We are just the "water-boys.' It's all about the precious Lord!

John 4:39-42 - *And many of the Samaritans of that city believed on him for the saying of the woman, which testified, He told me all that ever I did. So when the Samaritans were come unto him, they besought him that he would tarry with*

77

them: and he abode there two days. And many more
believed because of his own word; And said unto the
woman, Now we believe, not because of thy saying:
for we have heard him ourselves, and know that this
is indeed the Christ, the Saviour of the world.

Salvation came to the world through the Jews, but salvation was not for just the Jews. The revival lasted for several days and many more people of the city believed in Jesus as their Savior. Now, think about what a short time that Jesus had to fulfill His mission on earth, and here He stays *two more days.* It seems as though the disciples went back to Galilee and this separation in Samaria helps to explain why Jesus later calls the *same* disciples to *follow Him,* **Matt.4:18–22, Mark 1:16–20, Luke 5:2–11,** as we see in the synoptic gospels. This episode in Samaria was a mighty strong lesson for them to swallow and they would need to be called again.

"...for we have heard him ourselves, and know that this is indeed the Christ, the Saviour of the world." When the apostle John was writing this gospel, he was living in primarily a Gentile Christian community in Ephesus. Try to imagine how this brought great encouragement to them, knowing that Jesus was also the Savior of the world, not just of the Jews. There was a temple in Sebastia, just a few miles away from Shechem, built by Herod the Great to honor Caesar. One of the titles for Caesar was *Savior of the world* in a pagan context. But Caesar wasn't the real *Savior of the world,* Jesus was! This title encompasses the Gentile word as well as Israel.

Before we leave this all-important section of scripture,

we need to see that Jesus went from being a tired, weary *Jew*, to *Sir*, to *prophet*, to *Messiah*, to *I am*, to *Savior of the world* – all in this one chapter. Jesus, the Messiah of Israel, was the fulfillment of the covenant that God had given to Abraham, Isaac, *and* Jacob. That unconditional covenant would include *whosoever believes in Jesus!*

The Samaritan woman was identified in 47 AD. Her name was Phonita, and she was considered equal to the apostles. She led her sisters and two sons to Jesus. She led countless other people to Jesus and, after being shipped to Rome, she led Nero's daughter, Domnina, and all of her servants to Jesus. Nero became so angry that he had Phonita thrown to her death into a well in 66 AD. He chose this method of execution because she was always telling others how she met Jesus at a well.

JESUS LEAVES SAMARIA

John 4:43-45 – *Now after two days he departed thence, and went into Galilee. For Jesus himself testified, that a prophet hath no honour in his own country. Then when he was come into Galilee, the Galileans received him, having seen all the things that he did at Jerusalem at the feast: for they also went unto the feast.*

"...that a prophet hath no honour in his own country." Again, the apostle John is showing that Jesus was not well accepted in Judea, but was generally received in the Galilee. The synoptic gospels mention that Jesus mentioned a prophet not receiving honor when He was in Nazareth, in **Matt.13:54–57, Mark 6:1-4**, and **Luke 4:23-24**. Here John's gospel is referring to the Messiah not receiving honor from His *fatherland*, Judea (notice again - **John 4:1)**. Jesus was born in Bethlehem of Judea and the temple in Jerusalem was where the religious Jews were supposed to be worshipping the God of Israel. But, because of the corruptness of the Sadducees and the man-made traditions of the Pharisees, they were blinded to the time of their visitation. This also connects back to **John 1:11**, where it says: "He came unto His own, and his own received Him not."

Many of the Galileans, who came down to Jerusalem for the feasts, saw many of the miracles that Jesus did and they, in turn, received Him gladly. These strange paradoxical themes of rejection vs. receiving and Judea vs. Galilee are the backdrop of many of the miracles and parables throughout the ministry of Jesus.

> **John 4:46–54 -** *So Jesus came again into Cana of Galilee, where he made the water wine. And there was a certain nobleman, whose son was sick at Capernaum. When he heard that Jesus was come out of Judaea into Galilee, he went unto him, and besought him that he would come down, and heal his son: for he was at the point of death. Then said Jesus unto him, Except ye see signs and wonders, ye will not believe. The nobleman saith unto him, Sir, come down ere my child die. Jesus saith unto*

him, Go thy way; thy son liveth. And the man believed the word that Jesus had spoken unto him, and he went his way. And as he was now going down, his servants met him, and told him, saying, Thy son liveth. Then enquired he of them the hour when he began to amend. And they said unto him, Yesterday at the seventh hour the fever left him. So the father knew that it was at the same hour, in the which Jesus said unto him, Thy son liveth: and himself believed, and his whole house. This is again the second miracle that Jesus did, when he was come out of into Galilee.

"...where he made the water wine." The first miracle of Jesus was so powerful that John mentions it again when Jesus comes back to Cana. It would have taken at least a couple of days to walk from Samaria to Cana.

"And there was a certain nobleman, whose son was sick at Capernaum." Here a government official from Capernaum had walked close to twenty miles to see Jesus about his son. I find it very interesting that Jesus showed favor to three important people in Capernaum:

- *A nobleman -* **John 4:46**
- *A Roman centurion -* **Luke 7:2**
- *The ruler of the synagogue -* **Luke 8:41**

When we study everyday Jewish life in Galilee in Jesus' time, we find that there was a strong customary attitude of *reciprocity*: *If you help me, I will help you.* We have that attitude in our world today, but not as strong as it was in villages like Capernaum. So, because Jesus showed favor to these three different classes of people, He was given the returned favor of being allowed to live in Capernaum and have His headquarters there. He only needed about three and a half years to fulfill His mission. Jesus of Nazareth would also use common sense and move from Herod Antipas' territory in the western Galilee to Herod's Philip territory in the northeastern upper Galilee as the religious and political pressures mounted. This is not to say that Jesus the Son of God had to have any help, but that He humbled Himself to live among His people and to be subject to the customs of and attitudes of His day. The Holy Spirit, through John, wanted us to know that the first and second miracle that Jesus performed after he left Judea and entered into Galilee were both at Cana.

CHAPTER FIVE

John 5:1-9 - *After this there was a feast of the Jews; and Jesus went up to Jerusalem. Now there is at Jerusalem by the sheep market a pool, which is called in the Hebrew tongue Bethesda, having five porches. In these lay a great multitude of impotent folk, of blind, halt, withered, waiting for the moving of the water. For an angel went down at a certain season into the pool, and troubled the water: whosoever then first after the troubling of the water stepped in was made whole of whatsoever disease he had. And a certain man was there, which had an infirmity thirty and eight years. When Jesus saw him lie, and knew that he had been now a long time in that case, he saith unto him, Wilt thou be made whole? The impotent man answered him, Sir, I have no man, when the water is troubled, to put me into the pool: but while I am coming, another steppeth down before me. Jesus saith unto him, Rise, take up thy* *bed, and walk. And immediately the man was made whole, and took up his bed, and walked: and on the same day was the sabbath.*

"After this there was a feast of the Jews; and Jesus went up to Jerusalem." John was not writing his gospel to readers with a traditional, western-world mindset. Rather he was writing within a community that celebrated *Jewish Feasts*. If the gospel of John follows a chronological order then this feast would have been the Feast of Tabernacles. But chronology does not seem to be a high priority for John.

"Now there is at Jerusalem by the sheep market a pool, which is called in the Hebrew tongue, Bethesda, having five porches." *Bethesda* comes from two Hebrew words: *beit* for *house* and *chesed* for *mercy*. So it means the *house of mercy*. It is believed to be the same "upper pool," that is mentioned in **Isaiah 7:3** and **Isaiah 36:2**. I find it interesting that, within the context of **Isaiah 7**, faithless Ahaz refused to ask God for a sign to verify the word of the Lord from Isaiah. This is when Isaiah wrote the sign of the virgin birth in **Isaiah 7:14**. This sign was not given only to Ahaz, but to the entire house of David. The prophecy would later be fulfilled in Mary, who was from the house of David. Now the *Messiah Immanuel* has come to this upper pool where Isaiah and Ahaz had met seven hundred years prior.

The Bethesda pool was a double pool and served as the main water supply for the Temple Mount. In 1956, archaeologists found these double pools along with four porticoes and a fifth portico separating the upper pool from the lower pool. The archaeological find sits next to the Church of St. Anne, in Old City Jerusalem. In the process of uncovering the pools, they also found something very significant that relates back to the miracle: the 3rd century remains of a temple to *Asclepius*, the Greco-Roman god of healing. But the foundations of the temple were from an earlier temple to *Asclepius* dating back to Jesus' time. This helps to explain the reason for the five porches because, in Greek mythology, *Asclepius* had five daughters; two of which were Hygeia and Panacea. Snakes were connected to the cult and that is why we have snakes on a pole used as the symbol of modern medicine in our culture today.

There were over 400 *Asclepions* in the Roman empire. It is recorded in some rabbinical and historical writings that one of these pagan temples was in Jerusalem. So, from Isaiah's time, the pool was known as a house of mercy but, when Alexander the Great Hellenized Jerusalem, the pools became a place of pagan worship. So here we have a Hebrew name of a place, *Bethesda*, but probably a Greco-Roman *Asclepion* in the time of Jesus.

The crippled and blind would gather around this pagan site and wait for *an angel to come down and trouble the water.* This believed to have happened when the cultic priests would release the water from connecting pipes of the upper pool down to the lower pool and it would cause a stirring of the water. It was the pagan tradition that *whosoever stepped into the water first after the troubling of the water would be healed.*

"And a certain man was there, which had an infirmity thirty and eight years." Here is a picture of hopelessness! He had

been crippled for thirty-eight years and was trusting in a pagan god of healing. We need to also mention the importance of Jesus choosing to come to this pool during a Jewish feast because He knew this poor man would be there.

"When Jesus saw him lie, and knew that he had been now a long time in that case, he saith unto him, Wilt thou be made whole? The impotent man answered him, Sir, I have no man, when the water is troubled, to put me into the pool: but while I am coming, another steppeth down before me. Jesus saith unto him, Rise, take up thy bed, and walk." When the all-seeing eyes of Jesus saw the man lying around the pool, He asked the poor man if he wanted to *really* be made *whole*. The man was still focused on the troubling of the water and somebody helping him to get into the pool. Notice that Jesus did not demand faith from this poor man at this point because He knew the strong grip that the long-running *Asclepion* cult had on his mind Jesus knew that it needed to be revealed to this man that *Asclepius* could not heal anyone, but Israel's Messiah had power over all diseases! Jesus simply just spoke the word, "Rise, take up thy bed, and walk." It's interesting that Jesus told the man to do something that was prohibited by the religious traditions of the day. Jesus did not ask the man to wash in the pool, like He later told the blind man in **John 9**. The power in the words of Jesus was the same power that spoke creation into existence in **Genesis 1**.

"And immediately the man was made whole, and took up his bed, and walked: and on the same day was the sabbath." The power of the word of Israel's Messiah brought about

immediate healing! The man rolled up his bed and began to walk. Jesus deliberately healed this man on the Jewish Sabbath. Why?

> **John 5:10-13** - *The Jews therefore said unto him that was cured, It is the sabbath day: it is not lawful for thee to carry thy bed. He answered them, He that made me whole, the same said unto me, Take up thy bed, and walk. Then asked they him, What man is that which said unto thee, Take up thy bed, and walk? And he that was healed wist not who it was: for Jesus had conveyed himself away, a multitude being in that place.*

Within the realm of the rabbinical *halachah* (Talmudic interpretations of the law) it was not permitted to carry anything on the Sabbath day. But Jesus is not only going against the religious traditions of the day, He is also showing that there was nothing in the original definition of the Sabbath day that would prevent anyone from being healed, taking up his bed, and walking. We do not know if it was the Sadducees or the Pharisees but, when they told the man that it was unlawful to carry his bed on the Sabbath day, the man told them that the one who healed him had said that it was okay. So here again we have this background of Israel's Messiah going against some of the religious traditions of the day. At this moment, the man did not know who Jesus was and Jesus had disappeared into the crowd.

> **John 5:14** – *Afterward Jesus findeth him in the temple, and said unto him, Behold, thou art made whole: sin no more, lest a worse thing come unto thee.*

I find this verse to be commonly overlooked, and it holds a lot of interesting truths. It shows that the man was probably Jewish, because he went into the temple compound after he was healed. So Jesus most likely had set *free* a crippled Jewish man who had been led astray by a pagan cult. This would explain the strange response that Jesus gave: "sin no more, lest a worse thing come unto thee." Most of the time, when Jesus met someone who had a disease, it was not the result of his or her sin. But here it seems that this man's sin had contributed to his bad health. In other words: *if you go back into paganism, a worse thing will come upon you.* Can you think of a sin or sins that might result in someone having bad health?

> **John 5:15–18** – *The man departed, and told the Jews that it was Jesus, which had made him whole. And therefore did the Jews persecute Jesus, and sought to slay him, because he had done these things on the sabbath day. But Jesus answered them, My Father worketh hitherto, and I work. Therefore the Jews sought the more to kill him, because he not only had broken the sabbath, but said also that God was his Father, making himself equal with God.*

Look at the contrast: the man tells the Jews that it was Jesus who had healed him and then the Jews *persecute* Jesus.

Not only did they persecute Jesus, they also wanted to kill him because He had gone to a pagan temple site outside the walls of Jerusalem and also because He had broken their Sabbath *traditions*. Jesus the Messiah had found one of the lost sheep of the house of Israel and set him free on the Sabbath day and the religious leaders wanted to kill Jesus for it! But there is something deeper here. They really wanted to kill Jesus because He was healing people in Jerusalem like He had done in the Galilee. This caused a tremendous threat to the establishment and they were afraid of losing their positions of authority over the people. But there is still a deeper meaning of why they wanted to kill Jesus. Listen to the words of Jesus carefully: "My Father worketh hitherto, and I work." Jesus is putting himself on the same level as God! God rested on the seventh day during creation, but He continued to work every Sabbath day in the lives of His people. What about a baby who was born on the Sabbath day? What if the eighth day for circumcision landed on the Sabbath day? What about God protecting His people from evil on the Sabbath day? God was still working and so was Jesus.

An alternate understanding of this passage from the Jewish perspective is that Judaism recognizes the present era of history as *weekdays*. They divide history into six 1,000-year *days* (**Psalm 90:4**) and there is a *"Shabbat"* that is coming when the Messiah will reign in the Messianic kingdom, which will be the *seventh day*. While the following passage refers to the present *rest* that believers have in Jesus, the unbelieving Jew interprets it to be talking about the future rest.

> *There remaineth therefore a rest to the people of God. For he that is entered into his rest, he also hath ceased from his own works, as God did from his. Let us labour therefore to enter into that rest, lest any man fall after the same example of unbelief.*
> **—Hebrews 4:9-11**

But the Father and the Son will continue to work until the *day* comes when it will be the ultimate *Sabbath* in the one thousand-year reign of the Messiah. The anger that these religious leaders were showing was a perfect example of what Jesus had warned His followers about back in Galilee - **Matthew 5:31-32:**

> *Ye have heard that it was said of them of old time, Thou shalt not kill; and whosoever shall kill shall be in danger of the judgment: But I say unto you, That whosoever is angry with his brother without a cause shall be in danger of the judgment: and whosoever shall say to his brother, Raca, shall be in danger of the council: but whosoever shall say, Thou fool, shall be in danger of hell fire.*

This whole idea of Jesus breaking the Sabbath day is so ludicrous. Why would Jesus break His own law? The work of Jesus would not end until He had accomplished redemption for His people. His own resurrection would be on what day? The day *after* the Sabbath day, bringing about another new order! All who placed their faith in Jesus as the Son of God would be set free from the religious bondage of men!

The Jews would accept the fact that Jesus was a great teacher, even a miracle worker, but they could not accept the fact that Jesus was equal with God. This claim that Jesus made was followed by the very first reported effort of the religious establishment to kill Jesus. Remembering that they only had the Old Testament to read, here is a verse that might shed some light on how they felt. They were accusing Jesus of blasphemy.

And he that blasphemeth the name of the LORD, he shall surely be put to death, and all the congregation shall certainly stone him: as well the stranger, as he that is born in the land, when he blasphemeth the name of the Lord, shall be put to death.

—Leviticus 24:16

John 5:19-27 - *Then answered Jesus and said unto them, Verily, verily, I say unto you, The Son can do nothing of himself, but what he seeth the Father do: for what things soever he doeth, these also doeth the Son likewise. For the Father loveth the Son, and sheweth him all things that himself doeth: and he will shew him greater works than these, that ye may marvel. For as the Father raiseth up the dead, and quickeneth them; even so* *the Son quickeneth whom he will. For the Father judgeth no man, but hath committed all judgment unto the Son: That all men should honour the Son, even as they honour the Father. He that honoureth not the Son honoureth not the Father which hath sent him. Verily, verily, I say unto you, He that heareth my word, and believeth on him that sent me, hath everlasting life, and shall not come into condemnation; but is passed from death unto life. Verily, verily, I say unto you, The hour is coming, and now is, when the dead shall hear the voice of the Son of God: and they that hear shall live. For as the Father hath life in himself; so hath he given to the Son to have life in himself; And hath given him authority to execute judgment also, because he is the Son of man.*

Jesus lived in constant obedience to the Father and this demonstrated the perfection of God. We need to keep in mind the verse in **John 3:34**: "for God giveth not the Spirit by measure unto him." In this unusual passage of **John 5:19-27**, Jesus is simply stating how the *Son* and the *Father* relate to each other within the unity of the triune Godhead. Jesus is also using a Jewish style of teaching here where He begins by stating that He is equal with God, and then continues to make the same claim in a little different way. A good Old Testament example of this Hebrew style of writing is in **Joshua 1:5-9**, when God gives His assurance to Joshua at the beginning and at the end.

Notice several places in this passage where Jesus is equal with the God of the Old Testament:

- *Father raises the dead- Jesus raises the dead* **(vs.21)**
- *God was the judge in the Old Testament - Jesus is now the judge* **(vs.22, 27)**
- *Honour to the Father - Honour to the Son* **(vs.23)**
- *Father gives life- Jesus gives life* **(vs.26)**

Any time Jesus uses the words, *Verily, verily, I say unto you,* three times within seven verses we better pay close attention. The first time in **vs.19**, Jesus is talking about His mysterious vision: what He sees the Father do, those are the things that He does. The second time, in **vs.24**, Jesus is talking about the results of people who believe in Him: they will have everlasting life and not be condemned. The third time, in **vs.25**, He uses the important introduction to talk about the times that He will not only raise the dead during His earthly ministry, but the physical dead will hear His voice on judgment day and shall also live again.

A good parallel passage to help us connect the scriptures together is found in **I John 2:23**:

> *Whosoever denieth the Son, the same hath not the Father: he that acknowledgeth the Son hath the Father also.*

To summarize this all–important literary unit of scripture: the religious Jews hadn't seen anything yet. "The hour is coming." **(vs.25)** Raising the crippled man at the Pool of Bethesda was only a taste of what Jesus would finally accomplish. As the Second Person of the Trinity, the Son of God had come to do the Father's will: to die for the sins of the world and to rise again. Someone once said, "Only <u>God</u> could do something like that!" That is exactly the point that Jesus is making!

> **John 5:28-30** - *Marvel not at this: for the hour is coming, in the which all that are in the graves shall hear his voice, And shall come forth; they that have done good, unto the resurrection of life; and they that have done evil, unto the resurrection of damnation. I can of mine own self do nothing: as I hear, I judge: and my judgment is just; because I seek not mine own will, but the will of the Father which hath sent me.*

There is a constant tension in the gospels between the present *Kingdom of God* that is working in the lives of men, and the future *Kingdom of God* that is coming. So Jesus is taking the thought of the resurrection to an eschatological future. Jesus would refer to this climactic resurrection day again in **John 6:39-40**. It's interesting that Jesus mentions that He is the judge in **vs.22**, and here He states that he will be the judge at the last day. Judgment will be determined upon how people respond to Jesus. Those who have *done good* will be those who accepted Jesus, and those who have *done evil* will be those who rejected Jesus. Read what Paul preached on Mar's Hill in Athens, Greece a little over twenty years later:

> *Because he hath appointed a day, in the which he will judge the world in righteousness by that man whom he hath ordained; whereof he hath given assurance unto all men, in that he hath raised him from the dead.*
>
> **—Acts 17:31.**

Even early during the public ministry of Jesus and His confrontations with the religious leaders, He makes mention of the judgment that is to come. This idea of two resurrections reminds me of passages from the Old Testament and from the New Testament:

> *And many of them that sleep in the dust of the earth shall awake, some to everlasting life, and some to shame and everlasting contempt.*
>
> **—Daniel 12:2.**

> *And I saw thrones, and they sat upon them, and judgment was given unto them: and I saw the souls of them that were beheaded for the witness of Jesus, and for the word of God, and which had not worshipped the beast, neither his image, neither had received his mark upon their foreheads, or in their hands; and they lived and reigned with Christ a thousand years. But the rest of the dead lived not again until the thousand years were finished. This*

is the first resurrection. Blessed and holy is he that hath part in the first resurrection: on such the second death hath no power, but they shall be priests of God and of Christ, and shall reign with him a thousand years.

—**Revelation 20:4-6.**

And I saw the dead, small and great, stand before God; and the books were opened: and another book was opened, which is the book of life: and the dead were judged out of those things which were written in the books, according to their works. And the sea gave up the dead which were in it; and death and hell delivered up the dead which were in them: and they were judged every man according to their works. And death and hell were cast into the lake of fire. This is the second death. And whosoever was not found written in the book of life was cast into the lake of fire.

—**Revelation 20:12-15.**

Let's pick up the John account again:

John 5:31-39 - *If I bear witness of myself, my witness is not true. There is another that beareth witness of me; and I know that the witness which he witnesseth of me is true. Ye sent unto John, and he bare witness unto the truth. But I receive not testimony from man: but these things I say, that ye might be saved. He was a burning and a shining* *light: and ye were willing for a season to rejoice in his light. But I have greater witness than that of John: for the works which the Father hath given me to finish, the same works that I do, bear witness of me, that the Father hath sent me. And the Father himself, which hath sent me, hath borne witness of me. Ye have neither heard his voice at any time, nor seen his shape. And ye have not his word abiding in you: for whom he hath sent, him ye believe not. Search the scriptures; for in them ye think ye have eternal life: and they are they which testify of me.*

"*If I bear witness of myself, my witness is not true.*" Jesus, being a Jew in the flesh, knows the Jewish mind of the religious leaders. This idea of being a witness takes us back to **Deuteronomy 19:15:**

One witness shall not rise up against a man for any iniquity, or for any sin, in any sin that he sinneth: at the mouth of two witnesses, or at the mouth of three witnesses, shall the matter be established.

Jesus doesn't just give three more *witnesses* of Himself. He gives five:

- *John the Baptist –*   **vs.33–35**
- *Jesus' miracles –*   **vs.36**
- *The Father –*   **vs.37–38**
- *The Scriptures –*   **vs.39**
- *Moses –*   **vs.45–47**

When it comes to *searching the scriptures*, the Old Testament has hundreds of prophecies about the coming Messiah. The scriptures of the Torah, the Prophets, and the Psalms, all were filled with verses talking about Israel's Messiah. This is how Jesus explained who He was. (**Luke 24:44**) The religious Jews in Judea claimed to be experts on the sacred scriptures, but they didn't know the scriptures very well. There were three major messianic prophecies that *even* the non-Messianic Jews all regarded as referring to the Messiah:

> *The sceptre shall not depart from Judah, nor a lawgiver from between his feet, until Shiloh come; and unto him shall the gathering of the people be.*
> **—Genesis 49:10.**

> *I shall see him, but not now: I shall behold him, but not nigh: there shall come a Star out of Jacob, and a Sceptre shall rise out of Israel, and shall smite the corners of Moab, and destroy all the children of Sheth.*
> **—Numbers 24:17.**

> *The LORD thy God will raise up unto thee a Prophet from the midst of thee, of thy brethren, like unto me; unto him ye shall hearken; According to all that thou desiredst of the LORD thy God in Horeb in the day of the assembly, saying, Let me not hear again the voice of the LORD my God, neither let me see this great fire any more, that I die not. And*

the LORD said unto me, They have well spoken that which they have spoken. I will raise them up a Prophet from among their brethren, like unto thee, and will put my words in his mouth; and he shall speak unto them all that I shall command him.

—**Deut.18:15-18.**

John's gospel continues:

John 5:40-47 - *And ye will not come to me, that ye might have life. I receive not honour from men. But I know you, that ye have not the love of God in you. I am come in my Father's name, and ye receive me not: if another shall come in his own name, him ye will receive. How can ye believe, which receive honour one of another, and seek not the honour that cometh from God only? Do not think that I will accuse you to the Father: there is one that accuseth you, even Moses, in whom ye trust. For had ye believed Moses, ye would have believed me; for he wrote of me. But if ye believe not his writings, how shall ye believe my words?*

Notice that Jesus places the responsibility upon the people to *come* to Him. Our Calvinist friends would have us to believe that man has no choice and that everything has been pre-determined. Almighty God knows everything and He knows who the saved will be and who the lost will be, but the scriptures reveal that He desires for *all* to be saved. (**John**

1:7,9, John 3:16-17, Rom. 10:13, I Tim. 2:4, 2 Peter 3:9). People can be saved when the Holy Spirit, primarily through the preached word, draws them. (**Rom. 10:17**) But the Holy Spirit can be rejected as Stephen preached to the religious Jews in Jerusalem in **Acts 7:51.**

There are six negative things that Jesus says about these religious leaders in Jerusalem:

- *Ye will not come to me* – **vs.40**
- *Ye have not the love of God in you* – **vs.42**
- *Ye receive me not* – **vs.43**
- *If another comes in his own name, him ye will receive* – **vs.43**
- *Receive honour one of another* – **vs.44**
- *They did not believe the writings of Moses* – **vs.46–47**

Again, there seems to be this overarching contrast of the Jews in Judea who rejected Jesus and the Galilean Jews who received Jesus. The religious establishment was so bent on keeping their man-made traditions that they missed their Messiah. At the same time, the not-so-religious Jews from Galilee, the *people of the land*, received Jesus with open arms. The Jews in Jerusalem would sometimes believe the writings of some famous rabbi or some wicked priest and they sought honor for themselves. If the religious Jews in Jerusalem did not believe Moses (although they claimed they did), they would not believe even though one rose from the dead. (**Luke 16:31**)

CHAPTER SIX

John 6:1-15 – *After these things Jesus went over the sea of Galilee, which is the sea of Tiberias. And a great multitude followed him, because they saw his miracles which he did on them that were diseased. And Jesus went up into a mountain, and there he sat with his disciples. And the passover, a feast of the Jews, was nigh. When Jesus then lifted up his eyes, and saw a great company come unto him, he saith unto Philip, Whence shall we buy bread, that these may eat? And this he said to prove him: for he himself knew what he would do. Philip answered him, Two hundred pennyworth of bread is not sufficient for them, that every one of them may take a little. One of his disciples, Andrew, Simon Peter's brother, saith unto him, There is a lad here, which hath five barley loaves, and two small fishes: but what are they among so many? And Jesus said, Make the men sit down. Now there was much grass* *in the place. So the men sat down, in number about five thousand. And Jesus took the loaves; and when he had given thanks, he distributed to the disciples, and the disciples to them that were set down; and likewise of the fishes as much as they would. When they were filled, he said unto his disciples, Gather up the fragments that remain, that nothing be lost. Therefore they gathered them together, and filled twelve baskets with the fragments of the five barley loaves, which remained over and above unto them that had eaten. Then those men, when they had seen the miracle that Jesus did, said, This is of a truth that prophet that should come into the world. When Jesus therefore perceived that they would come and take him by force, to make him a king, he departed again into a mountain himself alone.*

In **John 6**, we find the very first time that John's gospel parallels the synoptic gospels. The feeding of the five thousand is recorded in all four gospels. However, John's account gives us some unusual and different points of interest. This shows us that John did not have to copy from the other gospels. He was there when it all happened. To show the importance of this miracle of Jesus, John's gospel includes it, even though he is more focused on the Judean ministry of the Messiah. There are a lot of miracles in the other gospels that occurred in Galilee that John does not mention, but he records the feeding of the five thousand.

On a personal note, every time we travel to Israel this

miracle seems to stand out to me as one of monumental importance. I think as we go through this chapter you will see why this miracle is recorded in all four gospels. But John is the only one to really explain the deeper meaning of the miracle. I always read the miracle from John's gospel when we are on location in Israel. I have done a lot of archaeological studies on the possible sites where this miracle happened. I seem to differ with many of the scholars on the location. Some say it happened at the southern end of the Sea of Galilee. Some say that it took place on the northern shore close to the Mt. of Beatitudes. According to **Luke 9:10**, the miracle took place across the lake at a place called *Bethsaida*, the hometown of *Peter, Andrew,* and *Philip.* (**John 1:44**) Some scholars think that *James* and *John* were from *Bethsaida* originally, and later moved to Capernaum. *Bethsaida* (which means *house of fishing* or *house of hunting*) was a fishing village in Jesus' time. It was later lifted to the place of a *polis*, or city, by Herod Philip, the tetrarch on that region (**Luke 3:1**) in 30-31 AD and re-named *Bethsaida-Julias.* Herod Philip, trying to gain favor with Tiberius Caesar in Rome, named the city after *Julias*, the daughter of Augustus Caesar who died in 14 AD, and in honor of *Livia*, the wife of Augustus who had just died in 29 AD. The ruins of *Bethsaida-Julias* were discovered on the northeastern shore between 1994–1996, a little less than a mile from the present-day shoreline. Tremendous earthquakes over the centuries shifted the course of the Jordan River more to the west and the filling-in of silt over the last two thousand years has caused confusion and different opinions about the exact place. This archaeological find is not visited by a lot of the groups who come to Galilee but I think it is one of the most interesting places. I mentioned all of this because there is a large grassy mountain that lies just north of the ruins, which could possibly be the mountain where Jesus fed the multitude. Every year when we go there, I can just visualize thousands and thousands of people sitting on the side of that mountain. The soil samples from just below the mountain revealed that water came up all the way to the bottom of the mountain in Jesus' time.

We know about there being about *five thousand men,* and that it was in the springtime because there was *much grass in the place.* It is also recorded in the other gospels that it would have taken *200 denarii,* (Over half of a year's wages) to feed the multitude. The other gospels tell us about the twelve baskets that were left over. But some of the different points that John records for us are:

- *The Sea of Galilee is also called the Sea of Tiberias.* - **vs.1**
- *The Passover, a feast of the Jews, was nigh,* (first part of April) *which adds even deeper meaning to the bread and Jesus being the Bread of Life, the true Passover lamb.* - **vs.4**
- *Jesus had conversations with Philip and Andrew.* - **vs.5–9**
- *A small boy is mentioned who had the five loaves and two fishes.* - **vs.9**
- *It was barley loaves, the poorest means of bread.* - **vs.9, 13**
- *Jesus gave the command to "Gather up the fragments that remain, that nothing be lost."* - **vs.12**

- *The men thought that Jesus was that prophet Moses wrote about in **Deut.18:15**, which connects us back to the subject of Moses in **John 5:46–47**,- **vs.14***
- *The multitude wanted to take Jesus by force and make him a king, because they were expecting a conquering Messiah to set them free from Roman oppression. - **vs.15***

I think that it is significant to mention that the Greek word for *fishes* is *opsarion*, which means *small, salted, or pickled fish.* This is the very same word for fish that is used in the last miracle of **John 21** when the risen Jesus prepared breakfast for the disciples on the shore of Galilee. John was probably referring to the small fish in the lake that the Jews call *lavnun,* in the Hebrew tongue. It's also significant that the Greek word for *baskets* is *kophinos,* which means *small baskets.* The Jews used the smaller baskets and the Gentiles used the larger size baskets. This tells us that it was primarily a *Jewish* crowd that day.

One of the important symbolisms of the miracle is that Jesus told them to "Gather up the fragments that remain, that nothing be lost," and they filled *twelve* leftover baskets. The twelve is no doubt connected to the *twelve* tribes of Israel that came from the patriarch Jacob in **Genesis 49**. The *twelve* gates in the New Jerusalem will be named after the *twelve* tribes of Israel. (**Ezek.49:31–34, Rev.21:12**) Jesus the Messiah would provide salvation that would be sufficient for any member of any tribe of Israel.

Jesus created bread without planting or harvesting barley. Jesus created fish without having to go fishing in the Sea of Galilee. It was truly a miracle from the Creator of heaven and earth. One has to wonder how many of those who were in the crowd that day became true followers of our Lord.

JESUS WALKS UPON THE SEA

> **John 6:16-21** - *And when even was now come, his disciples went down unto the sea, And entered into a ship, and went over the sea toward Capernaum. And it was now dark, and Jesus was not come to them. And the sea arose by reason of a great wind that blew. So when they had rowed about five and twenty or thirty furlongs, they see Jesus walking on the sea, and drawing nigh unto the ship: and they were afraid. But he saith unto them, It is I; be not afraid. Then they willingly received him into the ship: and immediately the ship was at the land whither they went.*

We must not miss the truth that John is conveying to his readers in the first century that Jesus of Nazareth is more than just a carpenter, the son of Joseph. He is more than just a great Rabbi. He is more than just a revolutionary figure. He is the Lord! This miracle shows His *lordship* over creation. He is the last Adam regaining the dominion that the first Adam had lost.

From Bethsaida, the disciples had gone out about three to four miles out into the sea. To give you a better understanding, the Sea of Galilee is about thirteen miles long and about seven miles wide. So the disciples were out in the deepest part of the lake, *and it was now dark.* The Sea of Galilee lies about 650 ft. *below* sea level and is completely surrounded by mountains. The cold wind that rushes down from Mt. Hermon, which is about 9,200 ft. *above* sea level, hits the warm wind on the water and can cause a sudden storm. The fishermen disciples knew very well about the storms on the lake, but this was not a normal storm, this was a *great (exceeding) wind that blew.* What adds even more thought to the picture is that Jesus was alone on *a mountain* somewhere on the northern shore and He knew that the disciples were going into a great storm. There has to be a lesson for the disciples and for us as well!

A boat was found near the shore of Galilee in 1985 that had been buried since the early first century. The boat is less than thirty feet in length and is made out of about ten different types of wood. So, to be in the middle of the Galilee, in a small fishing vessel, during a *great* storm, in the dark, must have been a terrifying experience!

"...*they see Jesus walking on the sea, and drawing nigh unto the ship: and they were afraid.*" They saw the form of a man walking on top of the water? The glory of Jesus shined in the night that allowed the disciples to see Him. According to bones that were found in the Galilee from Jesus' time, some scholars believe that Jesus was a medium-sized man of average height. Think about the disciples seeing Jesus coming closer to the boat. They were scared out of their skin! What is this? No one walks on water! I am reminded of **Job 9:8-11**: *Which alone spreadeth out the heavens, and treadeth upon the waves of the sea.* The psalmist said: *Thy way is in the sea, and thy path in the great waters, and thy footsteps are not known.* (**Psalm 77:19**)

"*It is I; be not afraid.*" Not only did Jesus walk on the water, He started to *speak* to the disciples! The disciples still had not fully understood just who Jesus was. If they had of known who it was that fed the multitude they would not have been so afraid. I'm reminded of **Isaiah 43:2**: *When thou passest through the waters, I will be with thee.* Jesus walking upon the waters of Galilee inspired me to write this little song:

> *It was night on Galilee; the disciples were out on the sea,*
> *A storm came out of nowhere, suddenly they were in despair,*
> *Jesus came walking the sea, they wondered Oh*
> *what could this be, then Jesus spoke tenderly,*
> *It is I, be not afraid, it is I,*
> *I've come to save, I am the Lord, and*
> *I've come to calm the storm.*
> *It is I walking the sea, it is I, have faith*
> *in me, you'll never die because,*
> *It is I.*

(From the musical album, "Jesus Isreal")

"*Then they willingly received him into the ship: and immediately the ship was at the land whither they went.*" According to the other gospel accounts, the wind ceased once Jesus planted His precious feet in the boat. Part of the miracle that has

108

been overlooked is that they were about eight to ten miles from Capernaum, and *immediately* the ship was back on the land. Jesus showed *lordship* over creation, time, and distance.

There seems to be an obvious *typology* from the Old Testament to Jesus walking on the water. Noah and his family were all saved during a time of judgment by the ark floating on top of the water.

> *And the flood was forty days upon the earth; and the waters increased, and bare up the ark, and it was lift up above the earth.*
> **—Gen.7:17.**

Jesus was the God of Noah in human form walking on the Sea of Galilee. As long as Jesus was in the boat, there was nothing to fear. The ark of Noah has long been seen as a wonderful *type* of Christ.

God parted the waters of the Red Sea for Moses and the children of Israel and I find this verse very intriguing:

> *And Moses said unto the people, Fear ye not, stand still, and see the salvation (yeshua) of the LORD, which he will shew to you to day: for the Egyptians whom ye have seen to day, ye shall see them again no more for ever.*
> **—Exodus 14:13.**

Jesus, *Yeshua*, was the God of Moses in human form walking on the Sea of Galilee. A raging storm had no power over the *Lord God* of Moses. The apostle John, through the inspiration of the Holy Spirit, had walked the dusty roads of Galilee with the very God of the patriarchs and prophets of ancient Israel. Wow!

JESUS IS THE BREAD OF LIFE

> **John 6:22–25** – *The day following, when the people which stood on the other side of the sea saw that there was none other boat there, save that one whereinto his disciples were entered, and that Jesus went not with his disciples into the boat, but that his disciples were gone away alone; (Howbeit there came other boats from Tiberias nigh unto the place where they did eat bread, after that the Lord had given thanks:) When the people therefore saw that Jesus was not there, neither his disciples, they also took shipping, and came to Capernaum, seeking for Jesus. And when they had found him on the other side of the sea, they said unto him, Rabbi, when camest thou hither?*

This is a rather confusing little passage of scripture that is different in nature to most of the gospel of John. But inspiration would have us to carefully study it as it leads us into a major discourse of our Lord. It seems that most of the crowd that had experienced the feeding of the loaves and fishes were anxiously waiting the following morning on the eastern side of the lake. Maybe they were still determined to make Jesus their earthly king, but they realized that the only boat that had been there on the shore carried the disciples away alone and they did not take Jesus with them. The miracle had caused such a noise in Tiberias, that other boats had traveled the seven to eight mile trek across the lake. When the crowd saw that Jesus was nowhere to be found they also got in their boats and came back up the northern shore about six miles to Capernaum. They worked hard to go against the western wind trying to find the strange person who had fed thousands the day before. They came to Capernaum and finally found Jesus, and they asked Him, "Rabbi, when camest thou hither?" If they only had known that, while they were sleeping through the stormy night in their villages and homes with their families in *Bethsaida*, Jesus was walking on the water to rescue His disciples. Three major miracles had happened on the sea that night: 1) *Jesus walked on the water,* 2) *He calmed the storm, and* 3) *the boat miraculously, suddenly went back to Capernaum.* That's how Jesus came to Capernaum!

"...*after that the Lord had given thanks.*" It's strange to me that this is mentioned again. We know the Lord gave thanks before He broke the bread in **John 6:11**, but I believe there was something special and heavenly about the words and the emotions when Jesus gave thanks. Have you ever heard anyone pray and you could just feel the presence of the Holy Spirit? Well, try to imagine hearing the Lord of Glory, who was filled with the Holy Spirit without measure, give thanks. Giving thanks was a normal Jewish practice, but they had never heard anyone give thanks like Jesus!

> **John 6:26-27 -** *Jesus answered them and said,*
> *Verily, verily, I say unto you, Ye seek me, not*
> *because ye saw the miracles, but because ye did eat of*
> *the loaves, and were filled. Labour not for the meat*
> *which perisheth, but for that meat which endureth*
> *unto everlasting life, which the Son of man shall*
> *give unto you: for him hath God the Father sealed.*

Here we find a hidden dichotomy between the *signs* and *miracles*. Jesus knew that they had worked hard to find Him in Capernaum, but they were seeking the physical bread that He had provided for them. They should have recognized the *sign* that this truly was their Messiah. Jesus was not saying that they were not supposed to work in order to have physical food, but that they needed to spend less time and energy on things that are temporary and more energy on things that will last eternally. This would be the spiritual bread that could only come from the *Son of man*. God the Father had certified and put His seal of approval on His Son's ministry.

> **John 6:28-29 -** *Then said they unto him, What*
> *shall we do, that we might work the works of God?*
> *Jesus answered and said unto them, This is the work*
> *of God, that ye believe on him whom he hath sent.*

These verses have been used over the centuries to prove *justification by faith and not by works*. While that is certainly a true, biblical statement, this verse is not supposed to be understood in this manner. Looking through the Jewish eyes of the first century, they were saying: *What works can we do to please the God of Israel?* Jesus told them that to *believe in Him* was how they could please the God of Israel, for the covenant-keeping God of Israel was in their midst.

> **John 6:30-33** - *They said therefore unto him, What sign shewest thou then, that we may see, and believe thee? what dost thou work? Our fathers did eat manna in the desert; as it is written, He gave them bread from heaven to eat. Then Jesus said unto them, Verily, verily, I say unto you, Moses gave you not that bread from heaven; but my Father giveth you the true bread from heaven. For the bread of God is he which cometh down from heaven, and giveth life unto the world.*

The same people who were asking for a *sign*, witnessed the feeding of the multitude just yesterday. The very next day they asked: *Can you give us a greater sign than what you did yesterday?* It's interesting that they brought up the subject of *manna in the desert* that had occurred over fifteen hundred years earlier, during the time of Moses. Was it because the miracle of feeding the multitude reminded them of *manna*? Was it because they considered the *manna* in Moses' time to be one of the greatest sings in the history of Israel? It was written in the Midrash Rabbah *(Great Talmudic Literature)* that the return of *manna* would be a major sign of the true Messiah. Some of the rabbis stated that, as the first *manna* descended from heaven, so also the Redeemer will cause the second *manna* to descend. They believed that the sign of the *manna* was second only to the Messiah riding on a donkey. (Compare **Exo. 4:20** to **Zech. 9:9** to **John 12:12-19**) It's amazing how many of the things that Jesus said and did also paralleled much of the ancient Jewish literature and they refused to believe in Him. They had not studied their own Jewish writings carefully enough. Tradition blinds and truth sets us free.

"Moses gave you not that bread from heaven; but my Father giveth you the true bread from heaven." Jesus let the people know that it was not Moses that gave them *manna* in the desert, but that it came from the Father in heaven. It wasn't just another prophet who gave you the loaves and fishes across the lake. It was the long-awaited Messiah that the Father had sent down from heaven. Jesus changes the *true bread* from heaven to be a <u>person</u> who comes down from heaven, and the *true bread, Jesus the Messiah,* will give spiritual life to the world.

> **John 6:34-35** - *Then said they unto him, Lord, evermore give us this bread. And Jesus said unto them, I am the bread of life: he that cometh to me shall never hunger; and he that believeth on me shall never thirst.*

What the people said parallels what the Samaritan woman said: *Sir, give me this water.* (**John 4:15**) The Samaritan woman saw no miracle and she believed. These people witnessed the feeding of the multitude and most of them did not believe. One of the most profound statements that Jesus ever gave was *Anee lechem ha chayim*, or *I am the bread of life*. Jesus using the words hunger and thirst reminds me of a passage in the Torah that will help explain:

> *And he humbled thee, and suffered thee to hunger,*
> *and fed thee with manna, which thou knewest not,*
> *neither did thy fathers know; that he might make*
> *thee know that man doth not live by bread only, but*
> *by every word that proceedeth out of the mouth of*
> *the LORD doth man live.*
>
> **—Deut.8:3**

The *word* that proceeds out of the mouth of the Lord is none other than Jesus the Messiah. He is the true *manna* from heaven. There is a spiritual *hunger* and *thirst* that is far greater than physical bread and water can satisfy. Through trusting and believing in Jesus the Christ, that spiritual *hunger* and *thirst* can be satisfied. Hallelujah! The Israelites of old were told a truth that applies to every one of us today.

John 6:36–40 - *But I said unto you, That ye also have seen me, and believe not. All that the Father giveth me shall come to me; and him that cometh to me I will in no wise cast out. For I came down from heaven, not to do mine own will, but the will of him that sent me. And this is the Father's will which hath sent me, that of all which he hath given me I* *should lose nothing, but should raise it up again at the last day. And this is the will of him that sent me, that every one which seeth the Son, and believeth on him, may have everlasting life: and I will raise him up at the last day.*

Again, we need to compare the acceptance of Jesus among the Samaritans (**John 4:40-42**) to the unbelief of many of the people who saw the miracles of Jesus. There was probably a group of Jews from Judea (who may have lived in Nazareth) in the crowd that day who were representatives of the establishment because the word *"Jews"* is used in **vs.41**.

"All that the Father giveth to me shall come to me; and him that cometh to me I will in no wise cast out." This is one of those verses that have been interpreted over the centuries on a personal level in an effort to prove the doctrine of Calvinism. Without going down the wrong road here, just let me say that the proper way to interpret the verse is from the Jewish worldview of Jesus' time. The Messiah had not only come for the Jews in Judea, but for the Samaritans and the Galileans as well. The call is universal, not just to the Judeans. All who come to Jesus are gifts that are given to Him by the Father. What a promise we have in the sacred scriptures that whosoever comes to Jesus will not be cast out! It is the Father's will for them to be saved, and Jesus came to do the Father's will. The *bread of life* gives *everlasting life* and the *bread of life* will be the same one who raises the dead at the resurrection. This thought connects us back to **John 5:28-29**. When we go deeper into the Jewish view

of that day, we find that only the God of Israel could raise the dead. Consider these verses:

> O LORD, *thou hast brought up my soul from the grave: thou hast kept me alive, that I should not go down to the pit.*
>
> **—Psalm 30:3**

> *After two days will he revive us: in the third day he will raise us up, and we shall live in his sight.*
>
> **—Hosea 6:2**

Yet again, Jesus is stating that He is equal with the God of the Old Testament. As a reminder, we must remember as we read the words *Father* and *Son* that there is only one God who operates in three distinct persons: *Father, Son,* and the *Holy Spirit.* Because our finite minds cannot understand such an infinite concept, many false churches and false doctrines have risen over the centuries.

"*...that every one which seeth the Son, and believeth on him, may have everlasting life.*" Think of Nicodemus who *saw* Jesus face to face in **John 3**; the Samaritan woman who *saw* Jesus face to face in **John 4**; the crippled man at the Pool of Bethesda who saw Jesus face to face in **John 5**. Now, this group of Jews in **John 6** is *seeing* Jesus face to face and is refusing to believe in Him.

John 6:41-44 - *The Jews then murmured at him, because he said, I am the bread which came down from heaven. And they said, Is not this Jesus, the*

> *son of Joseph, whose father and mother we know?*
> *how is it then that he saith, I came down from*
> *heaven? Jesus therefore answered and said unto*
> *them, Murmur not among yourselves. No man can*
> *come to me, except the Father which hath sent me*
> *draw him: and I will raise him up at the last day.*

It's interesting that the children of Israel murmured after they were fed manna from heaven (**Deut.1:27, Psalm 106:25**) and here these Jews are murmuring because Jesus said "I am bread which came down from heaven." To help us to better understand the situation, Jesus is in Galilee, but He is being attacked by a group of unbelieving Jews who evidently knew the earthly parents of Jesus in Nazareth. They could not see how Jesus could be the bread that came down from heaven when His earthly parents were Joseph and Mary from Nazareth. Jesus dismisses their grumbling and approaches them from another angle. Although Jesus the Messiah came for everyone, every tribe of Israel and every Gentile, each individual person has to be drawn by the Father before they will come to Jesus. This is not talking about some being drawn and others not being drawn. This is simply stating that true salvation is not of anyone's own volition. How does a person receive faith in Jesus? People are drawn to the Lord by hearing the preached word of God (**Rom. 10:17**) and these Jews were so favored to be standing in front of the very Word of God Himself! One has to wonder if many of them did not come to faith in Jesus later on in the book of Acts, but at this point they are still in unbelief. The ones who are drawn to Jesus, receive Him, and do not reject Him will be the ones that will be raised up in the last day.

> **John 6:45-51 -** *It is written in the prophets, And they shall be all taught of God. Every man therefore that hath heard, and hath learned of the Father, cometh unto me. Not that any man hath seen the Father, save he which is of God, he hath seen the Father. Verily, verily, I say unto you, He that believeth on me hath everlasting life. I am that bread of life. Your fathers did eat manna in the wilderness, and are dead. This is the bread which cometh down from heaven, that a man may eat thereof, and not die. I am the living bread which came down from heaven: if any man eat of this bread, he shall live for ever: and the bread that I will give is my flesh, which I will give for the life of the world.*

Jesus brings up a very unusual passage from the prophet Isaiah:

> *And all thy children shall be taught of the LORD;*
> *and great shall be the peace of thy children.*
> **—Isaiah 54:13**

All of the children of Israel shall be taught by the Lord? Then Jesus says that *no one has ever seen the Father;* so how is the Father going to teach them? In order for this scripture to be fulfilled, the Son of God, who sees the Father, has to come down to the earth and teach Israel's sons and daughters. Then Jesus goes back to the *manna* metaphor once again and tells them that their forefathers, who ate *manna* in the time of Moses, had all died. The old *manna* could not impart *everlasting life*, even though it gave them physical life for a time. Jesus is the *living bread* that came down from heaven to give them life and life more abundantly. He offered the woman at the well *living* water, and now He is offering the people *living* bread. A thought that has been overlooked many times is that Jesus is again connecting Himself to the God of the Old Testament.

> *But the* LORD *is the true God, he is the living God, and an everlasting king: at his wrath the earth shall tremble, and the nations shall not be able to abide his indignation.*
>
> **—Jeremiah 10:10**

Jesus goes a step farther and tells them that the way the bread will give them eternal life is that His *flesh* will be given for the life of the world. He is about to give them a metaphor that not only offended many of them, but it still offends many today.

> **John 6:52–59 –** *The Jews therefore strove among themselves, saying, How can this man give us his flesh to eat? Then Jesus said unto them, Verily, verily, I say unto you, Except ye eat the flesh of the Son of man, and drink his blood, ye have no life*

in you. Whoso eateth my flesh, and drinketh my blood, hath eternal life; and I will raise him up at the last day. For my flesh is meat indeed, and my blood is drink indeed. He that eateth my flesh, and drinketh my blood, dwelleth in me, and I in him. As the living Father hath sent me, and I live by the Father: so he that eateth me, even he shall live by me. This is that bread which came down from heaven: not as your fathers did eat manna, and are dead: he that eateth of this bread shall live for ever. These things said he in the synagogue, as he taught in Capernaum.

A misunderstanding of this passage has caused the Catholic Church to teach a doctrine called *transubstantiation*, which says that the Communion bread becomes the actual body of Jesus. But Jesus is speaking metaphorically about the *manna* and about the *feeding of the multitude.* As the children of Israel ate the manna and just like the people across the Sea of Galilee ate the loaves and fishes, one must *internalize* Jesus in order to have the life He offers. How could they do that?

- *The <u>work</u> required was to believe in the one God has sent.* - **vs.29**
- *<u>Come</u> to the Son of God, <u>look</u> to the Son, and <u>believe</u> in Him.* - **vs.35, 40**
- *<u>Listen</u> to the Father who is speaking through His Son.* - **vs.45**
- *He who <u>believes</u> has everlasting life.* – **vs.47**

The Jews were very familiar with this type of language. It was a Jewish thought in Jesus' time that eating the bread from heaven was a synonym for studying the sacred scriptures. Here are two of the verses where they gathered this thought:

> *O taste and see that the LORD is good: blessed is the man that trusteth in him.*
>
> **—Psalm 34:8**

> *There is nothing better for a man, than that he should eat and drink, and that he should make his soul enjoy good in his labour. This also I saw, that it was from the hand of God.*
>
> **—Eccl. 2:24**

Even in our western culture we say things like *drink it in, swallow the story,* or *devour that book.* So it wasn't only the *eating of His flesh and drinking of His blood* teaching that offended them, it was also Jesus' teaching that the Sanhedrin-led leadership in Jerusalem and the Pharisees in the synagogues were not the ones to lead the people to the God of Israel as they proclaimed themselves to be. Jesus the Messiah was only way to the Father! Jesus was in the *synagogue in Capernaum* when He spoke those words.

> **John 6:60-66** - *Many therefore of his disciples, when they had heard this, said, This is an hard saying; who can hear it? When Jesus knew in himself that his disciples murmured at it, he said unto them,*

Doth this offend you? What and if ye shall see the Son of man ascend up where he was before? It is the spirit that quickeneth; the flesh profiteth nothing: the words that I speak unto you, they are spirit, and they are life. But there are some of you that believe not. For Jesus knew from the beginning who they were that believed not, and who should betray him. And he said, Therefore said I unto you, that no man can come unto me, except it were given unto him of my Father. From that time many of his disciples went back, and walked no more with him.

Not only was the metaphorical teaching of the *flesh and blood* a hard teaching, it was this *coming down from heaven* thing again. Jesus is saying: *If this offends you, what would you think if you were to see the Son of man ascending back to heaven?* This verse is overlooked many times when talking about the *ascension* of the Messiah. Jesus is saying that He is none other than the Son of Man from the Old Testament.

I saw in the night visions, and, behold, one like the Son of man came with the clouds of heaven, and came to the Ancient of days, and they brought him near before him. And there was given him dominion, and glory, and a kingdom, that all people, nations, and languages, should serve him: his dominion is an everlasting dominion, which shall not pass away, and his kingdom that which shall not be destroyed.

—Daniel 7:13-14

"It is the spirit that quickeneth; the flesh profiteth nothing:" The people could not understand what Jesus was saying because they were thinking about His Nazareth family and how they knew Him from His childhood. The words that Jesus was giving were *spirit* and therefore they gave life to all who received His words.

"But there are some of you that believe not. For Jesus knew from the beginning who they were that believed not, and who should betray him." I believe a parallel to this verse is when Jesus explained to the disciples why He taught in parables:

> *He answered and said unto them, Because it is given*
> *unto you to know the mysteries of the kingdom of*
> *heaven, but to them it is not given.*
>
> **—Matthew 13:11**

Jesus, being God, knew from the beginning the ones would not believe in Him, and this is the backdrop to some of His teachings. The unbelief of the Jewish establishment would play into the hands of the historical crucifixion. All of this is part of the timing of the Messiah coming into the world. The Roman oppression and the unbelieving Jewish leaders were mere puppets in the hands of Almighty God. (**Acts 4:26–28**)

"From that time many of his disciples went back, and walked no more with him." Even some of the disciples, up to this point, were turned back by the difficult words of Jesus. Did Jesus make His words hard in order to sift out those who were not true believers? This thought too has caused much controversy over the centuries. If a person believes

in Jesus can they ever be lost again? The answer lies in the fact that, if the person is *truly* a believer in Jesus, they will not turn back. They will make mistakes, like Jesus' closest disciples, but they will keep on following Jesus. Jesus knew who would leave and who would stay. Many of the so-called disciples were only following Jesus for what they could receive from Him, not because they really believed that He was the Messiah of Israel.

> **John 6:67-71** - *Then said Jesus unto the twelve, Will ye also go away? Then Simon Peter answered him, Lord, to whom shall we go? thou hast the words of eternal life. And we believe and are sure that thou art that Christ, the Son of the living God. Jesus answered them, Have not I chosen you twelve, and one of you is a devil? He spake of Judas Iscariot the son of Simon: for he it was that should betray him, being one of the twelve.*

The crowded synagogue cleared out quickly and now Jesus was speaking only to the *twelve*. He was saying to them: *Do you want to leave me too?* Simon Peter speaks on behalf of the twelve, "Lord, to whom shall we go? thou hast the words of eternal life. And we believe and are sure that thou art the Christ, the Son of the living God." Later on, Peter would speak on behalf of the disciples near Caesarea Philippi and make the same confession. (**Matthew 16:13-16**) Peter is saying, *There is no other like you Lord!* If we had been in the synagogue that day in Capernaum, would we have followed those who walked away or would we be in the small group that followed Jesus?

"Jesus answered them, Have not I chosen you twelve, and one of you is a devil? He spake of Judas Iscariot the son of Simon: for he it was that should betray him, being one of the twelve." Scholars have debated over the centuries about this strange person called *Judas Iscariot, the son of Simon Iscariot.* Some say that his name comes from *Kerioth*, a town in Judea, while others think his name comes from the word *Sicarii*, which means that he was part of the nationalistic, zealot movement. If the latter is true, then the betrayal of Jesus was not just for thirty pieces of silver, but his betrayal was to force Jesus to lead a revolt against the Romans. If Judas was from Judea, then this joins him with the many unbelieving Jews from Judea. There are a few Hebrew scholars who believe that Judas was saved in his dying breath, but we have a biblical problem with that: Jesus called him *the devil!* But all of the things that Jesus said and did were in order to fulfill the sacred scriptures.

CHAPTER SEVEN

JESUS IN GALILEE

> **John 7:1-5 -** *After these things Jesus walked in Galilee: for he would not walk in Judaea, because the Jews sought to kill him. Now the Jews' feast of tabernacles was at hand. His brethren therefore said unto him, Depart hence, and go into Judaea, that thy disciples also may see the works that thou doest. For there is no man that doeth any thing in secret, and he himself seeketh to be known openly. If thou do these things, shew thyself to the world. For neither did his brethren believe in him.*

We find a summary here that confirms that Jesus spent most of His earthly ministry in the Galilee. Why? Because the Judean leadership *sought to kill him*. During the months of Jesus' ministry in Galilee between **John 6** and **John 7** that are not recorded by John, Jesus may have traveled north to Tyre and Sidon. We know that He went up to Caesarea Philippi for Peter's big confession, was transfigured before the disciples, came back down to the lake for the feeding of the *four thousand*, and was confronted by the Pharisees back in Capernaum. John's gospel focuses more on the Judean ministry of the Messiah and now he takes us back down to Jerusalem about seventy miles for another Jewish feast, where the events are recorded in **John 7-8**. This will begin the last six to seven months of Jesus' earthly ministry, ending in the crucifixion in Jerusalem. So, in John's account, we do not find Jesus back in Galilee until after the resurrection in **John 21**.

In **John 6:4**, the Feast of *Passover* was near. Here the Feast of *Sukkot* (Tabernacles) is near. Between the two would be a time of around six months, because the Feast of Tabernacles was in the latter part of September. There were *seven* Jewish feasts in a calendar year (**Lev.23**) but Jewish men were required to attend only three feasts: *Pesach* – Passover, *Shavuot* – weeks or Pentecost, and *Sukkot* – Booths or Tabernacles. There may be two reasons why John is showing that Jesus was faithful to attend the major Jewish feasts in Jerusalem:

1) *To show that Jesus was a law-keeping Jew, and His birth and identity were from Judea* (Bethlehem of Judea).
2) *To show that Jesus followed the religious, Jewish calendar of events, so the feasts would find their fulfillment in Jesus.*

Jesus knew that His time on earth was short and the timing and locations of His travels were crucial. He just didn't randomly go from place to place. It was all orchestrated before Jesus came into the world.

"If thou do these things, shew thyself to the world." His brothers from Nazareth still felt a little hostility toward Jesus because He had left Nazareth and came to live in Capernaum. Jesus had given His new followers in Galilee precedence over them. I can just imagine some of the things they were thinking: *Here is our brother out traveling these hills preaching that He is the Messiah and we are having to stay back home and work. Who does He think He is, claiming to do all these miracles and not going to Jerusalem and showing the whole world?* Maybe they thought that His claims of being the Messiah would collapse when He was faced with the Jews in Judea. His own family members were not followers at this point. Most of us can relate to our families being the hardest ones to reach but, in the case of Jesus and His family, they could not find any fault in Jesus. They just didn't believe that He was the Messiah. But, one day, they would!

> **John 7:6-13 -** *Then Jesus said unto them, My time is not yet come: but your time is alway ready. The world cannot hate you; but me it hateth, because I testify of it, that the works thereof are evil. Go ye up unto this feast: I go not up yet unto this feast: for my time is not yet come. When he had said these words unto them, he abode still in Galilee. But when his brethren were gone up, then went he also up unto the feast, not openly, but as it were in secret. Then the Jews sought him at the feast, and*

*said, Where is he? And there was much murmuring
among the people concerning him: for some said, He
is a good man: others said, Nay; but he deceiveth
the people. Howbeit no man spake openly of him
for fear of the Jews.*

"*My time is not yet come.*" (**vs.6**) "*Go ye up unto this feast: I go
not up yet unto this feast; for my time is not yet full come.*" (**vs.8**)
I think we have missed a great truth here by the translated
word *time*. It is very likely that the word that Jesus used for
time may have been the Hebrew word, *moed*, which is used
for *seasons*. In other words: *You can go up to the feast any time,
but for me, it's not the appointed time for me yet, but I will follow
later.* Also, Jesus may have been alluding to the *appointed
time* when He would go into Jerusalem during the Passover
to be crucified. John uses the phrases *my time is not yet come*
and *my time is come* several times in his gospel.

"*The world cannot hate you; but me it hateth, because I testify
of it, that the works thereof are evil.*" Judea could not hate the
brothers of Jesus now because they were not true believers.
Judea, or the *world*, would hate Jesus because He exposed
their evil deeds. This connects us back to **John 1:11** - "He
came unto his own, and is own received him not."

"*Howbeit no man spake openely of him for fear of the Jews.*"
Jesus waited until after His brothers had departed to
Jerusalem. He wanted to make a private trip with His
disciples. At this time, He wanted to keep a low profile.
Yeshua was on the lips of many of the people who were
attending the feast and some even thought that He was a

good man. But no one talked about Jesus out in the open because they knew how the religious leaders felt. Notice the word *Jews* here at the end of the verse. Were not the ones who were attending the feast *Jews* as well? This is another proof that the word *Jews* is used to refer to the Judean leadership in Jerusalem; namely the *Sanhedrin*, the *Priesthood*, and the *Herodians*.

JESUS AT THE FEAST OF TABERNACLES

> **John 7:14-16** – *Now about the midst of the feast Jesus went up into the temple, and taught. And the Jews marvelled, saying, How knoweth this man letters, having never learned? Jesus answered them, and said, My doctrine is not mine, but his that sent me.*

Jesus and His disciples may have stopped somewhere on the Mt. of Olives and slept under their *sukkah*, eating meals together, with the moon shining down through the partial open top of their little hut. This festival of joy and celebration lasted for eight days, so probably on the third or fourth day Jesus began to teach in the temple.

"How knoweth this man letters, having never learned?" The rabbis in the temple compound were amazed when they heard the Galilean preacher from Nazareth begin to teach the scriptures. Jesus had not studied in one of the schools of the rabbis, called *yeshivas*. Later on, the Jewish Talmud would mention that *Yeshu* (which was a mockery form of

Yeshua) was taught by one of the famous rabbis of the day. To show you how ridiculous this claim is, the rabbi they named as Y'hoshua ben-Perachyah lived a hundred years before Jesus came. The wisdom of Jesus transcended the religious schools of men. He did not come to represent one of the great rabbis of their day, but He came from heaven, as a representative of the God of Israel!

> **John 7:17-18** - *If any man will do his will, he shall know of the doctrine, whether it be of God, or whether I speak of myself. He that speaketh of himself seeketh his own glory: but he that seeketh his glory that sent him, the same is true, and no unrighteousness is in him.*

The language seems a little bit confusing, so maybe I can paraphrase it for you. There are two kinds of teachers. There are those who teach from their own wisdom and their own words. This kind of teacher seeks glory for himself, but his deeds will demonstrate that he is false. Then, there is the teacher who works for the honor of God. His words come from God because he is trying to do God's will. His works demonstrate that he is genuine.

> **John 7:19-20** - *Did not Moses give you the law, and yet none of you keepeth the law? Why go ye about to kill me? The people answered and said, Thou hast a devil: who goeth about to kill thee?*

The religious leaders were claiming that they kept the Law of Moses while they were planning to kill Jesus. What hypocrisy! This connects us back to what Jesus said in **John 5:45–47**. Jesus was revealing what they would not admit. Here is a group of Judean leaders who are supposed to be leading people to the God of Israel, and they say to their own Messiah, "Thou hast a devil." It cannot be over-emphasized how corrupt, man-made religious systems want to go against the true, biblical Jesus! This scenario has repeated itself countless times throughout the course of mankind.

> **John 7:21-24 –** *Jesus answered and said unto them, I have done one work, and ye all marvel. Moses therefore gave unto you circumcision; (not because it is of Moses, but of the fathers;) and ye on the sabbath day circumcise a man. If a man on the sabbath day receive circumcision, that the law of Moses should not be broken; are ye angry at me, because I have made a man every whit whole on the sabbath day? Judge not according to the appearance, but judge righteous judgment.*

What was the *one work* that Jesus was referring back to? It was the healing of the man at the Pool of Bethesda a few months ago back in **John 5:9**, on the *Sabbath* day. The Judean leaders are still harboring hate toward Jesus because He healed on the *Sabbath* day. Jesus said that it was in the Law of Moses to *circumcise* a Jewish boy even if the eighth day fell on the *Sabbath*. Why then is it wrong for Him to *completely* heal someone on the Sabbath? Jesus told them that they were judging only to make themselves look pious in the eyes of men. Jesus was really using the Hebrew *kalv'chomer*, comparing the healing of only one of the 248 parts of the human body to saving a whole body.

> **John 7:25-27** - *Then said some of them of Jerusalem, Is not this he, whom they seek to kill? But, lo, he speaketh boldly, and they say nothing unto him. Do the rulers know indeed that this is the very Christ? Howbeit we know this man whence he is: but when Christ cometh, no man knoweth whence he is.*

Notice the distinction that John makes between the Judean leaders and the *people* in Jerusalem. They could not understand how Jesus was speaking so *boldly* against the establishment and they were not saying anything back to Him. Did the leaders think that Jesus was the Christ? They did not know that the religious leaders were living in fear of Rome and they were afraid of losing their positions among the people. This group of common people also said that they knew where Jesus' origins were, and that He could not possibly be the Messiah. There was a Jewish belief in the early first century that the Messiah's coming would be shrouded in mystery and His coming would be in secret. They thought He would come suddenly and not in the simple Galilean way that Jesus had come. Just like many people today have different opinions about the second coming of Jesus, they had different opinions about His first coming. But if they had of known the scriptures better they would have known the prophecies like **Micah 5:2**, where it states that the Messiah will come to Bethlehem. Again, not knowing the scriptures causes traditional thinking to supersede the truth.

> **John 7:28-31** - *Then cried Jesus in the temple as he taught, saying, Ye both know me, and ye know whence I am: and I am not come of myself, but he that sent me is true, whom ye know not. But I know him: for I am from him, and he hath sent me. Then they sought to take him: but no man laid hands on him, because his hour was not yet come. And many of the people believed on him, and said, When Christ cometh, will he do more miracles than these which this man hath done?*

A seemingly paradoxical statement is made by Jesus: *You know where I came from but you do not know the one who sent me.* In other words, Jesus was telling them that they may know about Him being from Nazareth, but they did not really know that He came from heaven. If they had of truly known the God of Israel, they would have known who Jesus was and where He really came from. It's interesting that John's gospel does not connect Jesus to Bethlehem or the Davidic dynasty like the other three gospels. Why? Because John is writing to a different group of people who, like the Samaritans, maybe did not believe the Messiah would come through the house of David. John was more concerned about his audience knowing that Jesus was the Eternal God in human flesh. That is why this subject of Jesus coming down from the Father is mentioned so often. Of course this also connects us back to **John 1**. *In the beginning was the Word.*

"Then they sought to take him: but no man laid hands on him, because his hour was not yet come." The religious leaders wanted to take Jesus because, every time he taught, more people believed in Him. They were afraid that this revolutionary preacher from Nazareth was going to create such a following that it would lead into a revolt, not against Rome, but against their corrupt system. But the time was not yet for Jesus to be turned over to the Sanhedrin. Here we find again the phrase: *his hour was not yet come.* (Compare **John 2:4, 7:8, 7:30, 12:23, 17:1**)

"And many of the people believed on him, and said, When Christ cometh, will he do more miracles than these which this man hath done?" This is a treasure verse hidden in the gospel of John that is overlooked most of the time. Many of the people who started this whole thing back in **vs.25-27**, became followers of Jesus. Why? Because deep in their hearts they knew that the miracles that Jesus had performed were Messianic in nature. They even asked the rhetorical question: *When the Messiah comes, will he do more miracles that this man?* The same is true today even within the land of Israel. There are more Jews who do believe in Jesus than many would have us to think. We must keep in mind that God's Holy Spirit can reveal to people who Jesus is even

in the midst of vain traditions and man-made religious systems.

> **John 7:32-36** - *The Pharisees heard that the people murmured such things concerning him; and the Pharisees and the chief priests sent officers to take him. Then said Jesus unto them, Yet a little while am I with you, and then I go unto him that sent me. Ye shall seek me, and shall not find me: and where I am, thither ye cannot come. Then said the Jews among themselves, Whither will he go, that we shall not find him? will he go unto the dispersed among the Gentiles, and teach the Gentiles? What manner of saying is this that he said, Ye shall seek me, and shall not find me: and where I am, thither ye cannot come?*

Notice that the Pharisees of the Sanhedrin were working along with the priests of the Sadducees, who had the authority here to send temple guards to arrest Jesus. Jesus then changed the subject from the *religious* authority to *divine* authority. Jesus was telling them that He was sent by someone who had far more authority than they did. When Jesus talked about going somewhere they could not come, the Judean leaders thought that Jesus was talking about going to the Hellenized Jews, who were outside of the control of the temple authorities. It helps us to understand that there were factions within Judaism even in Jesus' time. They lived outside of Jerusalem, *(Places like the Qumran, and*

Egypt) and they saw the corruption of the temple leadership. This is why they thought that Jesus was talking about going to the Greek-speaking Jews outside of their jurisdiction. But Jesus was referring to His departure back to heaven once He had finished the will of the Father.

> **John 7:37-39** - *In the last day, that great day of the feast, Jesus stood and cried, saying, If any man thirst, let him come unto me, and drink. He that believeth on me, as the scripture hath said, out of his belly shall flow rivers of living water. (But this spake he of the Spirit, which they that believe on him should receive: for the Holy Ghost was not yet given; because that Jesus was not yet glorified.)*

This is such a rich and important passage of scripture that it deserves a little more time. (Please study about the Feast of Tabernacles in **Lev.23:33-44**) Throughout this feast in Jerusalem, the priests would carry a gold pitcher down to the *Pool of Siloam* and draw water each day for seven days. The priest would then bring it back up to the temple compound and pour the water at the foot of the altar. It not only symbolized a prayer for rain, but it also pointed to the day when the Holy Spirit would be poured out on the people of Israel. This custom was drawn from **Isaiah 12:3**:

Therefore with joy shall ye draw water out of the wells of salvation.

The *last day* of the Feast of Tabernacles was the pinnacle of the festival. There was music, dancing, and chanting of

Psalms 113-118. It was called *Hoshana Rabbah* or Great Hosanna. The feast climaxed with the blowing of gold trumpets. These customs were really pointed to the Messiah of Israel! This *last day* was also the final chance for the people to have their sins forgiven. On Rosh Hashanah the people ask *to be inscribed in the Book of Life* and on *Yom Kippur* (Day of Atonement) they hoped that their names would be sealed. We need to realize that Jesus did not discount or disregard what their customs were; He just wanted them to know that what they were doing was pointing to Him. What a time for Jesus to make such an announcement! So, during the greatest moment of the feast, while they were filled with ecstatic joy and the people were asking for forgiveness, in the presence of the 24 divisions of the priesthood, Jesus *cried*:

> *If any man thirst, let him come unto me, and drink.*
> *He that believeth on me, as the scripture hath said,*
> *out of his belly shall flow rivers of living water.*

Jesus didn't quietly say these words; He *cried* them out! There are several verses in the old, Hebrew scriptures that are connected with what Jesus said.

> *And all the congregation of the children of Israel journeyed from the wilderness of Sin, after their journeys, according to the commandment of the* LORD, *and pitched in Rephidim: and there was no water for the people to drink. Wherefore the people*

did chide with Moses, and said, Give us water that we may drink. And Moses said unto them, Why chide ye with me? wherefore do ye tempt the LORD? And the people thirsted there for water; and the people murmured against Moses, and said, Wherefore is this that thou hast brought us up out of Egypt, to kill us and our children and our cattle with thirst? And Moses cried unto the LORD, saying, What shall I do unto this people? they be almost ready to stone me. And the LORD said unto Moses, Go on before the people, and take with thee of the elders of Israel; and thy rod, wherewith thou smotest the river, take in thine hand, and go. Behold, I will stand before thee there upon the rock in Horeb; and thou shalt smite the rock, and there shall come water out of it, that the people may drink. And Moses did so in the sight of the elders of Israel.

—Exodus 17:1-6

For I will pour water upon him that is thirsty, and floods upon the dry ground: I will pour my spirit upon thy seed, and my blessing upon thine offspring:

—Isaiah 44:3

Ho, every one that thirsteth, come ye to the waters, and he that hath no money; come ye, buy, and eat; yea, come, buy wine and milk without money and without price.

—Isaiah 55:1

Afterward he brought me again unto the door of the house; and, behold, waters issued out from under the threshold of the house eastward: for the forefront of the house stood toward the east, and the waters came down from under from the right side of the house, at the south side of the altar.

—Ezekiel 47:1

This passage in **John 7** also needs to be paralleled with **John 4:10**:

Jesus answered and said unto her, If thou knewest the gift of God, and who it is that saith to thee, Give me to drink; thou wouldest have asked of him, and he would have given thee living water.

It also needs to be read along with the ultimate fulfillment in **Revelation 22:17**:

And the Spirit and the bride say, Come. And let him that heareth say, Come. And let him that is athirst come. And whosoever will, let him take the water of life freely.

Read **John 7:39** again:

(But this spake he of the Spirit, which they that believe on him should receive: for the Holy Ghost was not yet given; because that Jesus was not yet glorified.)

Now take some time to study **John 14:26, 15:26, 16:7-15, 17:5,** and also **Acts 1:8** and **2:4**.

Let's continue with **John 7**.

> **John 7:40-43** - *Many of the people therefore, when they heard this saying, said, Of a truth this is the Prophet. Others said, This is the Christ. But some said, Shall Christ come out of Galilee? Hath not the scripture said, That Christ cometh of the seed of David, and out of the town of Bethlehem, where David was? So there was a division among the people because of him.*

Apparently, the declaration that Jesus made had an impact on the people as a Messianic claim. Many thought that Jesus must be the Prophet that Moses wrote about in **Deut.18:15**. This was also what many thought after Jesus fed the multitude in **John 6:14**. Other people said that Jesus was the *Christ*, which comes from the Greek, *Christos*, for the Hebrew, *Messiah*. Some who knew that Jesus was from Nazareth said: *the Messiah will not come out of Galilee.* They went on to say that *the Messiah was to come from the seed of David out of the town of Bethlehem.* They were right. Jesus did come through the house of David and was born in Bethlehem. Why didn't John, the author of this gospel, make this correction here? He certainly knew that Jesus was born in Bethlehem. The answer is: because he was just showing what the different opinions were of the people.

There is a saying in Israel today: *where there are three Jews, there will be four opinions.*

> **John 7:44-46** - *And some of them would have taken him; but no man laid hands on him. Then came the officers to the chief priests and Pharisees; and they said unto them, Why have ye not brought him? The officers answered, Never man spake like this man.*

I personally love this passage of scripture. The Roman officers, who had a pagan background, were moved by what Jesus said. It wasn't only *what* Jesus said, but it was *how* He said it. Such compassion, such conviction, such power, and such truth proceeded out of His mouth. They had never heard anyone speak like Jesus. I'm reminded of what the people said in Galilee, after Jesus healed the paralytic, in **Luke 5:26** *We have seen strange things today.*

> **John 7:47-53** - *Then answered them the Pharisees, Are ye also deceived? Have any of the rulers or of the Pharisees believed on him? But this people who knoweth not the law are cursed. Nicodemus saith unto them, (he that came to Jesus by night, being one of them,) Doth our law judge any man, before it hear him, and know what he doeth? They answered and said unto him, Art thou also of Galilee? Search, and look: for out of Galilee ariseth no prophet. And every man went unto his own house.*

It is profoundly interesting that when the Pharisees said that the officers were deceived and that not any of the rulers had believed on Jesus, we find none other than *Nicodemus*, who we studied about in **John 3**. The conversation that he had with Jesus on that brisk, Passover *night* changed his life. He brought up a truth that was even mentioned in some of the rabbinic writings of the day:

> *Men pass judgment on a man if they hear his words;*
> *if they do not hear his words they cannot establish*
> *judgment on him.*
>
> **—Exodus Rabbah 21:3**

But the unbelieving Pharisees dismissed Nicodemus' words by throwing an anti-Galilean slur at him: *Are you also from Galilee?* They said that a prophet does not come out of Galilee, showing their animosity and prejudice toward the Galileans. If the had of only known the scriptures better, they would have understood that there had been a prophet who came out of Galilee. *Jonah*, who lived in the 9th century BC, came from *Gath-Hepher* (**2 Kings 14:25**) just a few miles from Nazareth. Jonah's time in the belly of the whale was a type of the Messiah that is even used by Jesus Himself, who would stay in the grave three days and three nights. (**Matthew 12:38–41**)

CHAPTER EIGHT

JESUS AND THE ADULTEROUS WOMAN

John 8:1-11 – *Jesus went unto the mount of Olives. And early in the morning he came again into the temple, and all the people came unto him; and he sat down, and taught them. And the scribes and Pharisees brought unto him a woman taken in adultery; and when they had set her in the midst, They say unto him, Master, this woman was taken in adultery, in the very act. Now Moses in the law commanded us, that such should be stoned: but what sayest thou? This they said, tempting him, that they might have to accuse him. But Jesus stooped down, and with his finger wrote on the ground, as though he heard them not. So when they continued asking him, he lifted up himself, and said unto them, He that is without sin among you, let him first cast a stone at her. And again he stooped down, and wrote on the ground. And they which heard it, being convicted by their own conscience, went* *out one by one, beginning at the eldest, even unto the last: and Jesus was left alone, and the woman standing in the midst. When Jesus had lifted up himself, and saw none but the woman, he said unto her, Woman, where are those thine accusers? hath no man condemned thee? She said, No man, Lord. And Jesus said unto her, Neither do I condemn thee: go, and sin no more.*

I need to mention that most scholars do not like to comment on this passage because it was not found in many of the earlier manuscripts. May I ask why? It was not found in some of the earliest manuscripts because the early church Fathers thought that Jesus was putting His okay on adultery and they took it out. In my opinion, this beautiful story is definitely an inspired part of the Word of God and there would be a lot of wonderful truths lost if we left it out. It has been so misunderstood but, when we study the passage from the Jewish mind of Jesus' time, then things began to unfold.

"Jesus went unto the mount of Olives." During the feast of Tabernacles, Jesus either spent the night on the Mt. of Olives in communion with the Father or He may have spent the night with His dear friends, Mary, Martha, and Lazarus, who lived in Bethany just over the summit of the Mt. of Olives.

Early the next morning, Jesus walked down the Mt. of Olives, crossed the *Kidron Valley*, and went back into the courts of the temple on Mt. Moriah. While He was teaching, the *scribes and Pharisees* brought a woman who had been taken in the very act of adultery and set her in the midst of the crowd. Even the old Jewish sages recognized that the feast of Tabernacles was leading people to be immoral because the seven-day festival was filled with music, dancing, and sleeping in tents. In attempt to avoid trouble, they began to separate the men from the women. Evidently, this woman was caught in the very act of adultery during this time of celebration.

"Now Moses in the law commanded us, that such should be stoned: but what sayest thou? This they said, tempting, him, that they might have to accuse him." So it was a trap! If Jesus condemned the woman, it would go against His ministry of mercy and compassion. If Jesus did not condemn the woman, then he was going against the Law of Moses. Either way, they were going to trap Jesus. So, let's search for what the Torah really had to say about adultery:

> *And the man that committeth adultery with another man's wife, even he that committeth adultery with his neighbour's wife, the adulterer and the adulteress shall surely be put to death.*
>
> **—Lev.20:10**

> *If a man be found lying with a woman married to an husband, then they shall both of them die, both the man that lay with the woman, and the woman: so shalt thou put away evil from Israel. If a damsel that is a virgin be betrothed unto an husband, and a man*

find her in the city, and lie with her; Then ye shall bring them both out unto the gate of that city, and ye shall stone them with stones that they die; the damsel, because she cried not, being in the city; and the man, because he hath humbled his neighbour's wife: so thou shalt put away evil from among you.

—Deut.22:22-24

And the Lord spake unto Moses, saying, Speak unto the children of Israel, and say unto them, If any man's wife go aside, and commit a trespass against him, And a man lie with her carnally, and it be hid from the eyes of her husband, and be kept close, and she be defiled, and there be no witness against her, neither she be taken with the manner; And the spirit of jealousy come upon him, and he be jealous of his wife, and she be defiled: or if the spirit of jealousy come upon him, and he be jealous of his wife, and she be not defiled: Then shall the man bring his wife unto the priest, and he shall bring her offering for her, the tenth part of an ephah of barley meal; he shall pour no oil upon it, nor put frankincense thereon; for it is an offering of jealousy, an offering of memorial, bringing iniquity to remembrance. And the priest shall bring her near, and set her before the Lord: And the priest shall take holy water in an earthen vessel; and of the dust that is in the floor of the tabernacle the priest shall take, and put it into the water: And the priest shall set the woman before the LORD, *and uncover the woman's head, and put the offering of memorial in her hands, which is the jealousy offering: and the priest shall have in his hand the bitter water that causeth the curse: And the priest shall charge her by an oath, and say unto the woman, If no man have lain with thee, and if thou hast not gone aside to uncleanness with another instead of thy husband, be thou free from this bitter water that causeth the curse: But if thou hast gone aside to another instead of thy husband, and if thou be defiled, and some man have lain with thee beside thine husband: Then the priest shall charge the woman with an oath of cursing, and the priest shall say unto the woman, The* LORD *make thee a curse and an oath among thy people, when the* LORD *doth make thy thigh to rot, and thy belly to swell; And this water that causeth the curse shall go into thy bowels, to make thy belly to swell, and thy thigh to rot: And the woman shall say, Amen, amen. And the priest shall write these curses in a book, and he shall blot them out with the bitter water: And he shall cause the woman to drink the bitter water that causeth the curse: and the water that causeth the curse shall enter into her, and become bitter. Then the priest shall take the jealousy offering out of the woman's hand, and shall wave the offering before the* LORD, *and offer it upon the altar: And the priest shall take an handful of the offering, even the memorial thereof, and burn it upon the altar, and afterward shall cause the woman to drink the water. And when he hath made her to drink the water, then it shall come to pass, that, if she be defiled, and have done trespass against her husband, that the water that causeth the curse shall enter into her, and become bitter, and her belly shall swell, and her thigh shall rot: and the woman shall be a curse among her people. And if the woman be not defiled, but be clean; then she shall be free, and shall conceive seed. This is the law of jealousies, when a wife goeth aside to another instead of her husband, and is defiled; Or when the spirit of jealousy cometh upon him, and he be jealous over his wife, and shall set the woman before the LORD, and the priest shall execute upon her all this law. Then shall the man be guiltless from iniquity, and this woman shall bear her iniquity.*

—Numbers 5:11–31

A couple of things stand out in my mind when I read these passages: 1) *both the man and the woman were to be stoned,* and 2) *how reputable the witnesses are supposed to be.* Stoning someone to death was not allowed by the Romans during Jesus' time, but this did not prevent isolated cases like the stoning of Stephen (**Acts 7:58–59**) and other attempts even at the very Son of God. (**John 8:59, 10:31**)

"*But Jesus stooped down, and with his finger wrote on the ground, as though he heard them not.*" I am reminded of the *finger of God* writing the law and giving it to Moses:

150

*And the L*ORD *delivered unto me two tables of stone*
written with the finger of God; and on them was
*written according to all the words, which the L*ORD
spake with you in the mount out of the midst of the
fire in the day of the assembly.

—Deut. 9:10

I am also reminded of what Jesus said in **Luke 11:20**:

But if I with the finger of God cast out devils, no
doubt the kingdom of God is come upon you.

The Hebrew word for *finger* is *tsebah* and it means *to dip.* So
the *finger of Jesus,* which was the *finger of God,* was dipped
into the ground in order to write. The One who wrote the
law of Moses on tablets of stone on Mt. Sinai, was writing
in the sand on Mt. Moriah. The *One* who took His *finger*
and pointed to the demon-possessed in order to cast out
demons, is now taking His *finger* and writing in the ground.

"*He that is without sin among you, let him first cast a stone*
at her." In the Torah, as well as in Jewish literature, the
accusers had to be qualified witnesses. Without the proper
witnesses there could be no condemnation. An old saying
goes: *He that lives in a glass house had better not start throwing*
stones.

"*And again he stooped down, and wrote on the ground. And*
they which heard it, being convicted by their own conscience, went
out one by one, beginning at the eldest, even unto the last." Did
Jesus write down verses from the Torah? Did He write

down the names of the accusers? Did He write down certain sins of the accusers? Whatever Jesus wrote on the ground brought conviction to the minds of the accusers. Could it be that some of the men in the crowd had been with the woman themselves? Jesus knew their hearts and Jesus knew everything that had happened. I find it interesting that Jesus wrote *twice* on the ground, and God wrote the Ten Commandments *twice* and gave them to Moses. The point is that Jesus would not go against His own law that He gave *twice* to Moses.

> *And the LORD said unto Moses, Hew thee two tables of stone like unto the first: and I will write upon these tables the words that were in the first tables, which thou brakest.*
>
> **—Exodus 34:1**

Jesus used the Torah to throw the case out! He disqualified the witnesses! They were trying to use the Law of Moses to trap the One who actually wrote the Law of Moses! Again, we can see that the religious leaders of the day did not know the scriptures in the way they professed to know them. They were imposters!

"*...and Jesus was left alone, and the woman standing in the midst. When Jesus had lifted up himself, and saw none but the woman, he said unto her, Woman, where are those thine accusers? hath no man condemned thee? She said, No man, Lord. And Jesus said unto her, Neither do I condemn thee: go, and sin no more.*" I find it absolutely astounding that the woman called

Him "Lord" when she saw how Jesus put her accusers on the run by whatever He wrote on the ground. Jesus wasn't approving of the woman's sin, but He saw the hypocrisy of the Judean leadership. He came to offer forgiveness to anyone who would truly recognize Him as the *Lord!*

"Neither do I condemn thee: go and sin no more." This also connects us back to what Jesus had said earlier in **John 5:24:**

> *Verily, verily, I say unto you, He that heareth*
> *my word, and believeth on him that sent me, hath*
> *everlasting life, and shall not come into condemnation;*
> *but is passed from death unto life.*

Isn't this exactly what the good Lord has done for us, dear reader? We are all guilty of grave sins: both the physical and the spiritual. Satan accuses us and we condemn ourselves, but then Jesus the Christ sets us free by His wonderful mercy! Hallelujah!

Before we leave this amazing story, there is another verse from the old Hebrew scriptures that comes to mind. Listen to these words and make the comparison:

> *O LORD, the hope of Israel, all that forsake thee*
> *shall be ashamed, and they that depart from me*
> *shall be written in the earth, because they have*
> *forsaken the LORD, the fountain of living waters.*
> **—Jeremiah 17:13**

John 8:12-18 - *Then spake Jesus again unto*
them, saying, I am the light of the world: he that

followeth me shall not walk in darkness, but shall have the light of life. The Pharisees therefore said unto him, Thou bearest record of thyself; thy record is not true. Jesus answered and said unto them, Though I bear record of myself, yet my record is true: for I know whence I came, and whither I go; but ye cannot tell whence I come, and whither I go. Ye judge after the flesh; I judge no man. And yet if I judge, my judgment is true: for I am not alone, but I and the Father that sent me. It is also written in your law, that the testimony of two men is true. I am one that bear witness of myself, and the Father that sent me beareth witness of me.

During the Jewish feast of Tabernacles, the Temple mount was lit up like a torch with four huge lamps of gold that were seventy-five ft. high. Each lamp had four basins that were filled with about 2 gallons of olive oil. There were ladders going up each lamp and young priests would climb up and use the worn out garments of the priests as wicks. There was not a courtyard in Jerusalem that was not glowing all through the night. These lights were a reminder of the pillar of fire that guided the children of Israel in the wilderness. It was a symbol of the *Shekinah* Glory of God that had once been seen in the Temple that Solomon had built.

"I am the light of the world," or in the Hebrew language of Jesus, *Anee or Ha O Lam.* What a time for Jesus to make this powerful proclamation! Just like the people could *see* where

they were walking on the Temple mount, Jesus was telling them that they could also be guided by His great *light* if they would follow Him. If there were no lamps shining in Jerusalem the people would be walking in darkness. When people tried to follow their own path in life, they too would walk in darkness. But there is a deeper meaning here. This idea of Jesus being the *light of the world*, takes us back to both **Genesis 1:3** and **John 1:5-9.** We have the awesome privilege of knowing what the apostle John wrote in **John 1**, while the people in Jerusalem that day did not know those mysterious truths about Jesus.

But this term, the *light of the world,* was also used in Jewish literature in those days to refer to the Torah, the teachers of the Torah, the Temple, and the Menorah in the Temple. So the people had heard those words before, but they had never heard it proclaimed with the "I am" of Jesus. Jesus is the personification of *light* who had come into a very dark world. Here is another passage that has a strong connection to what Jesus said:

> *Arise, shine; for thy light is come, and the glory of the* LORD *is risen upon thee. For, behold, the darkness shall cover the earth, and gross darkness the people: but the* LORD *shall arise upon thee, and his glory shall be seen upon thee. And the Gentiles shall come to thy light, and kings to the brightness of thy rising.*
> —**Isaiah 60:1-3**

"The Pharisees therefore said unto him, Thou bearest record of thyself; thy record is not true." The subject of witnesses comes up again because it was such an important part of Judaism in Jesus' time. They were saying that Jesus is giving this self-proclamation without any witnesses to back up what He is saying. But Jesus goes back the Torah again in **vs. 17** and mentions part of **Deut. 19:15**:

> *...at the mouth of two witnesses, or at the mouth of three witnesses, shall the matter be established.*

Jesus had already given a more serious argument about proper witnesses in **John 5:31-39**. Here, in **vs.18**, He tells them again that the *two* primary witnesses are the *heavenly Father* and *Himself.* He and His Father are *one*, but they are also *two* independent Persons serving as *two* witnesses.

"Ye judge after the flesh; I judge no man." Remember that Jesus has already disqualified the Pharisees' authority to *judge* in **John 7:40** and **John 8:9**. At His first coming, the Messiah would not act as a *judge* because He came to save the lost sheep of the house of Israel. But, when He comes the second time, He will certainly be the *Judge* of all!

> **John 8:19-24** - *Then said they unto him, Where is thy Father? Jesus answered, Ye neither know me, nor my Father: if ye had known me, ye should have known my Father also. These words spake Jesus in the treasury, as he taught in the temple: and no man laid hands on him; for his hour was not yet come.*

Then said Jesus again unto them, I go my way, and ye shall seek me, and shall die in your sins: whither I go, ye cannot come. Then said the Jews, Will he kill himself? because he saith, Whither I go, ye cannot come. And he said unto them, Ye are from beneath; I am from above: ye are of this world; I am not of this world. I said therefore unto you, that ye shall die in your sins: for if ye believe not that I am he, ye shall die in your sins.

Notice that Jesus never speaks of Joseph as His *Father.* He always speaks of God as His *Father.* They were trying to cast doubt on the two witnesses that Jesus had given by asking Jesus "Where is thy Father?" Jesus was now in the *treasury* of the Temple, which was in close proximity of the Temple officials. This would have been the Court of the Women, one of the three courts in the inner Temple compound. It was 200 ft. square and on the outer colonnaded walls around the court were thirteen trumpet-shaped treasury boxes where the people placed their coins. (**Matthew 6:2, Luke 21:1-4**) So the scene has gone from Galilee to Judea, from Judea to Jerusalem, from Jerusalem to the Temple courts, and from the Temple courts to the *treasury.*

"…for if ye believed not that I am he, ye shall die in your sins." There are a lot of the religious Jews and Messianic Jews today who believe that *all* of the Jews who have ever been born will one day be saved. They gather this from their interpretation of **Isa.59:20** and **Romans 11:26**:

And so all Israel shall be saved: as it is written,
There shall come out of Sion the Deliverer, and shall
turn away ungodliness from Jacob:

I believe these verses are referring to the end of the
tribulation period when the Messiah returns and *all* of the
Jews who are alive at that time will acknowledge Jesus.
(**Zech.12:10**) Paul was quoting from Isaiah within the
context of the regathering of Israel after the fullness of the
Gentiles is closed. I realize that, within the context of **John
8**, Jesus is talking to the Judean leaders specifically. But
still, if they could *die in their sins*, are they still not Jews? So
how could every Jew be saved one day when Jesus Himself
pronounces judgment on Jews here?

While I am a deep lover of the Jewish people, and a
strong believer in the covenant that God made with Israel,
it is clear to me that if Jews die without Jesus they will be
lost, just like Gentiles will be lost if they die without Jesus.
What's the need of preaching the gospel to the Jew if they
are going to all be saved in the end anyway? If they would
place their faith in Jesus as the Messiah then their sins
would be judged on the cross and they would be forgiven.
If they refused to believe in Jesus as the Messiah then they
would *die in their sins* and judgment was sure. What about
the burden of the apostle Paul in **Romans 9:1-3**:

I say the truth in Christ, I lie not, my conscience
also bearing me witness in the Holy Ghost, That
I have great heaviness and continual sorrow in my

heart. For I could wish that myself were accursed
from Christ for my brethren, my kinsmen according
to the flesh:

Does this sound like all Jews are automatically saved to you?
I am stating this fact because there is a major division even
among Messianic Jews about this subject.

"Ye are from beneath; I am from above: ye are of this world; I
am not of this world." Jesus had come from the Sea of Galilee,
which lies about 650 ft. *below* sea level. The religious leaders
were standing on Mt. Moriah, which was about 2500 ft.
above sea level. Yet, Jesus was from heaven and the Judean
leaders were from the world. Jesus was saying that the
religious leaders thought they were more spiritual because
of their high positions in the Temple. While the common
people had to walk up to Jerusalem and had trusted that the
Judean leaders would lead them to the God of Israel, the
leaders were corrupt and were blind leaders of the blind.

John 8:25-29 - *Then said they unto him, Who*
art thou? And Jesus saith unto them, Even the
same that I said unto you from the beginning. I
have many things to say and to judge of you: but he
that sent me is true; and I speak to the world those
things which I have heard of him. They understood
not that he spake to them of the Father. Then said
Jesus unto them, When ye have lifted up the Son
of man, then shall ye know that I am he, and that I
do nothing of myself; but as my Father hath taught

me, I speak these things. And he that sent me is with me: the Father hath not left me alone; for I do always those things that please him.

No one had ever told the religious rulers that they would die in their sins. What a question to ask the Son of God, "Who art thou?" *I have already told you from the very beginning who I am and you do not believe me,* Jesus replied. Jesus was the supreme, all-knowing God and He knew enough to condemn the religious rulers: their hypocrisy, their pride, their hatred of the light, and the unbelief in their hearts. Jesus was saying: *The God of your forefathers told the prophets how you would deny me, and His word is true.* But they did not understand that Jesus was talking about the Father.

"When ye have lifted up the Son of man, then shall ye know that I am he." Being *lifted up* connects us to **John 3:14** and **John 12:32** and refers to His crucifixion. Jesus was telling them that their sin ledger will be full and that the signs that they would see during and after His crucifixion would prove that He is truly the Messiah.

"And he that sent me is with me: the Father hath not left me alone; for I do always those things that please him." Even though they would crucify Jesus, He is letting them know that He would not die alone. Because He came to do the Father's will, the Father would be with Him. Little did they know that they were fulfilling the Hebrew scriptures. Again, Jesus came when He knew the religious establishment would reject Him, but it was all in the Father's plan. I am reminded of a passage in **Psalms 40:7-8:**

Then said I, Lo, I come: in the volume of the book
it is written of me, I delight to do thy will, O my
God: yea, thy law is within my heart.

John 8:30 – *As he spake these words, many*
believed on him.

Though most of the Jewish rulers rejected Jesus' claim, His words started to have an impact on many. The same message of Jesus that brings people to faith can also be rejected. But it is encouraging to read the words, *many believed on him*. However, listen to the rest of the story.

John 8:31-32 – *Then said Jesus to those Jews*
which believed on him, If ye continue in my word,
then are ye my disciples indeed; And ye shall know
the truth, and the truth shall make you free.

Even though there was a remnant within the Judean establishment that did believe in Jesus, they needed to *continue in His word* if they wanted to be His disciples. There is a common faith that brings salvation and then there is an uncommon faith that turns believers into disciples. If they continued to listen and to obey Jesus, then they would be *set free* from the group of unbelieving Jews and they would be able to *know* more truth. There are many people who have an intellectual belief in Jesus, but they have never truly committed themselves to be His servants. May you and I *continue* in God's word and become genuine disciples of Jesus of Nazareth. Look again at **John 2:23-24**:

> *Now when he was in Jerusalem at the passover,*
> *in the feast day, many believed in his name, when*
> *they saw the miracles which he did. But Jesus did*
> *not commit himself unto them, because he knew*
> *all men.*

John continues:

> **John 8:33-34 -** *They answered him, We be*
> *Abraham's seed, and were never in bondage to any*
> *man: how sayest thou, Ye shall be made free? Jesus*
> *answered them, Verily, verily, I say unto you,*
> *Whosoever committeth sin is the servant of sin.*

These are not the ones who believed in Him, but the leaders from the previous verses. They were descendants of Abraham, but they were not the true children of Abraham. Listen to what John the Baptist said:

> *And think not to say within yourselves, We have*
> *Abraham to our father: for I say unto you, that God is*
> *able of these stones to raise up children unto Abraham.*
> **—Matt.3:9**

That group of Jews may not have been actual slaves but the nation of Israel had been slaves several times over the centuries. But Jesus turns their argument and tells them that real slavery is the slavery of sin - *Rome may give you the temporary freedom to live your Jewish lifestyle* (under Roman

162

jurisdiction), *but you are under the bondage of sin and don't even know it.*

> **John 8:35-36** – *And the servant abideth not in the house for ever: but the Son abideth ever. If the Son therefore shall make you free, ye shall be free indeed.*

Jesus may have been using the law of the servant in the Torah as a backdrop. Read **Exodus 21:2-6**:

> *If thou buy an Hebrew servant, six years he shall serve: and in the seventh he shall go out free for nothing. If he came in by himself, he shall go out by himself: if he were married, then his wife shall go out with him. If his master have given him a wife, and she have born him sons or daughters; the wife and her children shall be her master's, and he shall go out by himself. And if the servant shall plainly say, I love my master, my wife, and my children; I will not go out free: Then his master shall bring him unto the judges; he shall also bring him to the door, or unto the door post; and his master shall bore his ear through with an aul; and he shall serve him for ever.*

A servant would be set free after six years, but the servant could choose to stay a servant because he loved his master and family so much. They would make a hole in his ear lobe and this would be the sign that he was a servant forever.

Jesus chose to come to this earth and to be crucified. Throughout all eternity, He will bear the marks of His crucifixion. He chose to be a servant of the Father, even to become the perfect sacrifice on a tree, in order for His people to be truly set free from their sins.

> **John 8:37-38** - *I know that ye are Abraham's seed; but ye seek to kill me, because my word hath no place in you. I speak that which I have seen with my Father: and ye do that which ye have seen with your father.*

What a word of condemnation: "my word hath no place in you." The reason they were plotting to kill Jesus was because the word of God was not in them. They were a part of natural Israel but they were not spiritual Israelites. Jesus contrasted God being His Father with their father, the devil. They were of the seed of the serpent, and they would *bruise the heel* of the Messiah. (**Gen.3:15**)

> **John 8:39-41** - *They answered and said unto him, Abraham is our father. Jesus saith unto them, If ye were Abraham's children, ye would do the works of Abraham. But now ye seek to kill me, a man that hath told you the truth, which I have heard of God: this did not Abraham. Ye do the deeds of your father. Then said they to him, We be not born of fornication; we have one Father, even God.*

When Abraham heard the word of God he obeyed the word of God. When the Judean leaders heard their Messiah they did not obey, therefore, they were not true children of Abraham. The true seed of Abraham, the fulfillment of the Abrahamic Covenant, was in their midst and they did not believe in Him. When they heard Him speak, they sought to kill Him. They were doing the works of their evil father.

There was a rumor going around that Jesus was an illegitimate child and they were probably accusing Him of being born of *fornication*. They may have heard about the strange birth of Jesus but they neither knew nor believed the scriptures enough to even consider the virgin birth prophesied in **Isaiah 7:14**. Jesus said that they were seeking to kill the *man* that had told them the truth. John's gospel says that Jesus even said that He was a *man*, but He also said that He was *God*.

> **John 8:42–45 -** *Jesus said unto them, If God were your Father, ye would love me: for I proceeded forth and came from God; neither came I of myself, but he sent me. Why do ye not understand my speech? even because ye cannot hear my word. Ye are of your father the devil, and the lusts of your father ye will do. He was a murderer from the beginning, and abode not in the truth, because there is no truth in him. When he speaketh a lie, he speaketh of his own: for he is a liar, and the father of it. And because I tell you the truth, ye believe me not.*

Here, the righteous indignation is beginning to show even more in the words of our Lord. The Judean leaders kept saying that God was their Father but, if that were true, then they would have loved Jesus. The reason they could not understand the speech of Jesus was because they were a product of the devil. The one who deceived the world had deceived them. The serpent is against God and His kingdom and the serpent was living in the hearts of those religious leaders. What strong words coming from the precious mouth of the Lord Jesus! He was telling them: *The devil is a murderer and does not know the truth. He is the father of lies, and because you are his children; that is the reason why you will not believe my words.*

> **John 8:46–47** – *Which of you convinceth me of sin? And if I say the truth, why do ye not believe me? He that is of God heareth God's words: ye therefore hear them not, because ye are not of God.*

Jesus told them that they could not find any fault in His life or His deeds. His life and works proved that He was telling them the truth. Jesus makes the statement here that His words are *God's words.* It sounds redundant to keep saying it, but the reason they did not hear God's words was because they were *not of God.* Think on this again: Jesus is talking to Judean leaders in Jerusalem who were supposed to be the spiritual leaders of the Jewish people. They were in charge of the Temple! All of this repeated dialogue between Jesus the Messiah and these religious leaders is one of the unique things about John's gospel.

> **John 8:48-49 -** *Then answered the Jews, and said unto him, Say we not well that thou art a Samaritan, and hast a devil? Jesus answered, I have not a devil; but I honour my Father, and ye do dishonour me.*

They are throwing an insult to Jesus by calling Him a *Samaritan.* In other words, they are saying that you live among us but you are not one of us. The hatred between the Jews and the Samaritans is probably one reason why the Gospels contain both the account of Jesus introducing Himself to the Samaritan woman (**John 4)** and the story of the good Samaritan (**Luke 10:30-37).** These religious leaders in Jerusalem were not only dishonoring Jesus, they were also dishonoring the God who they claimed to represent by saying that Jesus was filled with demons after He had told them that their father was the devil.

> **John 8:50 -** *And I seek not mine own glory: there is one that seeketh and judgeth.*

The humble Jesus allowed Himself to have no reputation and to be slandered by His own people. We can see the depravity of mankind as these religious leaders say that Jesus has a devil. Jesus lets them know that He was not in their midst to receive honor and glory, but the God whom they claimed to worship would *seek* them out and be their *Judge.*

> **John 8:51-53** - *Verily, verily, I say unto you, If a man keep my saying, he shall never see death. Then said the Jews unto him, Now we know that thou hast a devil. Abraham is dead, and the prophets; and thou sayest, If a man keep my saying, he shall never taste of death. Art thou greater than our father Abraham, which is dead? and the prophets are dead: whom makest thou thyself?*

Jesus mentions the victory over *death* once again to the Jews who *keep,* or obey, His words. Jesus mentions this promise in **John 5:24** and **John 11:26** as well. He knew that *His* coming resurrection would provide *His* eternal life for *His* children. In the midst of the religious leaders showing their hatred for Jesus, He inserted a glorious truth. Of course, Jesus was not talking about physical death, but spiritual death that will *never* come to those who obey His words. They only understood what Jesus was saying from the perspective of physical death and they said, "Now we know that thou hast a devil." They were saying: *our father Abraham died and so did the prophets of Israel, and now you are telling us that if we believe in you we shall never die!*

"Art thou greater than our father Abraham?" Jesus is placing Himself on a higher level than *Abraham* and the ancient prophets. Little did these self-righteous rulers know that they were talking face to face to the One who Isaiah called *The Mighty God, The Everlasting Father.* (**Isa.9:6**) I am reminded of a similar question that the Samaritan woman asked Jesus; "Art thou greater than our father Jacob?" (**John 4:12**)

John 8:54–56 – *Jesus answered, If I honour myself, my honour is nothing: it is my Father that honoureth me; of whom ye say, that he is your God: Yet ye have not known him; but I know him: and if I should say, I know him not, I shall be a liar like unto you: but I know him, and keep his saying. Your father Abraham rejoiced to see my day: and he saw it, and was glad.*

Jesus cites the *Son/Father* relationship once again in reply to their question, "whom makest thou thyself?" Jesus is saying that He has to tell the truth about knowing the *Father* or He will be a *liar* like them. Jesus brings up a very powerful truth. When the Lord spoke to Abraham, it was the *Word of God* and Jesus is the *Word*. (**Gen. 12:1, John 1:1**) When the Lord appeared to Abraham, like in **Gen. 12:7** and **18:1,** it was the pre-incarnate *Son of God*, Jesus. This is why John's gospel presents Jesus in this light. He is the *Word* become flesh and He is the One Abraham knew and *saw*. It was commonly believed among many of the rabbis in Jesus' time that Abraham was able to see the days of the Messiah. Paul went a step farther and said that God preached the gospel to Abraham:

And the scripture, foreseeing that God would justify the heathen through faith, preached before the gospel unto Abraham, saying, In thee shall all nations be blessed.

—Galatians 3:8

> **John 8:57–59** – *Then said the Jews unto him,*
> *Thou art not yet fifty years old, and hast thou seen*
> *Abraham? Jesus said unto them, Verily, verily, I say*
> *unto you, Before Abraham was, I am. Then took*
> *they up stones to cast at him: but Jesus hid himself,*
> *and went out of the temple, going through the midst*
> *of them, and so passed by.*

Why did they say *fifty years old*? Did Jesus look *fifty* while He was only about thirty-three? Was *fifty years old* considered to be the age requirement for one to be able to serve in the congregation of Israel? It is just a conjecture, but it does deserve to be considered as a reason why they used this particular age. Consider these verses concerning the age limit of the priests that could serve in the tabernacle:

> *From thirty years old and upward even until fifty*
> *years old, all that enter into the host, to do the work*
> *in the tabernacle of the congregation."*
> **—Numbers 4:3** and **4:39**

> *And from the age of fifty years they shall cease waiting*
> *upon the service thereof, and shall serve no more:*
> **—Numbers 8:25**

Jesus said something that is many times overlooked among the great *I am* statements that He gave: "Before Abraham was, I am." Jesus is giving a clear announcement of His divinity like He later would do in **John 10:30**. This claim simply stated that Jesus was God! This was blasphemy in the eyes of the religious Jews, so they *took up stones to cast at him*. Their misplaced motivation was taken from this verse:

> *And he that blasphemeth the name of the* LORD, *he shall surely be put to death, and all the congregation shall certainly stone him: as well the stranger, as he that is born in the land, when he blasphemeth the name of the Lord, shall be put to death.*
> **—Lev.24:16**

"*...but Jesus hid himself, and went out of the temple, going through the midst of them, and so passed by.*" I'm reminded of Jesus having to do the very same thing in Nazareth. (**Luke 4:30**) But the real reason why they could not kill Jesus was because *His hour had not yet come.*

CHAPTER NINE

John 9:1-7 - *And as Jesus passed by, he saw a man which was blind from his birth. And his disciples asked him, saying, Master, who did sin, this man, or his parents, that he was born blind? Jesus answered, Neither hath this man sinned, nor his parents: but that the works of God should be made manifest in him. I must work the works of him that sent me, while it is day: the night cometh, when no man can work. As long as I am in the world, I am the light of the world. When he had thus spoken, he spat on the ground, and made clay of the spittle, and he anointed the eyes of the blind man with the clay, And said unto him, Go, wash in the pool of Siloam, (which is by interpretation, Sent.) He went his way therefore, and washed, and came seeing.*

"And as Jesus passed by, he saw a man which was blind from his birth." We do not know how much time had gone by since the previous chapter, but it was probably not very much. The overarching theme is still that Jesus is the light of the world (**John 8:12**) and that is contrasted with the Judean leadership being in spiritual darkness. So, to hopefully press home this thought deeper into their hearts, here is a man that was in physical darkness who needed a miracle in order to be able to see for the first time and then the favor to be able to see Jesus. Jesus knew He would meet the blind man when He casually *passed by* but the disciples did not know. Jesus didn't see people the way we do. *He saw a man* who needed a touch from God. This first verse gives us three simple, but important facts:

1. *And as Jesus passed by...*
2. *...He saw a man...*
3. *...Which was blind from his birth.*

"And his disciples asked him, saying, Master, who did sin, this man, or his parents, that he was born blind? Jesus answered, Neither hath this man sinned, nor his parents: but that the works of God should be made manifest in him." There was a false theology in Jesus' time that held that bad things always happen to bad people; that one's personal sins result in punishment. This prejudice was so widespread that even Jesus' own disciples believed it. It is true that sometimes our personal sins do affect our health but that is not always the case. If bad things happen to sinners then all of us

should expect the worst, because we are *all* sinners. In a fallen world, sometimes the wicked prosper (**Psalm 73**) and the righteous suffer. The sun rises on the just as well as the unjust. (**Matt. 5:45**) The prejudice that the religious people and the disciples had toward this blind man probably stemmed from passages like **Exodus 20:5**:

> *Thou shalt not bow down thyself to them, nor serve them: for I the* LORD *thy God am a jealous God, <u>visiting the iniquity of the fathers upon the children unto the third and fourth generation of them that hate me</u>;*

But the Master dispels this simplistic view of human suffering. The blindness wasn't caused by either this poor man's personal sins or the sins of his parents. Jesus said that the healing of this blind man would be something that would bring glory to God.

"I must work the works of him that sent me, while it is day: the night cometh, when no man can work. As long as I am in the world, I am the light of the world." Jesus was God, but He was also man. He knew that He only had a small window of time to fulfill His mission. Soon *the night was coming* when His quivering hands would be nailed to a tree outside the walls of Jerusalem. But, as long as Jesus walked the earth, He personified the *light* of the world.

"When he had thus spoken, he spat on the ground, and made clay of the spittle, and he anointed the eyes of the blind man with the clay, And said unto him, Go, wash in the pool of Siloam,

(which is by interpretation, Sent.) He went his way therefore, and washed, and came seeing." There is much more to what Jesus did than meets the eye, no pun intended! Jesus could have just spoken a single word or touched the man, but He took His own saliva and spit on the ground to knead a clay-like substance and placed it on the man's eyes. I find it interesting that Jesus wrote on the ground back in **John 8:8** in order to free a sinful woman and here He uses the ground again, but this time it is to free a man from darkness. There was the written law in Jesus' time and then there was the *oral* law. One of the Jewish *oral* laws stated that it was prohibited on the Sabbath to knead two things together in order to build any kind of material. It was also a violation of the *oral* law for Jesus to put the clay on the man's eyes. So it seems as though our Lord is deliberately healing this blind man in a way that shows that the Pharisaic *oral* laws of the day had gone too far and were placing people under religious bondage. Jesus wasn't against the *oral* laws, but He went against them when they were placing a yoke of bondage on the people. But the way Jesus used His saliva has even a deeper, more profound message. It was also in the Jewish *oral* laws that the spittle of a firstborn son had supernatural power. Jesus was showing that He was the ultimate *Firstborn Son*. The *Firstborn* Son of Mary and the *Firstborn* Son of God!

"Go, wash in the pool of Siloam." This is identified as the lower pool of *Shiloach* in the old city of David that is mentioned in **Neh. 3:15** and **Isa. 8:6**. The pool of *Shiloach*, or *Siloam*, was designed by Hezekiah around 700 BC to

bring water from the Gihon Spring in the Kidron Valley down to the old city of David. (**2 Kings 20:20**) The apostle John was inspired by the Holy Spirit to inform his readers that the word *Shiloach*, or translated *Siloam*, means *Sent*. There seems to be a real connection here to the origin of the word *Shiloach*, which is *Shiloh*, in one of the major prophecies concerning the first coming of the Messiah, in **Gen. 49:10**:

> *The sceptre shall not depart from Judah, nor a lawgiver from between his feet, until Shiloh come; and unto him shall the gathering of the people be.*

Shiloh was a title of the coming Messiah who would be *sent* by God! The meaning could also include the fact that Jesus *sent* the blind man down to the pool of *Shiloach* to wash his eyes. I also find it interesting that one of the major customs during the time of the Feast of Tabernacles, back in **John 7**, was to go and fetch a golden pitcher of water from the *Pool of Shiloach* and bring it back to the altar at the Temple. Jesus didn't have to use the *Pool of Shiloach* to heal this man, but He was using a place that held a deep, spiritual meaning to the Judean leaders.

> **John 9:8–25** - *The neighbours therefore, and they which before had seen him that he was blind, said, Is not this he that sat and begged? Some said, This is he: others said, He is like him: but he said, I am he. Therefore said they unto him, How were thine eyes*

opened? He answered and said, A man that is called Jesus made clay, and anointed mine eyes, and said unto me, Go to the pool of Siloam, and wash: and I went and washed, and I received sight. Then said they unto him, Where is he? He said, I know not. They brought to the Pharisees him that aforetime was blind. And it was the sabbath day when Jesus made the clay, and opened his eyes. Then again the Pharisees also asked him how he had received his sight. He said unto them, He put clay upon mine eyes, and I washed, and do see. Therefore said some of the Pharisees, This man is not of God, because he keepeth not the sabbath day. Others said, How can a man that is a sinner do such miracles? And there was a division among them. They say unto the blind man again, What sayest thou of him, that he hath opened thine eyes? He said, He is a prophet. But the Jews did not believe concerning him, that he had been blind, and received his sight, until they called the parents of him that had received his sight. And they asked them, saying, Is this your son, who ye say was born blind? how then doth he now see? His parents answered them and said, We know that this is our son, and that he was born blind: But by what means he now seeth, we know not; or who hath opened his eyes, we know not: he is of age; ask him: he shall speak for himself. These words spake his parents, because they feared the Jews: for the Jews had agreed already, that if any man did confess that he was Christ, he should be put out of the synagogue. Therefore said his parents, He is of age; ask him. Then again called they the man that was blind, and said unto him, Give God the praise: we know that this man is a sinner. He answered and said, Whether he be a sinner or no, I know not: one thing I know, that, whereas I was blind, now I see.

The neighbors arrange a meeting with the healed man and the Judean Pharisees. Try to imagine the once blind man who was healed and how he began to see the colors, shapes, and pictures of the whole world before him. He was able to see the Temple for the very first time. He must have been awestruck to say the least. The neighbors are excited to prove to the leaders that a *bona fide* miracle has taken place. Like we have been hearing for several chapters, these religious people are more concerned about their interpretations of the Sabbath Day than they are the spiritual and physical needs of the people of Israel. They are quick to pronounce judgment on Jesus because He *intentionally* did this on the Sabbath. A *sinner* could not do such miracles. There was a division among the leaders.

So the religious Jews called for the man's parents and wanted to ask them if this was truly their son. His parents told them that they knew that this was their son but they did not know *how* he was able to see. They were afraid of the Jews because anyone that confessed that Jesus was the Messiah would be cast out of the synagogue. So the parents just told the Pharisees to ask the man. "He is of age," they said. This tells us that the man was a young man; just how young we are not told. This group of Pharisees was so much against Jesus and wanted to prove legally that He was a *sinner*. This poor young man had been set free from total darkness and was anxious to go and see all that he had missed in his life, but religion called him to testify against Jesus. The leaders did it with the pious statement, "Give God the praise." This young man was running out of patience and he gave them an answer that the rulers or no one could ever deny: "One thing I know, that, whereas I was blind, now I see."

There are a lot of questions that people can ask someone who has been saved: Where were you when you received Christ? What was the prayer that you prayed when you were saved? Who was the preacher when you were born again? Have you been baptized? What is your denominational background? What is your theology? I've even heard self-righteous church people say things like, "Well, I've known him for many years and I'm just not sure that he is saved. They have lived a sinful life." But this answer will shut them up: "There may be a lot of questions that I cannot answer, but all I know is that I am not the same person I used to be, and it all happened when I asked Jesus to be my Savior!" End of conversation!

John 9:26-34 - *Then said they to him again, What did he to thee? how opened he thine eyes? He answered them, I have told you already, and ye did not hear: wherefore would ye hear it again?*

179

will ye also be his disciples? Then they reviled him, and said, Thou art his disciple; but we are Moses' disciples. We know that God spake unto Moses: as for this fellow, we know not from whence he is. The man answered and said unto them, Why herein is a marvellous thing, that ye know not from whence he is, and yet he hath opened mine eyes. Now we know that God heareth not sinners: but if any man be a worshipper of God, and doeth his will, him he heareth. Since the world began was it not heard that any man opened the eyes of one that was born blind. If this man were not of God, he could do nothing. They answered and said unto him, Thou wast altogether born in sins, and dost thou teach us? And they cast him out.

I love the reply the young man gives the Pharisees this time: "Will ye also be his disciples?" They certainly were not going to be the *disciples* of a maverick preacher from Galilee who made clay on the Sabbath Day (*which proved in their eyes that He was a sinner*) and healed a man that was born blind. They told the man that he was a *disciple* of Jesus but they were *disciples of Moses*. The young man told them that it was a mysterious thing why they would not believe in Jesus because He had truly opened his eyes. A truly marvelous thing had happened: a young man was born blind and now he is able to see. But the Pharisees were still in unbelief.

According to **vs.31**, this young man was a worshipper of God, even when he was yet blind. God had heard his prayer. He knew that God did not hear the prayers of people who lived in open sin. He knew this from the Hebrew Scriptures:

> *And ye shall cry out in that day because of your king which ye shall have chosen you; and the LORD will not hear you in that day.*
> **—I Sam. 8:18**

> *Then shall they call upon me, but I will not answer; they shall seek me early, but they shall not find me:*
> **—Prov. 1:28**

> *And when ye spread forth your hands, I will hide mine eyes from you: yea, when ye make many prayers, I will not hear: your hands are full of blood.*
> **—Isa. 1:15**

> *But your iniquities have separated between you and your God, and your sins have hid his face from you, that he will not hear.*
> **—Isa. 59:2**

There were and are certain prayers that God hears from sinners when they repent of their sins but the prayers of someone who lives in stubborn rebellion, like these Pharisees, God does not hear.

"Since the world began was it not heard that any man opened the eyes of one that was born blind. If this man were not of God, he could do nothing. They answered and said unto him, Thou

wast altogether born in sins, and dost thou teach us? And they cast him out." This man lets the religious leaders know that the healing of someone who had been *born* blind had never happened in the history of the world. Healing a man that had been *born* blind was a true Messianic miracle. This was a fulfillment of **Isaiah 35:5**:

> *Then the eyes of the blind shall be opened, and the ears of the deaf shall be unstopped.*

The Pharisees went back to their traditional thinking that this poor young man had been born blind because he was a sinner and they cast him out. This was called *cherem*, which means that he was treated like one who was dead. The Pharisees were saying that they were the rabbis here and the young man had no right to lecture them. They were teachers of the law. No one who was born blind was going to tell them anything about God.

> **John 9:35–41** – *Jesus heard that they had cast him out; and when he had found him, he said unto him, Dost thou believe on the Son of God? He answered and said, Who is he, Lord, that I might believe on him? And Jesus said unto him, Thou hast both seen him, and it is he that talketh with thee. And he said, Lord, I believe. And he worshipped him.And Jesus said, For judgment I am come into this world, that they which see not might see; and that they which see might be made*

blind. And some of the Pharisees which were with him heard these words, and said unto him, Are we blind also? Jesus said unto them, If ye were blind, ye should have no sin: but now ye say, We see; therefore your sin remaineth.

This poor man had been cast out and, even though he was able to see for the first time, he had not yet seen the *Great Physician* that had healed Him. So what happens? Jesus found him! And the very first words Jesus said to him were: "Dost thou believe on the Son of God?" Faith in Jesus being the *Son of God* is the prerequisite for salvation. (**John 1:49, 3:16, 11:27, 20:31**) For anyone to have the assurance that they are truly saved, they must believe that Jesus is the *Son of God*. (**I John 5:13**)

"Who is he, Lord, that I might believe on him?" This man did not yet know that Jesus was the Son of God but he did believe in the *Lord*. I believe this is one of the primary reasons why Jesus healed the man and why Jesus is revealing Himself as the *Son of God* to him. Remember, this man was a *worshipper of God* back in **vs.31**. He just needed to know that the One who healed him is the Messiah of Israel, the *Son of God*! Just like when Jesus revealed Himself to the Samaritan woman who believed in the coming Messiah (**John 4:25**), this man knew that only the God of Israel could open the eyes of anyone that was born blind. (**vs.32**)

"And Jesus said unto him, Thou hast both seen him, and it is he that talketh with thee. And he said, Lord, I believe. And he worshipped him." Not only was he blessed to *see* the Son of

God, but he was also highly favored in that the Son of God was *talking* with him. Notice the man called Jesus *Lord* once more and *worshipped him*. He had been a worshipper of the God of Israel and now he worshiped God who had come in the flesh. Wow!

"And Jesus said, For judgment I am come into this world, that they which see not might see; and that they which see might be made blind." Here we find the spiritual meaning of why Jesus healed this man who was born blind. It was so those who did believe in Him would be given spiritual sight and those who did not believe in Him (*unbelieving religious rulers*) would be made spiritually blind.

"And some of the Pharisees which were with him heard these words, and said unto him, Are we blind also? Jesus said unto them, If ye were blind, ye should have no sin: but now ye say, We see; therefore your sin remaineth." The chapter closes with an unusual ending. At the beginning of the chapter, we find the disciples thinking that a man was *physically* blind because he was a sinner. At the end of the chapter we find Jesus saying that the Pharisees were *spiritually* blind because they were sinners. (**John 9:2, 9:41**)

Israel had a long history of thinking that God would not judge them because they were His chosen people. Many times throughout their history they thought they were innocent when they were guilty, like in **Jeremiah 2:35**:

> *Yet thou sayest, Because I am innocent, surely his anger shall turn from me.*

CHAPTER TEN

John 10:1-6 - *Verily, verily, I say unto you, He that entereth not by the door into the sheepfold, but climbeth up some other way, the same is a thief and a robber. But he that entereth in by the door is the shepherd of the sheep. To him the porter openeth; and the sheep hear his voice: and he calleth his own sheep by name, and leadeth them out. And when he putteth forth his own sheep, he goeth before them, and the sheep follow him: for they know his voice. And a stranger will they not follow, but will flee from him: for they know not the voice of strangers. This parable spake Jesus unto them: but they understood not what things they were which he spake unto them.*

For us to properly understand this chapter, we must keep in mind what has happened in the previous chapter. The false shepherds of Israel had cast out a man that was healed by the Son of God. Jesus, the *Good Shepherd*, had come to gather the lost sheep of the house of Israel and the false shepherds in Jerusalem were trying to hinder His mission. The *shepherd and the sheep* (or *flock*) is the most common used *metaphor* in the Bible. It is used in a positive way and a negative way. Let's begin with some of the positive verses:

> *The* LORD *is my shepherd; I shall not want. He maketh me to lie down in green pastures: he leadeth me beside the still waters. He restoreth my soul: he leadeth me in the paths of righteousness for his name's sake. Yea, though I walk through the valley of the shadow of death, I will fear no evil: for thou art with me; thy rod and thy staff they comfort me. Thou preparest a table before me in the presence of mine enemies: thou anointest my head with oil; my cup runneth over. Surely goodness and mercy shall follow me all the days of my life: and I will dwell in the house of the* LORD *for ever.*
>
> **—Psalm 23**

> *Thou leddest thy people like a flock by the hand of Moses and Aaron.*
>
> **—Psalm 77:20**

> *He chose David also his servant, and took him from the sheepfolds: From following the ewes great with young he brought him to feed Jacob his people, and Israel his inheritance. So he fed them according to*

the integrity of his heart; and guided them by the skilfulness of his hands.

—Psalm 78:70-72

Give ear, O Shepherd of Israel, thou that leadest Joseph like a flock; thou that dwellest between the cherubims, shine forth.

—Psalm 80:1

He shall feed his flock like a shepherd: he shall gather the lambs with his arm, and carry them in his bosom, and shall gently lead those that are with young.

—Isa. 40:11

And I will set up one shepherd over them, and he shall feed them, even my servant David; he shall feed them, and he shall be their shepherd.

—Ezekiel 34:23

Now let's read some of the verses that are using the shepherd/sheep *metaphor* in a negative way:

Woe be unto the pastors that destroy and scatter the sheep of my pasture! saith the LORD. Therefore thus saith the LORD God of Israel against the pastors that feed my people; Ye have scattered my flock, and driven them away, and have not visited them: behold, I will visit upon you the evil of your doings, saith the LORD.

—Jeremiah 23:1-2

And the word of the LORD came unto me, saying, Son of man, prophesy against the shepherds of Israel, prophesy, and say unto them, Thus saith the Lord GOD unto the shepherds; Woe be to the shepherds of Israel that do feed themselves! should not the shepherds feed the flocks? Ye eat the fat, and ye clothe you with the wool, ye kill them that are fed: but ye feed not the flock. The diseased have ye not strengthened, neither have ye healed that which was sick, neither have ye bound up that which was broken, neither have ye brought again that which was driven away, neither have ye sought that which was lost; but with force and with cruelty have ye ruled them. And they were scattered, because there is no shepherd: and they became meat to all the beasts of the field, when they were scattered. My sheep wandered through all the mountains, and upon every high hill: yea, my flock was scattered upon all the face of the earth, and none did search or seek after them. Therefore, ye shepherds, hear the word of the LORD; As I live, saith the Lord GOD, surely because my flock became a prey, and my flock became meat to every beast of the field, because there was no shepherd, neither did my shepherds search for my flock, but the shepherds fed themselves, and fed not my flock; Therefore, O ye shepherds, hear the word of the LORD; Thus saith the Lord GOD; Behold, I am against the shepherds; and I will require my flock at their hand, and cause them to cease from feeding the flock; neither shall the shepherds feed themselves any more; for I will deliver my flock from their mouth, that they may not be meat for them. For thus saith the Lord GOD; Behold, I, even I, will both search my sheep, and seek them out. As a shepherd seeketh out his flock in the day that he is among his sheep that are scattered; so will I seek out my sheep, and will deliver them out of all places where they have been scattered in the cloudy and dark day. And I will bring them out from the people, and gather them from the countries, and will bring them to their own land, and feed them upon the mountains of Israel by the rivers, and in all the inhabited places of the country. I will feed them in a good pasture, and upon the high mountains of Israel shall their fold be: there shall they lie in a good fold, and in a fat pasture shall they feed upon the mountains of Israel. I will feed my flock, and I will cause them to lie down, saith the Lord GOD. I will seek that which was lost, and bring again that which was driven away, and will bind up that which was broken, and will strengthen that which was sick: but I will destroy the fat and the strong; I will feed them with judgment. And as for you, O my flock, thus saith the Lord GOD; Behold, I judge between cattle and cattle, between the rams and the he goats. Seemeth it a small thing unto you to have eaten up the good pasture, but ye must tread down with your feet the residue of your pastures? and to have drunk of the deep waters, but ye must foul the residue with your feet? And as for my flock, they eat that which ye have trodden with your feet; and they drink that which ye have fouled with your feet. Therefore thus saith the Lord GOD unto them; Behold, I, even I, will judge between the fat cattle and between the lean cattle. Because ye have thrust with side and with shoulder, and pushed all the diseased with your horns, till ye have scattered them abroad; Therefore will I save my flock, and they shall no more be a prey; and I will judge between cattle and cattle.

—**Ezekiel 34:1-22**

So, when Jesus gives three parables comparing the *Good Shepherd* and the false shepherds, He is connecting this familiar *metaphor* in a positive and negative way, *together*. But He is also saying that He is the fulfillment of the *Messiah/ Shepherd* prophecies of the Old Testament. (**Psalm 23, Isa.40:11, Eze.34:23,** etc.) It was also a Jewish style of teaching to tell a parable and then retell the parable in a little different way in order to explain different facets of the main message. Now to simplify these first six verses of **John 10:1-6** let's try to explain just who Jesus is talking about:

The door into the sheepfold = *Jesus*

Thieves and robbers = *The Jewish Rulers*

Shepherd of the sheep = *Jesus*

The porter = *John the Baptist*

Sheep = *Jews and Gentiles who believed in Jesus*

Stranger = *The Jewish Rulers*

John 10:7-10 - *Then said Jesus unto them again, Verily, verily, I say unto you, I am the door of the sheep. All that ever came before me are thieves and robbers: but the sheep did not hear them. I am the door: by me if any man enter in, he shall be saved, and shall go in and out, and find pasture. The thief cometh not, but for to steal, and to kill, and to destroy: I am come that they might have life, and that they might have it more abundantly.*

Here is another one of the great "I am" statements of Jesus: "I am the door." In the language of Jesus: *Anee Ha Shaar.* In everyday village life, when a shepherd would gather his sheep in for the night, he would sometimes block the opening of the sheep pen with his own body. Thus the shepherd becomes the *door* of the sheep. When the morning comes, the shepherd gets out of the opening, and the sheep run over each other trying to go out and find pasture. This imagery is also hidden away in **Micah 2:12-13** :

> *I will surely assemble, O Jacob, all of thee; I will surely gather the remnant of Israel; I will put them together as the sheep of Bozrah, as the flock in the midst of their fold: they shall make great noise by*

reason of the multitude of men. The breaker is come up before them: they have broken up, and have passed through the gate, and are gone out by it: and their king shall pass before them, and the LORD on the head of them."

This imagery is also seen in the ministry of John the Baptist opening the way for the Messiah's earthly ministry as we read in **Matthew 11:12**:

And from the days of John the Baptist until now the kingdom of heaven suffereth violence, and the violent take it by force.

This verse carries a two-fold message. John the Baptist *suffered violence* and Jesus the Messiah would also *suffer violence*. But there was a *holy violence* as well when many of the lost sheep of the house of Israel would run like sheep coming out of the sheepfold to hear and to see Jesus during His ministry. Try to imagine the scene in **Luke 12:1**:

In the mean time, when there were gathered together an innumerable multitude of people, insomuch that they trode one upon another.

There is another passage with this imagery where Moses was talking to the Lord about the congregation of Israel that is found in **Numbers 27:15-17**:

And Moses spake unto the LORD, saying, Let the LORD, the God of the spirits of all flesh, set a man over the congregation, Which may go out before them, and which may go in before them, and which may lead them out, and which may bring them in; that the congregation of the LORD be not as sheep which have no shepherd.

So Jesus is the *door*, and He is opening the sheepfold so His sheep can go in and out to find *pasture*, which probably is a metaphor here the *kingdom life.*

"The thief cometh not, but for to steal, and to kill, and to destroy: I am come that they might have life, and that they might have it more abundantly." We need to think back to **John 8:44** where Jesus said the corrupt religious leaders were *children of the devil.* The Judean rulers were being used as instruments of the devil. They are the *thieves* who are *stealing* the sheep, *killing* the sheep, and ultimately *destroying* the sheep. Listen to what Jesus said in **Matthew 23:15** :

Woe unto you, scribes and Pharisees, hypocrites! for ye compass sea and land to make one proselyte, and when he is made, ye make him twofold more the child of hell than yourselves.

Not only were they leading the common people astray, they were also placing man-made traditions upon the people. They were telling the people that Jesus was a sinner, a heretic from Nazareth, and that He was committing blasphemy. Now contrast the *thieves* to Jesus. He came to give His sheep *abundant life* on earth that is filled with peace and joy and to give them His eternal life! We too need to listen to what our Lord is saying. In the midst of a very dark world with its man-made religious systems, we can enjoy the abundant life that Jesus wants to give to His sheep! Hallelujah!

> **John 10:11-15-** *"I am the good shepherd: the good shepherd giveth his life for the sheep. But he that is an hireling, and not the shepherd, whose own the sheep are not, seeth the wolf coming, and leaveth the sheep, and fleeth: and the wolf catcheth them, and scattereth the sheep. The hireling fleeth, because he is an hireling, and careth not for the sheep. I am the good shepherd, and know my sheep, and am known of mine. As the Father knoweth me, even so know I the Father: and I lay down my life for the sheep."*

Here we find another great "I am" statement by our Lord: "I am the good shepherd." In the Hebrew tongue: *Anee Ha Roi Ha Tov.* Jesus is again contrasting Himself, the *Good Shepherd,* with the false shepherds of Israel by stating that He even gives His life for His sheep while the false shepherds leave the sheep when the wolf (the devil). Jesus uses another word to describe the false shepherds: *hireling.* The religious system was so corrupt that the position of the high priest in Jerusalem went to the person who could pay the highest price to Rome. They were puppets of Rome, and they were lovers of money. It was a big cover-up job. I am reminded of the vast difference between these *hirelings* and our precious Lord:

> *For ye know the grace of our Lord Jesus Christ, that, though he was rich, yet for your sakes he became poor, that ye through his poverty might be rich.*
>
> **—2 Cor. 8:9**

Jesus, the *Good Shepherd*, left the glories of heaven, was born in a cave, lived in obscurity, preached to the poor, and then He sacrificially gave His life for the sheep. This is why He is called the *Shepherd* in other places in the New Testament:

> *Now the God of peace, that brought again from the dead our Lord Jesus, that great shepherd of the sheep, through the blood of the everlasting covenant.*
>
> **—Hebrews 13:20**

> *And when the chief Shepherd shall appear, ye shall receive a crown of glory that fadeth not away.*
>
> **—I Peter 5:4**

"I am the good shepherd, and know my sheep, and am known of mine. As the Father knoweth me, even so know I the Father: and I lay down my life for the sheep." Jesus again uses the mysterious Father/Son relationship to illustrate that the *Good Shepherd* knows His sheep and His sheep know Him. What a blessing to know that I do know the *Good Shepherd* and praise God, the *Good Shepherd* knows me!

> **John 10:16** – *And other sheep I have, which are not of this fold: them also I must bring, and they shall hear my voice; and there shall be one fold, and one shepherd."*

This has to be one of the most thought-provoking verses in the Bible. It deserves a little more of our time. The "other sheep" are the Gentiles who will come to faith in Jesus. There will not be *two* folds but *one fold*. Notice there is only *one shepherd*. The Gentiles who believe in Jesus are in the fold *with Israel*, not Israel in the fold of the Gentiles. It all started with Israel and the first sheep were Jews. But the Gentiles are not considered second-class sheep. They help to make up the *one fold*. Over the last two thousand years, the Gentile sheep have been millions more in number compared to the Jewish sheep. This connects us back to many of the Old Testament prophecies:

> *And I will bless them that bless thee, and curse him that curseth thee: <u>and in thee shall all families of the earth be blessed</u>.*
>
> **—Gen.12:3**

> *And I will make thy seed to multiply as the stars of heaven, and will give unto thy seed all these countries; and in thy seed shall <u>all the nations of the earth be blessed</u>;*
>
> **—Gen.26:4**

196

And in that day there shall be a root of Jesse, which shall stand for an ensign of the people; to it <u>shall the Gentiles seek</u>: and his rest shall be glorious.

—Isa.11:10

Sing, O barren, thou that didst not bear; break forth into singing, and cry aloud, thou that didst not travail with child: <u>for more are the children of the desolate than the children of the married wife</u>, saith the LORD. *Enlarge the place of thy tent, and let them stretch forth the curtains of thine habitations: spare not, lengthen thy cords, and strengthen thy stakes; For thou shalt break forth on the right hand and on the left; and <u>thy seed shall inherit the Gentiles</u>, and make the desolate cities to be inhabited.*

—Isa.54:1-3

The Lord GOD, *which gathereth the outcasts of Israel saith, <u>Yet will I gather others to him</u>, beside those that are gathered unto him.*

—Isa.56:8

And the <u>Gentiles shall come to thy light</u>, and kings to the brightness of thy rising.

—Isa.60:3

Yet the number of the children of Israel shall be as the sand of the sea, which cannot be measured nor numbered; and it shall come to pass, that in the place where it was said unto them, <u>Ye are not my people,</u>

there it shall be said unto them, Ye are the sons of the living God.

—Hosea 1:10

For from the rising of the sun even unto the going down of the same my name shall be great among the Gentiles; and in every place incense shall be offered unto my name, and a pure offering: for my name shall be great among the heathen, saith the LORD of hosts.

—Malachi 1:11

And the LORD shall be king over all the earth: in that day shall there be one LORD, and his name one.

—Zechariah 14:9

We can also see this mystery of the Gentiles being in the fold of Israel as we study the earthly ministry of the Messiah, the Roman centurion in **Luke 7:1-10**, the Syrophenician woman's daughter in **Matt.15:21-28**, the woman of Samaria in **John 4:1-39**, and the maniac of Gadara in **Mark 5:1-20**. Jesus even said these powerful words about other people coming to faith in Him outside of Israel who will be joined with the Patriarchs of old:

And I say unto you, That many shall come from the east and west, and shall sit down with Abraham, and Isaac, and Jacob, in the kingdom of heaven.

—Matt.8:11

This idea of *other sheep,* or Gentiles coming to faith in the Jewish Messiah, is a major theme in the book of Acts, Romans, Galatians, Ephesians, and the book of the Revelation.

In **vs.16**, the Hebrew idiom, "they shall hear my voice," means simply those who *obey my voice.* This was probably gathered from verses like **Exodus 19:5**:

> *Now therefore, if ye will obey my voice indeed, and keep my covenant, then ye shall be a peculiar treasure unto me above all people: for all the earth is mine:*

> **John 10:17–18** – *Therefore doth my Father love me, because I lay down my life, that I might take it again. No man taketh it from me, but I lay it down of myself. I have power to lay it down, and I have power to take it again. This commandment have I received of my Father.*

Jesus was not a martyr or the victim of any religious plot. He fulfilled God's eternal plan. Jesus came to this earth in the fullness of time knowing very well when He would die and how He would die. While we need to study about the historical situation of the politics and the religion during Jesus' time, we must never forget that there was an overarching purpose in the crucifixion of Jesus. Jesus had *the power to lay down His life and He had the power to take it again.* Jesus even predicted His own death and resurrection.

If we just look only in the gospel of John we find verses like these:

> *And Jesus answered them, saying, The hour is come, that the Son of man should be glorified. Verily, verily, I say unto you, Except a corn of wheat fall into the ground and die, it abideth alone: but if it die, it bringeth forth much fruit.*
>
> **—John 12:23-24**

> *Little children, yet a little while I am with you. Ye shall seek me: and as I said unto the Jews, Whither I go, ye cannot come; so now I say to you.*
>
> **—John 13:33**

> *I came forth from the Father, and am come into the world: again, I leave the world, and go to the Father.*
>
> **—John 16:28**

Jesus mentions several times in John's gospel that He has received a *commandment from the Father.* In the mysterious, eternal counsels of the triune Godhead, God The Father gave His Son the commandment to come down from heaven and to provide eternal salvation for His sheep. What a thought!

> **John 10:19-21** - *There was a division therefore again among the Jews for these sayings. And many of them said, He hath a devil, and is mad; why hear ye him? Others said, These are not the words*

of him that hath a devil. Can a devil open the eyes
of the blind?

We find where there was a division also in **John 7:43** and
John 9:16. It was to this extreme: "He hath a devil, and is
mad," while others said, "Can a devil open the eyes of the
blind?" Jesus is the great divider among men. Because the
sinful nature of man is to be stubborn and rebellious, so
many refuse to surrender to their Creator. After serving in
the Lord's work for well over thirty years, it never ceases
to amaze me how sinful we really are. The message of our
merciful Lord can be proclaimed time and time again and
some people willingly refuse His offer of eternal life. As
I have already asked a similar question, I will ask it again:
If you and I were in the crowd that day in Jerusalem, and heard
these words of Jesus, would we have followed him? Or would we
have said that He was just a rabble rouser from Nazareth? What
are your thoughts about Him today?

> **John 10:22-23** - *And it was at Jerusalem the*
> *feast of the dedication, and it was winter. And Jesus*
> *walked in the temple in Solomon's porch.*

This is the only time that the Jewish *feast of dedication* is
mentioned in the scriptures. It is called the feast of *Chanukkah*,
which means *to dedicate*. This feast began in 164 BC, when
the *Maccabees*, who were *Hasmonean* priests, revolted against
the pagan Greek ruler, Antiochus Epiphanes, for placing
the temple to Zeus in the Temple in Jerusalem. The real

Maccabean period of Jewish independence was from about 142-63 BC, even though the revolt started in 164 BC.

This tells that us that Jesus was in Jerusalem during the winter months, maybe late November or sometime in December. Without spending a lot of time and space to explain the customs of the feast, let me just say that today the unbelieving religious Jews celebrate *Channukah* as a reminder of their Jewish independence, while the Messianic Jews celebrate Jesus their Messiah as the light of the world (**John 8:12**) who came to give light to everyone (**John 1:9**) and to make His followers a light to the world (**Matt. 5:14**). *Channukah* is also a Jewish refuge against assimilating into the Gentile traditional Christmas in December.

"And Jesus walked in the temple in Solomon's porch." This area called *Solomon's porch* was on the east side of the Temple and it faced the Mt. of Olives. The Eastern gate opened into this area. There was a long-running belief that the Messiah of Israel would come from the east, from the Mt. of Olives and through the Eastern Gate into the Temple. Listen to these verses:

> *Afterward he brought me to the gate, even the gate that looketh toward the east: And, behold, the glory of the God of Israel came from the way of the east: and his voice was like a noise of many waters: and the earth shined with his glory. And it was according to the appearance of the vision which I saw, even according to the vision that I saw when I came to destroy the city: and the visions were like the vision that I saw by the*

river Chebar; and I fell upon my face. And the glory of the LORD *came into the house by the way of the gate whose prospect is toward the east.*

—Ezekiel 43:1-4

And his feet shall stand in that day upon the mount of Olives, which is before Jerusalem on the east, and the mount of Olives shall cleave in the midst thereof toward the east and toward the west, and there shall be a very great valley; and half of the mountain shall remove toward the north, and half of it toward the south.

—Zechariah 14:4

This is why the first church on Mt. Zion gathered in *Solomon's porch.* We find this place mentioned again in **Acts 3:11** and **Acts 5:12**.

John 10:24-26 - *Then came the Jews round about him, and said unto him, How long dost thou make us to doubt? If thou be the Christ, tell us plainly. Jesus answered them, I told you, and ye believed not: the works that I do in my Father's name, they bear witness of me. But ye believe not, because ye are not of my sheep, as I said unto you.*

I think the emphasis here should be placed on the word *us.* In other words, the Jewish authorities thought that Jesus should tell *them* that he was the Messiah because they were the leaders of the nation. But Jesus told them that His works in Galilee and Jerusalem had already been a *witness* that He truly is the Messiah and they would not obey His voice. They were not his *sheep*, not because they were elected to be lost, but because of their unbelief. (**Romans 11:19–20**)

> **John 10:27–29** – *My sheep hear my voice, and I know them, and they follow me: And I give unto them eternal life; and they shall never perish, neither shall any man pluck them out of my hand. My Father, which gave them me, is greater than all; and no man is able to pluck them out of my Father's hand.*

This assurance is mentioned in **John 10:10, 10:14, 10:28, and 10:29.** I would like to also call your attention to what Isaiah said:

> *And the work of righteousness shall be peace; and the effect of righteousness quietness and assurance for ever.*
> **—Isa. 32:17**

Listen to the words of Jude, the half brother of Jesus:

> *Jude, the servant of Jesus Christ, and brother of James, to them that are sanctified by God the Father, and preserved in Jesus Christ, and called:*
> **—Jude 1**

The Jews of Jesus' day that believed in Him, as well as all of those Jews and Gentiles today who believe in Jesus as the Son of God, can have the *peace* and the *assurance* that *eternal life* belongs to them. Eternal life is not a work of the flesh and is not based on our performance. It is a *gift* from our precious Lord Jesus Christ through the finished work of the cross! Eternal life is our gift *from* Jesus, and we are the Father's gift *to* Jesus.

> **John 10:30-33 -** *I and my Father are one. Then the Jews took up stones again to stone him. Jesus answered them, Many good works have I shewed you from my Father; for which of those works do ye stone me? The Jews answered him, saying, For a good work we stone thee not; but for blasphemy; and because that thou, being a man, makest thyself God.*

What a statement by Jesus! *Anee veha'av echad anachnu.* This idea of saying that Jesus and the Father are *one* has a direct correlation to the Jewish belief of *one* God:

Hear, O Israel: The LORD our God is one LORD: - **Deut.6:4**

While the *Son of God* walked this earth, He prayed to the *Father*, and was empowered by the *Holy Spirit*. There is only *one* God! It took all three manifestations of God to provide salvation for lost humanity. Jesus has just said that no one can pluck the sheep out of *His hand* (**vs.28**) nor can anyone pluck them out of His *Father's hand* (**vs.29**). This gives the believers in Jesus the assurance that nothing will be able to separate them from God. While in the upper room Jesus would say: "he that hath seen me hath seen the Father." (**John 14:9**) Jesus would later say that, when the religious rulers hated Him, they also hated the Father.

(**John 15:23**) Jesus prayed in the high priestly prayer that all believers *may be one even as He and the Father were one.* (**John 17:21**) At the very end of Matthew's gospel we find Jesus giving these instructions to His disciples:

> *Go ye therefore, and teach all nations, baptizing them in the <u>name</u> of the Father, and of the Son, and of the Holy Ghost:*
>
> **—Matt. 28:19**

Notice that Jesus did not say *names,* but *name.* The final *name* of the one true God is *Father, Son,* and *Holy Spirit.* When we want to see what God is like, we look at Jesus. When we want to see the works of God, we see the works of Jesus. When Jesus walked the hills of Galilee, it was God walking the hills. When Jesus walked on the water, it was God walking on the water. When Jesus healed a man that was born blind, it was God who healed the man born blind. *Jesus is God!* Again, we need to connect John's prologue in **John 1** to everything that happens in the rest of the gospel. The Word had become flesh and was walking among men, so we can see Him doing and saying things that only God would say and do.

"*Then the Jews took up stones again to stone him. Jesus answered them, Many good works have I shewed you from my Father; for which of those works do ye stone me? The Jews answered him, saying, For a good work we stone thee not; but for blasphemy; and because that thou, being a man, makest thyself God.*" The self-identification as being one with the Father caused the

Judeans to pick of stones to kill Jesus. Back when Jesus said, "Before Abraham was, I am," they also wanted to stone Him. (**John 8:59**) Jesus had performed many sign miracles that were works directly from the Father. It wasn't His *good works* that angered them; it was His teaching that He was *God*, yet He was *man*. To them, this was *blasphemy*, which called for stoning under the Jewish law.

> **John 10:33–36** - *Jesus answered them, Is it not written in your law, I said, Ye are gods? If he called them gods, unto whom the word of God came, and the scripture cannot be broken; Say ye of him, whom the Father hath sanctified, and sent into the world, Thou blasphemest; because I said, I am the Son of God?*

Jesus is referring to **Psalm 82** that was sung in the Temple by the Levites every Tuesday:

> *God standeth in the congregation of the mighty; he judgeth among the gods. How long will ye judge unjustly, and accept the persons of the wicked? Selah. Defend the poor and fatherless: do justice to the afflicted and needy. Deliver the poor and needy: rid them out of the hand of the wicked. They know not, neither will they understand; they walk on in darkness: all the foundations of the earth are out of course. I have said, Ye are gods; and all of you are children of the most High. But ye shall die like men,*

and fall like one of the princes. Arise, O God, judge
the earth: for thou shalt inherit all nations.

How strange is this? Why would Jesus be alluding to the word *gods* in this context? Let's see if we can unravel this double meaning of *elohim* and *Elohim*. The Israelites who were given the sacred scriptures were called *gods* because they had been set apart to not only represent God in this world, but to also righteously *judge* His people. But, within the context of **Psalm 82**, the *judges* were not judging righteously. They were under the indictment of God and, as a result, they would die like other men. So Jesus is using the Hebrew *kol v'homer* style of teaching again, comparing the light to the heavy. If the judges of Israel were called *gods*, the how much more should the *One* that was sent from the Father in heaven be called *God*? Putting it another way: if the Jewish leaders, who were evil, were called *sons of God*, how much more should the Good Shepherd, the Messiah of Israel, call Himself the *Son of God*? These Judean rulers would die like other men because they were not leading the people righteously.

> **John 10:37-39** - *If I do not the works of my Father, believe me not. But if I do, though ye believe not me, believe the works: that ye may know, and believe, that the Father is in me, and I in him. Therefore they sought again to take him: but he escaped out of their hand,*

Examine my *works*! Is giving sight to a man that was born blind a *work of God*? If it is, then believe in me as a result of *my works*. This is how important it is to know why Jesus performed His miracles and what they really meant in the early first century. His works vindicated His claim that He was the Son of God! In Jewish thought, one could not just *say* that he was the Messiah. He had to prove it by His works and that is exactly what Jesus did. They sought to take Jesus again, like in **Luke 4:30** and **John 8:59**.

> **John 10:40-42** - *And went away again beyond Jordan into the place where John at first baptized; and there he abode. And many resorted unto him, and said, John did no miracle: but all things that John spake of this man were true. And many believed on him there.*

Most of the time, this passage is just skipped over or just considered an afterthought. But it holds a great deal of hidden truths. Jesus left Jerusalem, walked back down toward Jericho, and continued on across *beyond Jordan (Land of Perea, that was governed by Herod Antipas)*. This was over a twenty-mile walk from over 2500 ft. above sea level to about 1100 ft. below sea level. Jesus just didn't go to any place but the place where *John at first baptized*. Many followed Him and *believed on Him* at the very place where John the Baptist baptized Jesus. How refreshing this must have been for our precious Lord! He was being rejected by the Jews in Judea and then went back to the place where

He was baptized by John to renew His strength. All of us need a time of spiritual renewal in our lives and we need to come away from the traditions of men and meditate on how good the Lord has been to us!

CHAPTER ELEVEN

THE RAISING OF LAZARUS

John 11:1-16 – *Now a certain man was sick, named Lazarus, of Bethany, the town of Mary and her sister Martha. (It was that Mary which anointed the Lord with ointment, and wiped his feet with her hair, whose brother Lazarus was sick.) Therefore his sisters sent unto him, saying, Lord, behold, he whom thou lovest is sick. When Jesus heard that, he said, This sickness is not unto death, but for the glory of God, that the Son of God might be glorified thereby. Now Jesus loved Martha, and her sister, and Lazarus. When he had heard therefore that he was sick, he abode two days still in the same place where he was. Then after that saith he to his disciples, Let us go into Judaea again. His disciples say unto him, Master, the Jews of late sought to stone thee; and goest thou thither again. Jesus answered, Are there not twelve hours in the day? If any man walk in the day, he stumbleth not,* *because he seeth the light of this world. But if a man walk in the night, he stumbleth, because there is no light in him. These things said he: and after that he saith unto them, Our friend Lazarus sleepeth; but I go, that I may awake him out of sleep. Then said his disciples, Lord, if he sleep, he shall do well. Howbeit Jesus spake of his death: but they thought that he had spoken of taking of rest in sleep. Then said Jesus unto them plainly, Lazarus is dead. And I am glad for your sakes that I was not there, to the intent ye may believe; nevertheless let us go unto him. Then said Thomas, which is called Didymus, unto his fellowdisciples, Let us also go, that we may die with him.*

By way of introduction to the transitional story and the last sign miracle of the Messiah, we need to ask ourselves a question: What does it mean to have eternal life if we still have to die? The apostle John is writing this letter, we believe, to the second generation of believers in Ephesus. Try to imagine how they must have felt to be taught by one of Jesus' closest disciples. He was the only one to live to be old, would he escape physical death? No! John would have to die physically as well because flesh and blood shall not inherit the kingdom of God.

Jesus probably raised many from the dead throughout His ministry (**Matt.11:5**), but it is written in the gospel accounts that He had raised the widow's son from Nain (**Luke 7**) and Jairus' daughter in Capernaum (**Luke 8**).

Raising Lazarus would be the most dramatic because it would contrast the resurrection of Jesus. Before we get into the context of Jesus raising Lazarus, there are several connections back to the previous chapters that I find interesting. Here are a few:

- *Light -* **John 8-9** and **John 11:9-10**
- *Jesus is life and light in* **John 1:4**. *He gives life to Lazarus and light to the man born blind in* **John 9:39**
- *Purpose of man born blind and the death of Lazarus is to bring glory to God.* – **John 9:3** *and* **John 11:4**
- *The healing of the man born blind is even mentioned in* **John 11:37**
- *The Jews trying to stone Jesus is mentioned again in* **John 11:8**
- *Turning the water into wine was the <u>first</u> sign miracle and the raising of Lazarus was the <u>last</u> before Jesus's own resurrection in Jerusalem.* – **John 2:11** and **John 11:4**
- *The raising of Lazarus took place sometime during the four months between the winter Feast of Dedication in* **John 10:22** *and the Feast of Passover that was only a few days away* (**John 12:1**).

The Hebrew name for *Lazarus* is *Eleazar,* which means *God will help.* Lazarus lived with his two sisters, *Mary* and *Martha,* in the little village of *Beit Anya, house of poverty,* about two miles east of Jerusalem, along the Jericho road on the eastern slopes of the Mount of Olives. Here we can learn a little bit more about the personal life of our dear Lord. He spent time at the home of Mary and Martha in

Luke 10:38–42. Jesus must have felt at home there because He is at their home again six days before Passover in **John 12:1.** So they were not only His disciples, they were his friends.

"It was that Mary which anointed the Lord with ointment." Since the gospel of John was written decades after the other gospel narratives, the anointing of Jesus by Mary was a well already known by his readers.

"Lord, behold, he whom thou lovest is sick." Most of the miracles that Jesus performed were on people that He certainly loved, but He didn't have a deep relationship with most of them like He did Lazarus. Jesus loved Lazarus, yet He lingered two extra days back near the Jordan River after He heard the news. **(vs.6)** Jesus also loved Martha and Mary. **(vs.5)** After two days, Jesus said, "Let us go into Judea again." The disciples could not believe that Jesus was going back to Judea after the Pharisees had tried to stone Him. **(vs.7–8)** Jesus reminds them of His previous teaching about the approaching night, **(John 9:4)** and the disciples have nothing to fear as long as the light is with them. **(vs.9–10)**

"Our friend Lazarus sleepeth; but I go, that I may awake him out of sleep." The metaphor *sleep* was used in Bible times for *death.* **(I Cor.15:51)** Even though the disciples still thought that Jesus meant Lazarus was alive, Jesus knew that Lazarus had died. **(vs.11–14)**

"And I am glad for your sakes that I was not there, to the intent ye may believe; nevertheless let us go unto him. Then said Thomas, which is called Didymus, unto his fellowdisciples, Let

us also go, that we may die with him." So not only was the death of Lazarus going to bring glory to God, it was going to teach the disciples a powerful lesson as well. *Thomas,* or *T'oma,* meaning *twin* (*Didymus* in the Greek), realized the dangers of Jesus going back to Judea, and told the other disciples that they needed to go to Jerusalem and die with Jesus. Little did these disciples know that their fear of dying would be reversed when they saw the risen Jesus. I also find it very interesting that *Thomas* is mentioned in John's gospel several times: **John 11:16, 14:5, 20:28,** and **21:2.** I believe this proves that Thomas should not be called *doubting Thomas.* He just always wanted to be wherever Jesus was.

John 10:17-27 - *Then when Jesus came, he found that he had lain in the grave four days already. Now Bethany was nigh unto Jerusalem, about fifteen furlongs off: And many of the Jews came to Martha and Mary, to comfort them concerning their brother. Then Martha, as soon as she heard that Jesus was coming, went and met him: but Mary sat still in the house. Then said Martha unto Jesus, Lord, if thou hadst been here, my brother had not died. But I know, that even now, whatsoever thou wilt ask of God, God will give it thee. Jesus saith unto her, Thy brother shall rise again. Martha saith unto him, I know that he shall rise again in the resurrection at the last day. Jesus said unto her, I am the resurrection, and the life: he that believeth*

in me, though he were dead, yet shall he live: And
whosoever liveth and believeth in me shall never die.
Believest thou this? She saith unto him, Yea, Lord:
I believe that thou art the Christ, the Son of God,
which should come into the world.

Jesus came to Bethany in the middle of the seven-day mourning period, *shiva*. This type of mourning was the custom in His day. It was the Jewish belief that the spirit hovered over a dead body for three days. They believed that on the fourth day the spirit departed and resurrection was impossible. Jesus deliberately waited until Lazarus had been in the grave for *four days*. Jesus knew exactly how long it would take to walk from the other side of Jordan to Bethany and, as always, the eternal Jesus was the Master over *time*. He wanted to show that this was truly a sign miracle that He was the giver of life.

"Many of the Jews came to Martha and Mary." Some Hebrew scholars believe that this family was friends to many of the Judeans. This even makes the miracle more important. It stands to reason because Bethany was not far from Jerusalem and was certainly in the precincts of Judea. If this conjecture is true, then Jesus is about to raise a Judean Jew from the grave in plain view of the religious establishment. Mary stayed back at the house with the mourners while Martha ran out to meet Jesus. While Martha is grieving and telling Jesus that Lazarus would have not died if he had been there, she also had the faith

that whatever Jesus asked the Father for would be done. So here we see that Martha's was mixed with fear and realism.

"Jesus saith unto her, Thy brother shall rise again. Martha saith unto him, I know that he shall rise again in the resurrection at the last day." It was a common belief among religious Jews that the coming of the Messiah would include a resurrection. Jesus was talking about raising Lazarus now while Martha thought that He was referring to the resurrection of the dead in the Messianic Age. Why did she believe this? She knew the prophecy:

> *And many of them that sleep in the dust of the earth shall awake, some to everlasting life, and some to shame and everlasting contempt.*
>
> **—Daniel 12:2**

"Jesus said unto her, I am the resurrection, and the life: he that believeth in me, though he were dead, yet shall he live: And whosoever liveth and believeth in me shall never die. Believest thou this? She saith unto him, Yea, Lord: I believe that thou art the Christ, the Son of God, which should come into the world." Here is another one of the great "I am" statements of Jesus: *Anee Ha Te Chee Ya Veh Ha Chayim.* Resurrection is not just something that Jesus will *do. He is the resurrection!* The eternal life that Jesus gives is so much greater compared to our earthly life. It is a *life on earth* to *life in heaven* journey. The ones who believe in Jesus *shall never die.* Physical death is but a moment compared to the glory that God's children will enjoy throughout all of eternity. Martha gives one the

great confessions in the gospels, she not only confesses that Jesus is the Messiah of Israel, but also that He is the *Son of God which should come into the world*. A remnant of Jews believed that God had a *Son* and that He would come into the world that He created. (**Isa.9:6, Prov.30:4**)

> **John 11:28-37** - *And when she had so said, she went her way, and called Mary her sister secretly, saying, The Master is come, and calleth for thee. As soon as she heard that, she arose quickly, and came unto him. Now Jesus was not yet come into the town, but was in that place where Martha met him. The Jews then which were with her in the house, and comforted her, when they saw Mary, that she rose up hastily and went out, followed her, saying, She goeth unto the grave to weep there. Then when Mary was come where Jesus was, and saw him, she fell down at his feet, saying unto him, Lord, if thou hadst been here, my brother had not died. When Jesus therefore saw her weeping, and the Jews also weeping which came with her, he groaned in the spirit, and was troubled. And said, Where have ye laid him? They said unto him, Lord, come and see. Jesus wept. Then said the Jews, Behold how he loved him! And some of them said, Could not this man, which opened the eyes of the blind, have caused that even this man should not have died?*

Martha went and called her sister Mary, who was back at the house mourning, and told her that the *Master is here* and calling for her. Try to imagine the mixed feelings of Mary who had sat the feet of Jesus and heard His words. Mary knew Jesus was her Lord, but why did He allow her brother Lazarus to die? The Jews who were in the house comforting Mary *followed her*, not to the grave of Lazarus, but to meet Jesus. Here again we see a *group* of the Jews from Judea mourning with Mary and they see her fall down at the feet of Jesus and say: "Lord, if thou hadst been here, my brother had not died." Jesus not only saw Mary *weeping*, but He also saw this group of Jews from Judea *weeping* with her. This is one of the few times that it mentions in the gospels that *Jesus groaned in his spirit*. It is written that *He sighed* (**Mark 7:34, 8:12**) but here in Bethany *He groaned*. Jesus asked, "Where have ye laid him?" They said, "Lord, come and see." The look on their faces and the grieving was so intense, that *Jesus wept!* He didn't just *cry. Jesus wept!* The humanity of Jesus comes out as He sees the genuine sorrow that has broken the hearts of His close friends and the mourners from Judea. I don't think we need to try to read anything else into this powerful emotion that Jesus felt. He was going to prove that He was God by raising Lazarus, but here we can see that he was a man of deep compassion. It helps us to also understand that in Jesus' time, when a righteous person died, the whole community suffered the loss. This was because this righteous person was not only a great help to many within the community; they were also a spiritual influence to so many others. This was a sad day in the little village of Bethany and Jesus joined in their grief. Jesus wept so much that even this group of Jews said, "Behold how he loved him."

"*And some of them said, Could not this man, which opened the eyes of the blind, have caused that even this man should not have died?*" Some of the Jews really began to take notice and thought that, if Jesus could open the eyes of a man that had been born blind, He could have certainly healed a man that was sick and kept him from dying.

> **John 11:38-43** - *Jesus therefore again groaning in himself cometh to the grave. It was a cave, and a stone lay upon it. Jesus said, Take ye away the stone. Martha, the sister of him that was dead, saith unto him, Lord, by this time he stinketh: for he hath been dead four days. Jesus saith unto her, Said I not unto thee, that, if thou wouldest believe, thou shouldest see the glory of God? Then they took away the stone from the place where the dead was laid. And Jesus lifted up his eyes, and said, Father, I thank thee that thou hast heard me. And I knew that thou hearest me always: but because of the people which stand by I said it, that they may believe that thou hast sent me. And when he thus had spoken, he cried with a loud voice, Lazarus, come forth.*

Jesus is still groaning within Himself and now He comes to the grave. It was a first-century family tomb where a stone was rolled in front of the cave. Jesus said, "Take ye away the stone." Martha said, "Lord, by this time he stinketh: for he hath been dead four days." Lazarus's body had started to see corruption. This is one of the major differences between the resurrection of Lazarus and Jesus' own resurrection: Jesus' body would *not* see corruption. (**Psalm 16:10**, **Acts 2:27**) So, in Jewish belief, the spirit had left the decayed body of Lazarus. Jesus brings up the fact that, if they would believe, they would see the *glory*, or the revelation, of God.

"Father, I thank thee that thou hast heard me." Jesus began to pray to the Father so the people that were standing by would know that it was the Father who had sent Him into the world. I'm reminded of how Jesus prayed and thanked the Father for hiding His mysteries from the wise and prudent in **Matt. 11:25**. I'm also reminded of how Jesus prayed before feeding the five thousand in **John 6:11**. Before this last sign miracle of raising Lazarus, Jesus prayed to the Father.

"...he cried with a loud voice, Lazarus, come forth," or *"Eleazar, come out!"* Two reasons why Jesus may have cried out with a loud voice:

1. *It was unlawful under the Jewish law to touch a dead body* (**Numbers 19:11**) *and, even though Jesus had touched dead bodies in the Galilee, He was now in the religious territory of Judea.*
2. *It is believed that the tomb of Lazarus was built with a long tunnel or stairs leading down to the grave, so Jesus wanted Lazarus to hear His voice.*

> **John 11:44 –** *And he that was dead came forth, bound hand and foot with graveclothes: and his face was bound about with a napkin. Jesus saith unto them, Loose him, and let him go.*

Here we find another major difference between the resurrection of Lazarus and the resurrection of Jesus. Lazarus came forth "bound hand and foot with grave clothes: and his face was still bound with a napkin." John's gospel tells us that when Jesus arose He left the grave clothes and face napkin behind in the tomb. (**John 20:6–7**) What could this tell us? It says that Lazarus still was mortal and that he would have to die again. But Jesus arose and left mortality in the tomb, to never again face death. Jesus conquered death once and for all! Hallelujah! When our Lord comes to gather His children away, we too will never have to face death again. Think on this verse:

> *So when this corruptible shall have put on incorruption, and this mortal shall have put on immortality, then shall be brought to pass the saying that is written, Death is swallowed up in victory.*
>
> **—I Corinthians 15:54**

*Ossuaries were small stone boxes filled with bones of the deceased after they had been dead for about one year. They were only used from around 30 BC- 70 AD; this includes the time of the earthly ministry of Jesus. In 1873, a French archaeologist, Claremont-Gannueau, discovered a cave on the Mount of Olives east of

Jerusalem with several ossuaries. Three of the ossuaries that they found had the Hebrew names of Eleazar, Marta, and Miriam.

> **John 11:45–54** – *Then many of the Jews which came to Mary, and had seen the things which Jesus did, believed on him. But some of them went their ways to the Pharisees, and told them what things Jesus had done. Then gathered the chief priests and the Pharisees a council, and said, What do we? for this man doeth many miracles. If we let him thus alone, all men will believe on him: and the Romans shall come and take away both our place and nation. And one of them, named Caiaphas, being the high priest that same year, said unto them, Ye know nothing at all, Nor consider that it is expedient for us, that one man should die for the people, and that the whole nation perish not. And this spake he not of himself: but being high priest that year, he prophesied that Jesus should die for that nation; And not for that nation only, but that also he should gather together in one the children of God that were scattered abroad. Then from that day forth they took counsel together for to put him to death. Jesus therefore walked no more openly among the Jews; but went thence unto a country near to the wilderness, into a city called Ephraim, and there continued with his disciples.*

The enthusiasm for Jesus had reached a crescendo. Anyone could go and talk to Lazarus in Bethany and see that a real miracle of raising a dead man had occurred. Many of the Jews from Judea, who had come to comfort Mary after they saw Lazarus walk out of the grave, began to believe on Jesus. But there were some who did not believe, and they went into Jerusalem to tell the Pharisees of the Sanhedrin. (**vs.46**) So we have to differentiate between the *believing* religious Jews in Judea and the *unbelieving* religious Jews. The chief priests called a special council (**vs.47**) not to show faith in Jesus, but to see what they could do to stop Jesus because the raising of Lazarus was so monumental. They thought that if they didn't stop Jesus then a revolt would start and Rome would come, take away their power and positions, and do away with the nation of Israel. (**vs.48**) That particular year, the high priest was named *Caiaphas,* or the Hebrew *Kayafa,* and he served from 18–36 AD. He was the son-in-law of Annas. Even though he was an evil high priest, the Lord used him to speak a prophecy: "that one man should die for the people, and that the whole nation perish not." Caiaphas, trying to avoid a political crisis, was saying that it was better for one man to die than for Rome to kill all of them. Little did he know that he was prophesying about Jesus sacrificially dying for the nation of Israel. (**vs.51**) Not only was Jesus dying for the nation of Israel but Jesus was also dying for all of those who were *scattered abroad,* including the Jews in the diaspora and the Gentile believers. (**vs.52**) This was the last straw. Jesus was causing too much of stir and His popularity was growing. He had to be put to death. (**vs.53**) Jesus then left Bethany and went back into the desert to a place called *Ephraim.*

This was about fifteen miles northwest of Jerusalem, not far from the border of Samaria. Today is had been identified with the town of *Taybeh*. Jesus stayed there until it was time to go back into Jerusalem for the feast of Passover.

> **John 11:55-57** - *And the Jews' passover was nigh at hand: and many went out of the country up to Jerusalem before the passover, to purify themselves. Then sought they for Jesus, and spake among themselves, as they stood in the temple, What think ye, that he will not come to the feast? Now both the chief priests and the Pharisees had given a commandment, that, if any man knew where he were, he should shew it, that they might take him.*

There was a seven-day process of Jewish purification before they could celebrate the feast of Passover. One of the primary reasons why they had to be cleansed before the feast was to purify themselves if they had been exposed to corpse contamination. Isn't that interesting that this purifying is mentioned after the raising of a dead man in Bethany? *Then sought they for Jesus.* Many who were in the Temple were talking among themselves: *Is Jesus going to come to the Passover? We haven't seen Him in since the feast of Tabernacles* (**John 7-8**), *or maybe He will not obey the laws of the Jews and come to Jerusalem for the feast this year.* The people who wanted to see Jesus did not know that the Jewish authorities had already decided that Jesus must be arrested and killed.

CHAPTER TWELVE

SUPPER AT BETHANY

John 12:1-11 - *Then Jesus six days before the passover came to Bethany, where Lazarus was, which had been dead, whom he raised from the dead. There they made him a supper; and Martha served: but Lazarus was one of them that sat at the table with him. Then took Mary a pound of ointment of spikenard, very costly, and anointed the feet of Jesus, and wiped his feet with her hair: and the house was filled with the odour of the ointment. Then saith one of his disciples, Judas Iscariot, Simon's son, which should betray him, Why was not this ointment sold for three hundred pence, and given to the poor? This he said, not that he cared for the poor; but because he was a thief, and had the bag, and bare what was put therein. Then said Jesus, Let her alone: against the day of my burying hath she kept this. For the poor always ye have with you; but me ye have not always. Much people of the Jews therefore knew that he was there: and they*

came not for Jesus' sake only, but that they might see
Lazarus also, whom he had raised from the dead. But
the chief priests consulted that they might put Lazarus
also to death; Because that by reason of him many of
the Jews went away, and believed on Jesus.

If the Passover that year was on Thursday, as many Hebrew scholars believe, then *six days before Passover* would make this setting what the Jews called *Shabbat Hagadol,* or the *big Sabbath* before the feast began. A meal was given in honor of Jesus raising Lazarus and now Jesus was the famous man who raised a man from the dead in Bethany. There are three beautiful moments that we find in **vs. 2-3**:

- *Martha is serving Jesus*
- *Lazarus is having fellowship with Jesus*
- *Mary is worshipping Jesus*

Although it sounds confusing, I need to mention that many have asked over the centuries if Mary was the same woman who anointed the feet of Jesus in **Mark 14:3**? The same story in **Mark** is given in **Luke 7:36-50** where this woman is described as a *sinful woman*. It doesn't seem to fit the gospel accounts to portray Mary of Bethany as a prostitute. Could there have been two different women who anointed the feet of Jesus? Possibly so! However, it was the Jewish custom to have *three meals* on the Sabbath, so there could have been more than one house where the Sabbath was celebrated with Jesus.

But it does need to be mentioned here that Jesus was in

Bethany in **John 12.** He was in the house of *Simon the leper* in **Mark 14:3.** Judas Iscariot is called *Simon's son* in **John 12:4.** This Simon could be *Simon the leper.* This is why some scholars believe that there was only one anointing.

The very costly *spikenard,* worth *three hundred pence* (a year's wages), seemed to be a waste to *Judas Iscariot,* but Mary evidently knew about the soon-coming death of her Messiah and she was preparing Jesus for His burial in Jerusalem. Mary had learned much by sitting at the feet of Jesus. (**Luke 10:39**) As the fragrance from the ointment filled the house, what emotions and thoughts must have been going through their minds! What was Mary doing with such an expensive jar of ointment? Were they wealthy, or was this something that had been saved for years and was the most costly item she had? When I think of the tears that she must have cried, I think of this passage of **Psalm 56:8**:

> *Thou tellest my wanderings:* <u>*put thou my tears into*</u>
> <u>*thy bottle*</u>*: are they not in thy book?*

Jesus is quoting from **Deut. 15:11** when He says, "For the poor always have with you."

> *For the poor shall never cease out of the land:*
> *therefore I command thee, saying, Thou shalt open*
> *thine hand wide unto thy brother, to thy poor, and*
> *to thy needy, in thy land.*

Just imagine! The disciples had walked with Jesus for over three years and had lived with only the necessities of life.

Here, Mary is pouring this expensive ointment on *the feet of Jesus* and *wiping them with her hair*. It's interesting that *Judas Iscariot*, who kept the coins for the travels of Jesus and the disciples, was a *thief.* Anywhere there is true worship, Satan seems to be hiding in the shadows and is always wanting someone to focus on the money. Sadly, that ungodly scenario still goes on today.

"Much people of the Jews therefore knew that he was there: and they came not for Jesus' sake only, but that they might see Lazarus also, whom he had raised from the dead. But the chief priests consulted that they might put Lazarus also to death; Because that by reason of him many of the Jews went away, and believed on Jesus." Many were coming from Jerusalem to Bethany not only to see Jesus, but to see Lazarus as well. Maybe they wanted to ask him questions like: *Eleazar, what was it like to be dead, and then come back to life?* Keep in mind that there were many witnesses to the raising of Lazarus in Bethany. The *chief priests* were really worried now not only because the raising of Lazarus had been eye-witnessed by many, but also because *many had believed on Jesus.* They were so angry that they even wanted to *put Lazarus also to death.*

What contrasts we find in these few eleven verses:

- *Martha served Jesus.*
- *Lazarus had fellowship with Jesus.*
- *Mary worshipped Jesus.*
- *The burial of Jesus is mentioned.*
- *Judas Iscariot was a thief.*

- *Many Jews believed on Jesus.*
- *The chief priests wanted to kill Lazarus.*

When we consider the powerful story of the raising of Lazarus and the *positive* and *negative* effect that it had on the people of Judea, we can possibly assume that this may have been the reason why the name *Lazarus* is also used by Jesus in the story of the rich man who died and went to hell and the beggar who died and went to Abraham's bosom. (**Luke 16:19-31**) Could this be a parallel connection? The *Lazarus* of **John 11-12** had to have gone to Abraham's bosom also. The story in **Luke 16** closes by alluding to the resurrection:

> *And he said unto him, If they hear not Moses and the prophets, neither will they be persuaded, though one rose from the dead.*
>
> **—Luke 16:31**

THE TRIUMPHAL ENTRY OF THE MESSIAH

John 12:12-19 - *On the next day much people that were come to the feast, when they heard that Jesus was coming to Jerusalem, Took branches of palm trees, and went forth to meet him, and cried, Hosanna: Blessed is the King of Israel that cometh in the name of the Lord. And Jesus, when he had found a young ass, sat thereon; as it is written, Fear not, daughter of Sion: behold, thy King cometh, sitting on an ass's colt. These things understood* *not his disciples at the first: but when Jesus was glorified, then remembered they that these things were written of him, and that they had done these things unto him. The people therefore that was with him when he called Lazarus out of his grave, and raised him from the dead, bare record. For this cause the people also met him, for that they heard that he had done this miracle. The Pharisees therefore said among themselves, Perceive ye how ye prevail nothing? behold, the world is gone after him.*

Many people came to the feast of Passover because they heard that Jesus was going to be there. *(The estimated population during the feast of Passover was about 200,000 or more. Later in the first century, Josephus wrote that there were several million, but he was known to over-exaggerate his numbers)* Think of the people who were convinced that Jesus was the Messiah just six months earlier at the feast of Tabernacles in **John 7:41-43**. Remember all of the Galileans who had followed Jesus from the north along with all of the people who became believers in Jesus at the raising of Lazarus. (**John 12:17-18**) There was a Messianic fire like never before! Everything had reached a crescendo in the ministry of the Messiah. Now He is offering peace to Jerusalem, including even His enemies. Even though the religious leaders did not accept Jesus that day, the Mt. of Olives has never been the same since Jesus made that triumphal ride on a lowly donkey!

There are many Old Testament connections to the Triumphal Entry of the Messiah. "Hosanna: Blessed is the

King of Israel that cometh in the name of the Lord." They are *crying* out to Jesus, the *King of Israel*, to save them from the Romans. This is a clear Messianic title that they are giving to Jesus. We need to contrast the cries of the people here to the times when Jesus told people to not tell anyone. (**Matt.8:4, 16:20, Mark 7:36**) Now was the time. The hour had come for the Messiah of Israel to ride a donkey into Jerusalem. What a sight! What jubilation! What joy filled the hearts of His followers! They are quoting from **Psalm 118:26**:

> *Blessed be he that cometh in the name of the* LORD:
> *we have blessed you out of the house of the* LORD.

The fact that the *King of Israel* would ride on a donkey has hundreds of references to the history of Israel. The word *donkey* is used over 140 times and the word *ass* is used over 4oo times in the Bible. Here are some of the most important:

> *And Abraham rose up early in the morning, and saddled his ass, and took two of his young men with him, and Isaac his son, and clave the wood for the burnt offering, and rose up, and went unto the place of which God had told him.*
> **—Genesis 22:3**

> *Binding his foal unto the vine, and his ass's colt unto the choice vine; he washed his garments in wine, and his clothes in the blood of grapes:*
> **—Genesis 49:11**

And Moses took his wife and his sons, and set them upon an ass, and he returned to the land of Egypt: and Moses took the rod of God in his hand.
                                    —Exodus 4:20

Rejoice greatly, O daughter of Zion; shout, O daughter of Jerusalem: behold, thy King cometh unto thee: he is just, and having salvation; lowly, and riding upon an ass, and upon a colt the foal of an ass.
                                    —Zechariah 9:9

Even though it is not mentioned in the gospels, it is believed that Mary rode on a donkey from Nazareth all the way down to Bethlehem when she was pregnant with Jesus. The disciples of Jesus did not know at this moment in time about the connection to the Old Testament prophecies, but after Jesus spent forty days with the disciples after the resurrection, then they understood. (**vs.16**)

"*The Pharisees therefore said among themselves, Perceive ye how ye prevail nothing? behold, the world is gone after him.*" The Pharisees in Jerusalem who hated Jesus knew they were getting nowhere with the people. They said in a *hyperbolic* way: *The whole world is gone after him.* But the apostle John intends these words as a form of *irony*, because he knows that the world will go after Jesus in a very short while. We must not leave this all-important passage without stating the contrast between the humble Jesus riding a donkey and the ruling and reigning Jesus who will come the second time riding on a white horse:

And I saw heaven opened, and behold a white horse; and he that sat upon him was called Faithful and True, and in righteousness he doth judge and make war. His eyes were as a flame of fire, and on his head were many crowns; and he had a name written, that no man knew, but he himself. And he was clothed with a vesture dipped in blood: and his name is called The Word of God. And the armies which were in heaven followed him upon white horses, clothed in fine linen, white and clean. And out of his mouth goeth a sharp sword, that with it he should smite the nations: and he shall rule them with a rod of iron: and he treadeth the winepress of the fierceness and wrath of Almighty God. And he hath on his vesture and on his thigh a name written, KING OF KINGS, AND LORD OF LORDS.

—Revelation 19:11-16

GREEKS COMING TO SEE JESUS

John 12:20-22 - *And there were certain Greeks among them that came up to worship at the feast: The same came therefore to Philip, which was of Bethsaida of Galilee, and desired him, saying, Sir, we would see Jesus. Philip cometh and telleth Andrew: and again Andrew and Philip tell Jesus.*

There has been an ongoing debate for centuries about who these *Greeks* really were. Were they God-fearing Gentiles, or were they Hellenized, Greek-speaking Jews? I think the latter, because it says that they had come to Jerusalem for the Jewish feast of Passover. While there were many Gentiles who came up to Jerusalem for the feast, the majority of the people in the crowd were Jews. There were *certain Greeks* of the large Jewish population that had been scattered in the Roman Empire. Calling Hellenized Jews *Greeks* is also repeated in **Acts 6:1** and **Acts 9:29**. It's also interesting that they came to *Philip*, and *Philip* told *Andrew*. *Philip* and *Andrew* had Greek names and possibly spoke Greek better than the other disciples. These Hellenized Jews wanted to *see Jesus*. Did they want Jesus to come to their part of the world? It is not recorded where Jesus gave them His time. He probably didn't. His answer to the disciples is a cryptic description of His pending death and exaltation. John wanted the Greek-speaking people of Ephesus, who were the first to read this gospel, to know that the time was coming soon for the preaching of the gospel to be launched into the known world.

JESUS' ANSWER

John 12:23-26 – *And Jesus answered them, saying, The hour is come, that the Son of man should be glorified. Verily, verily, I say unto you, Except a corn of wheat fall into the ground and die, it abideth alone: but if it die, it bringeth forth much fruit. He that loveth his life shall lose it; and he that hateth his life in this world shall keep it unto life*

235

> *eternal. If any man serve me, let him follow me; and*
> *where I am, there shall also my servant be: if any*
> *man serve me, him will my Father honour.*

The hour is come for the *Son of man* to be revealed. This will be accomplished by the death, burial, resurrection, and ascension of the Messiah. Jesus uses the metaphor of a *kernel of wheat*. Just like a kernel of wheat must be placed in the ground before it can rise forth from the earth, so to Jesus would be buried before His glorious victory. His glorification would bring *forth much fruit*, just like a harvest of wheat. The apostle Paul would later use this same metaphor when speaking about the resurrection. (**I Cor. 15:35-40**) Many of the Jewish Sages of old said that the children of God will not be resurrected naked, but they will be clothed because a naked kernel of wheat comes forth from the ground clothed. They gathered this thought from **Psalm 72:16** :

> *There shall be an handful of corn in the earth upon*
> *the top of the mountains; the fruit thereof shall shake*
> *like Lebanon: and they of the city shall flourish like*
> *grass of the earth.*

Jesus gave the strange paradox: "He that loveth his life shall lose it; and he that hateth his life in this world shall keep it unto life eternal." This simply means that we should value our life in the world to come more than our life in this present world. This **vs.25** parallels verses like **Matthew 10:39, 16:25, Mark 8:35**, and **Luke 9:24, 17:33**.

"If any man serve me, let him follow me; and where I am, there shall also my servant be: if any man serve me, him will my Father honour." Jesus is saying that all those who follow Him may have to die as well. The good news is that, if they *follow the Son*, they will be *honored by the Father* because they were not ashamed to be *servants* of Christ. The *servants* of the Lord will be *where the Lord is* one day. Wouldn't it be wonderful to be remembered as one of our Lord's choicest servants?

> **John 12:27-30** - *Now is my soul troubled; and what shall I say? Father, save me from this hour: but for this cause came I unto this hour. Father, glorify thy name. Then came there a voice from heaven, saying, I have both glorified it, and will glorify it again. The people therefore, that stood by, and heard it, said that it thundered: others said, An angel spake to him. Jesus answered and said, This voice came not because of me, but for your sakes.*

Here we see the full humanity of Jesus. He asks the Father to "save me from this hour" and then He reverses and says, "but for this cause came I unto this hour." It is good to remember here that God is an Eternal Spirit; He cannot die! Jesus of Nazareth was God in the form of a man in order to even be capable of dying. The man Christ Jesus was facing death for the first time and His *soul was troubled*.

A parallel verse is found in **Matthew 26:38**, when Jesus was praying in the Garden of Gethsemane.

"Father, glorify thy name." Jesus is not giving a request for the Father to literally announce His name. In Hebrew thought it means to reveal the character or the essence of the person. Through the death, burial, resurrection, and ascension of Jesus, the Father would accurately reveal His character to the world.

"Then came there a voice from heaven, saying, I have both glorified it, and will glorify it again. The people therefore, that stood by, and heard it, said that it thundered: others said, An angel spake to him." The Father had glorified His name many times throughout the history of Israel, and the incarnation of the Messiah brought glory to the Father's name. He would glorify His name once again through the resurrection of the Son of God. So the glorification of the Son of God would also glorify the Father's name. The *voice from heaven* sounded like *thunder* (*bat qol* in Hebrew). This idea of the *voice* of God sounding like *thunder* comes from **Exodus 19:16-19**:

> *And it came to pass on the third day in the morning, that there were thunders and lightnings, and a thick cloud upon the mount, and the voice of the trumpet exceeding loud; so that all the people that was in the camp trembled. And Moses brought forth the people out of the camp to meet with God; and they stood at the nether part of the mount. And mount Sinai was altogether on a smoke, because the LORD descended upon it in fire: and the smoke thereof ascended as*

the smoke of a furnace, and the whole mount quaked
greatly. And when the voice of the trumpet sounded
long, and waxed louder and louder, Moses spake,
and God answered him by a voice.

Many of the rabbis during the intertestamental period believed that they still received communications from God through the *bat gol*, even though Malachi was the last prophet. *"Jesus answered and said, This voice came not because of me, but for your sakes."* Jesus understood what the Father said, but the people thought that they heard *thunder*. Some even thought an *angel* was speaking to Jesus. But the purpose was also to assure the people that the Father had sent Jesus into the world. If you recall, just before Jesus raised Lazarus from the grave, He prayed out loud to the Father in order for those standing by to know that He came forth from God. (**John 11:41–42**)

John 12:31 – *Now is the judgment of this world: now shall the prince of this world be cast out.*

Not only is the glorification of the Son of Man going to bring glory to the Father's name, but it will also mean the hour of judgment has arrived for the *prince of this world*. Satan's rebellion and all of his evil schemes to destroy Israel will be defeated at the cross. Even though Satan is still active in the lives of God's children, he is defeated foe. Here are a few verses that pertain to the purpose of the Messiah coming into the world and the results of His death and resurrection:

"And I will put enmity between thee and the woman, and between thy seed and her seed; it shall bruise thy head, and thou shalt bruise his heel."

—Genesis 3:15

Forasmuch then as the children are partakers of flesh and blood, he also himself likewise took part of the same; that through death he might destroy him that had the power of death, that is, the devil.

—Hebrews 2:14

Blotting out the handwriting of ordinances that was against us, which was contrary to us, and took it out of the way, nailing it to his cross; And having spoiled principalities and powers, he made a shew of them openly, triumphing over them in it.

—Colossians 2:14–15

He that committeth sin is of the devil; for the devil sinneth from the beginning. For this purpose the Son of God was manifested, that he might destroy the works of the devil.

—I John 3:8

Jesus continues:

John 12:32-33 - *And I, if I be lifted up from the earth, will draw all men unto me. This he said, signifying what death he should die."*

The *lifting up* of the Son of Man is a theme that is built throughout the gospel of John. The *lifting up* of the Messiah connects us back to **John 3:14** and **John 8:28**. It is not only referring to His resurrection and His ascension, but also to His pending death in Jerusalem. Jesus being lifted up *will draw all men unto Him* just like the Greeks were drawn to Him back in **John 12:20-21.** No one can argue the fact that countless people have been drawn to Jesus down through the centuries of time from all different races and cultural backgrounds. *(Each year at the Garden Tomb in Jerusalem, we are able to see and to hear many groups from all over the world praising Jesus in their native language. This verse always comes came to my mind when I am in Israel.)*

> **John 12:34-36 –** *The people answered him, We have heard out of the law that Christ abideth for ever: and how sayest thou, The Son of man must be lifted up? who is this Son of man? Then Jesus said unto them, Yet a little while is the light with you. Walk while ye have the light, lest darkness come upon you: for he that walketh in darkness knoweth not whither he goeth. While ye have light, believe in the light, that ye may be the children of light. These things spake Jesus, and departed, and did hide himself from them.*

The people could not understand how the Messiah could *endure forever* and be *lifted up* at the same time. Where was it written in the Old Testament that the Messiah would endure forever? Here are a few verses to consider:

> *And thine house and thy kingdom shall be established for ever before thee: thy throne shall be established for ever.*
>
> **—2 Samuel 7:16**

> *His name shall endure for ever: his name shall be continued as long as the sun: and men shall be blessed in him: all nations shall call him blessed.*
>
> **—Psalm 72:17**

> *Of old hast thou laid the foundation of the earth: and the heavens are the work of thy hands. They shall perish, but thou shalt endure: yea, all of them shall wax old like a garment; as a vesture shalt thou change them, and they shall be changed: But thou art the same, and thy years shall have no end.*
>
> **—Psalm 102:25–27**

> *"For unto us a child is born, unto us a son is given: and the government shall be upon his shoulder: and his name shall be called Wonderful, Counsellor, The mighty God, The everlasting Father, The Prince of Peace. Of the increase of his government and peace there shall be no end, upon the throne of David, and upon his kingdom, to order it, and to establish it with judgment and with justice from*

henceforth even for ever. The zeal of the LORD *of hosts will perform this.*

—**Isaiah 9:6-7**

The majority of the Jews in Jesus' time did not understand the suffering Messiah passages like **Isaiah 53, Psalm 22, and Zechariah 12:10.** They interpreted those kinds of verses to be talking about the nation of Israel. Their thoughts were on *one* coming of the Messiah and the Messiah would rule and reign forever. The misunderstanding of the Old Testament concerning the *suffering* Messiah and the *ruling* Messiah still goes on today within Judaism. The fact that Satan is still active in the world and that everything is not *yet* under the feet of the Messiah causes problems among some Gentile believers. Listen to **Hebrews 2:8**:

> *Thou hast put all things in subjection under his feet. For in that he put all in subjection under him, he left nothing that is not put under him. But now we see not yet all things put under him.*

Jesus again uses the imagery of *light and darkness.* His physical presence is compared to the *light* being with them, and His ministry coming to an end is compared to *darkness.* (**John 9:4-5**) There is urgency in the voice of the Messiah here. He is urging the people to put their trust in Him while He is yet with them. After His death on the cross, things will change and darkness will fall, making it even more difficult for them to believe. The true believers will be persecuted and the

Romans will come and destroy Jerusalem in just a few years. As long as a person is in darkness, they cannot see where they are going. Walking in the light of Christ meant that they would be the *children of light*! Jesus departed and hid Himself like He had previously done in **John 8:59** and **John 11:54**.

THE JEWISH REJECTION

> **John 12:37–43** – *But though he had done so many miracles before them, yet they believed not on him: That the saying of Esaias the prophet might be fulfilled, which he spake, Lord, who hath believed our report? and to whom hath the arm of the Lord been revealed? Therefore they could not believe, because that Esaias said again, He hath blinded their eyes, and hardened their heart; that they should not see with their eyes, nor understand with their heart, and be converted, and I should heal them. These things said Esaias, when he saw his glory, and spake of him. Nevertheless among the chief rulers also many believed on him; but because of the Pharisees they did not confess him, lest they should be put out of the synagogue: For they loved the praise of men more than the praise of God.*

We have entered into a very controversial section of John's gospel. After these people had rejected Jesus out of their own stubbornness, the Lord hardened their hearts so they *could not* believe. The Holy Bible declares that God desires for all to come to repentance, but the scriptures also declare that people can reject the precious Savior so long that they never feel the Holy Spirit's conviction any longer. (**Romans 1:24-28**) But within the context of this chapter, John reveals that the prophecies of Isaiah, written some seven hundred years before, had to be fulfilled. What makes it even more mysterious is that Jesus came *when the fullness of time was come* (**Gal. 4:4**) so the scriptures would be fulfilled. In other words, Jesus loved those religious leaders or He would have never offered Himself to them. But the Father sent His Son into the world when He knew that the religious establishment was corrupt. God even used their blindness and unbelief to fulfill the sacred scriptures. Here we can see clearly the two-sided coin of the *free will of man* and the *sovereignty of God*. It is a serious thing when we hear the message of Christ and reject it. While there was a vast number of Jews who did believe in Jesus, Judaism for the most part, even unto this day, has rejected her Messiah. There were some of the Jewish leaders who *believed on Him*, but they were afraid of being cast out of the synagogue. *They loved the praise of men more than the praise of God.* It was not genuine faith. This rejection led to a partial blindness on Israel. (Study **Romans 11:25**) It is very important to see why John connected Isaiah's prophecies to the Jewish rejection. Compare these verses to **John 12:38-40**:

> *Who hath believed our report? and to whom is the arm of the LORD revealed?*
>
> **—Isaiah 53:1**

> *Make the heart of this people fat, and make their ears heavy, and shut their eyes; lest they see with their eyes, and hear with their ears, and understand with their heart, and convert, and be healed.*
>
> **—Isaiah 6:10**

"These things said Esaias, when he saw his glory, and spake of him." I believe this is one of the most astounding verses in John's gospel that has been overlooked by so many scholars over the years. Let's read the passage in Isaiah that John is referring too:

> *"In the year that king Uzziah died I saw also the LORD sitting upon a throne, high and lifted up, and his train filled the temple. Above it stood the seraphims: each one had six wings; with twain he covered his face, and with twain he covered his feet, and with twain he did fly. And one cried unto another, and said, Holy, holy, holy, is the LORD of hosts: the whole earth is full of his glory.*
>
> **—Isaiah 6:1-3**

What John's gospel is telling us is that the glory that Isaiah saw was the glory of Jesus the Messiah! Most of the time, we separate the glory of the God of the Old Testament from Jesus, but they are the same one true God! Isaiah even saw the *future glory* of the Messiah and this passage is connected to the unbelief of the Jews. Wow! John's gospel is the only one to mention this. When I consider the depth and the mystery of this passage of John, I am reminded of this verse in **Romans 11:33:**

> *O the depth of the riches both of the wisdom and knowledge of God! how unsearchable are his judgments, and his ways past finding out!*

> **John 12:44-50** - *Jesus cried and said, He that believeth on me, believeth not on me, but on him that sent me. And he that seeth me seeth him that sent me. I am come a light into the world, that whosoever believeth on me should not abide in darkness. And if any man hear my words, and believe not, I judge him not: for I came not to judge the world, but to save the world. He that rejecteth me, and receiveth not my words, hath one that judgeth him: the word that I have spoken, the same shall judge him in the last day. For I have not spoken of myself; but the Father which sent me, he gave me a commandment, what I should say, and what I should speak. And I know that his commandment is life everlasting: whatsoever I speak therefore, even as the Father said unto me, so I speak.*

Jesus had already hidden Himself back in **John 12:36**, so John is giving us a summary of what Jesus had already stated. If they believe in Jesus, they believe in God. When they hear the words of Jesus, they are hearing the words of God. If they reject the words of Jesus, the very Word of God will judge them in the last day.

When God spoke through the prophets of old, He used dreams, visions, oracles, and signs but now, God has manifested Himself in human flesh. When Jesus is walking in the midst of the Judean leadership, it is Almighty God walking in their midst. As great as Moses was, who even saw God face to face (**Exodus 33:11**), Jesus was far greater than Moses. (**Hebrews 3:1-6**)

Dear reader! Before we leave this chapter, please examine yourself to see if you have truly believed on the Son of God. If so, please confess Him publicly and do not reject His love and mercy. He is such a longsuffering Savior, but if we choose to deny Him, one day He will deny us! Maybe a simple prayer like this: *Heavenly Father, if I have never truly surrendered to Christ, I do now. I truly believe that Jesus is the Son of God, that He died for my sins, and arose the third day. Come into my heart, Lord Jesus, and save me forever. Help me to never be ashamed of you. Thank you Lord for hearing my prayer.*

CHAPTER THIRTEEN

John 13:1-5 - *Now before the feast of the passover, when Jesus knew that his hour was come that he should depart out of this world unto the Father, having loved his own which were in the world, he loved them unto the end. And supper being ended, the devil having now put into the heart of Judas Iscariot, Simon's son, to betray him; Jesus knowing that the Father had given all things into his hands, and that he was come from God, and went to God; He riseth from supper, and laid aside his garments; and took a towel, and girded himself. After that he poureth water into a bason, and began to wash the disciples' feet, and to wipe them with the towel wherewith he was girded.*

We have already seen how the Good Shepherd loves His sheep and that He will lay down His life for the sheep. Here it is given in the words, *having loved his own which were in the world, he loved them unto the very end.* Many times we fail to see that the next several chapters of John actually only cover the remaining hours of Jesus in Jerusalem, just before He *would depart out of this world unto the Father.* There is so much for our minds and hearts to comprehend within these next few chapters.

The setting is the springtime in Jerusalem, with all of the smells of spring flowers, fresh wine, ovens baking bread, and the feeling of the warm Mediterranean breeze coming from the west. Within this setting, we can imagine how the crowds were growing in Jerusalem as the dusty roads were filled with people rushing over the Mt. of Olives from the east and from the old city of David in the south. Pilgrims were filled with joy as they were coming down from the north and from across the western coastal plains of Israel, walking and riding camels and donkeys into the holy city. People in Jerusalem were chanting many of the Jewish blessings as Jesus and His disciples prepared for this last Passover meal together. But the most important thing going on in Jerusalem were the conversations and the examples that Jesus was about to leave with His disciples.

After the supper, the *devil* started working in the heart of Judas to betray the Son of God. There was something about *Judas Iscariot, Simon's son,* that the devil thought he could use, but it was all part of the divine plan. The *devil* knows, but he is not *all-knowing.* The *devil* thinks that all of this is going to lead into a victory for his kingdom of darkness, but the Almighty God is using it to bring about the fulfillment of the scriptures and salvation to mankind.

What a contrast we find here! Jesus knows that the Father has sent Him into the world and He knows that He is going back to the Father. But He is the *Suffering Servant Messiah!* The Master begins to wash the dirt off of the disciple's feet: even the filthy, betrayal dirt from Judas' feet. It was the custom in Jesus' time to have a basin of water at the front door of the house and a servant would wash the dust from the feet of the guests. Even if they had recently bathed, their feet would still get dirty from wearing sandals along the dusty roads of Israel. But there is a much deeper meaning to Jesus washing the disciples' feet.

As we think back on the previous chapters in John, the Judean leaders were evil shepherds and had no love or concern for others. They were not leading the people in the ways of the God of Israel. Jesus is showing the disciples here that they are to follow His example as they become the *new* leaders of the community of believers. They are going to be the *new* leaders! It's all about serving others and not being self-righteous or trying to hold a higher position like the religious rulers. Many modern-day believers think that the foot washing should be an ordinance in the church and they understand it as a beautiful act of humility. But we need to interpret it within the context of Jesus being the *true Servant*; His disciples, who would be His servants; and the leaders who were pretending to be God's servants.

John 13:6–11 – *Then cometh he to Simon Peter: and Peter saith unto him, Lord, dost thou wash my feet? Jesus answered and said unto him, What*

I do thou knowest not now; but thou shalt know
hereafter. Peter saith unto him, Thou shalt never
wash my feet. Jesus answered him, If I wash thee
not, thou hast no part with me. Simon Peter saith
unto him, Lord, not my feet only, but also my
hands and my head. Jesus saith to him, He that
is washed needeth not save to wash his feet, but is
clean every whit: and ye are clean, but not all. For
he knew who should betray him; therefore said he,
Ye are not all clean.

Simon Peter felt ashamed and he knew the lowly task of washing feet was even beneath a normal Jewish slave in their culture. We assume from the customs of the day that the disciples had probably just immersed in a Jewish bath, a *mikveh*, before entering into the Passover meal with Jesus. Jesus is using this humble custom to show a deep spiritual meaning to His disciples. In other words, the disciples had already been cleansed through the word that Jesus had spoken to them. What they did not yet know was that His death on the cross was going to provide eternal salvation for them. But before they could be shepherds of the flock, they needed a daily cleansing for their sins. Before the priests of the Old Testament could minister to the people, they had to wash with water:

When they go into the tabernacle of the congregation,
they shall wash with water, that they die not; or

when they come near to the altar to minister, to burn
offering made by fire unto the LORD:

—Exodus 30:20

What Jesus was doing was not understood by the disciples
and many people today still do not understand. We must
humble ourselves at the foot of the cross before we can be
saved. We must allow the Messiah to *serve* us by giving us
His eternal salvation. It is what He does for us! Then, as we
began to *serve* others, we need to receive forgiveness for our
sins on a daily basis. Each day we sin, either in the spirit or
in the flesh, sometimes unknowingly, but we need to be
clean before we can be effective in God's kingdom. This
is the meaning of what the apostle John would later write
in **I John 1:7-10**:

> *But if we walk in the light, as he is in the light,*
> *we have fellowship one with another, and the blood*
> *of Jesus Christ his Son cleanseth us from all sin. If*
> *we say that we have no sin, we deceive ourselves,*
> *and the truth is not in us. If we confess our sins,*
> *he is faithful and just to forgive us our sins, and to*
> *cleanse us from all unrighteousness. If we say that*
> *we have not sinned, we make him a liar, and his*
> *word is not in us.*

John 13:12-17 - *So after he had washed their*
feet, and had taken his garments, and was set down
again, he said unto them, Know ye what I have

done to you? Ye call me Master and Lord: and ye say well; for so I am. If I then, your Lord and Master, have washed your feet; ye also ought to wash one another's feet. For I have given you an example, that ye should do as I have done to you. Verily, verily, I say unto you, The servant is not greater than his lord; neither he that is sent greater than he that sent him. If ye know these things, happy are ye if ye do them.

In Jesus' time, a student, or a *talmid*, was to imitate his rabbi. As they walked with the rabbi, they would follow his teachings and his example of caring for others. Because they walked behind their rabbi, *the dust of his feet* would surround them. This is where the term *talmid* originated. Here, Jesus is the great Rabbi and His disciples are to follow and pattern themselves after Him. He was using the Jewish *kal v'homer* style of teaching once again: *if the Master is washing your feet, how much more should you wash one another's feet.* In the process of obeying what Jesus had told them, it would bring great *joy* to their lives.

> **John 13:18** – *I speak not of you all: I know whom I have chosen: but that the scripture may be fulfilled, He that eateth bread with me hath lifted up his heel against me.*

There was one at the table that would never be a servant of the Lord. Judas could be a soldier. He could be a revolutionary. He could be a teacher. He could be a leader. But he would never be a servant. Here we see the reason why Jesus chose Judas Iscariot, in order to fulfill the sacred scriptures. What scripture?

> *Yea, mine own familiar friend, in whom I trusted, which did eat of my bread, hath lifted up his heel against me.*
>
> **—Psalm 41:9**

John 13:19-20 - *Now I tell you before it come, that, when it is come to pass, ye may believe that I am he. Verily, verily, I say unto you, He that receiveth whomsoever I send receiveth me; and he that receiveth me receiveth him that sent me.*

The little italicized word *he* shows to us that the word was placed there by the translators, but it should be simply *I am*. This is one of the "I am" statements of Jesus that is missed most of the time. Jesus is the representative of God. The disciples were to be representatives of Jesus. One of the major themes of John's gospel is the chain of authority: The Father to the Son, the Son to His disciples, the disciples to their followers. There is also something very powerful about what Jesus said. When the people *received* the disciples, they were also *receiving* Jesus.

John 13:21-28 - *When Jesus had thus said, he was troubled in spirit, and testified, and said, Verily, verily, I say unto you, that one of you shall* *betray me. Then the disciples looked one on another, doubting of whom he spake. Now there was leaning on Jesus' bosom one of his disciples, whom Jesus loved. Simon Peter therefore beckoned to him, that he should ask who it should be of whom he spake. He then lying on Jesus' breast saith unto him, Lord, who is it? Jesus answered, He it is, to whom I shall give a sop, when I have dipped it. And when he had dipped the sop, he gave it to Judas Iscariot, the son of Simon. And after the sop Satan entered into him. Then said Jesus unto him, That thou doest, do quickly. Now no man at the table knew for what intent he spake this unto him.*

In the midst of the Passover celebration with His disciples, Jesus is *troubled in spirit*. The sting of betrayal is reclining at the table. The one disciple that they thought would never betray their Lord was Judas. Why? Because he was the one who had been trusted with the treasury bag. It was Matthew who had been a tax collector. The aged apostle John never did forget the time when he leaned on the bosom of the very Son of God. Peter knew that John was closer to Jesus than anyone else, so Peter asked John to find out who the betrayer would be. Try to imagine the picture of John leaning on the breast of Jesus and asking, *Lord, who is it?* What Jesus did was a customary act of friendship and it didn't seem unusual to the other disciples. He took a piece of *matzah* bread, dipped it either in the bitter herbs or the sweet *charoset*, and gave it to Judas. Notice this is the third time that Judas is called the son of Simon. (**John 12:4, 13:2, 13:26**) Again, it is believed that Judas was the son of Simon the leper. (**Mark 14:3**) I find it so disturbing that while Jesus and His disciples are enjoying their last supper together, the name of *Satan* appears. He enters into Judas. Satan saw something in Judas that he thought could be used for his kingdom of darkness. But little did Satan know that it was all part of the divine plan. Jesus, knowing that His hour is soon approaching, tells Judas to go about his evil business *quickly.*

> **John 13:29** – *For some of them thought, because Judas had the bag, that Jesus had said unto him, Buy those things that we have need of against the feast; or, that he should give something to the poor.*

Other than the apostle John, the disciples did not understand what Jesus had told Judas. They thought that Jesus was sending Judas out to purchase their needs for the Passover feast. This verse seems to imply that the Passover meal that Jesus celebrated with His disciples did not occur on the traditional night and that they might have followed a different calendar. Some Hebrew scholars think that Jesus was following the Essene Solar calendar, which would have been one night earlier than the Pharisees in Jerusalem.

> **John 13:30** – *He then having received the sop went immediately out: and it was night.*

How fitting that this hour was for the power of darkness. (**Luke 22:53**) It was *night* literally and it was *night* spiritually in the heart of Judas Iscariot. The one whom Satan entered would betray the *Light of the world.*

> **John 13:31-32** - *Therefore, when he was gone out, Jesus said, Now is the Son of man glorified, and God is glorified in him. If God be glorified in him, God shall also glorify him in himself, and shall straightway glorify him.*

Jesus is speaking of His pending death, burial, resurrection, and ascension, in advance. *Now is the Son of man glorified, and God is glorified in him.* Although the hour of darkness had arrived, the hour for the Son of Man to be revealed had also arrived. Jesus the Son would reveal that He is God. It would be a glorification! The cross would bring *glory* to the Father, *glory* to the Son, and *glory* to the Holy Spirit. The corrupt Judean leaders, the pagan Romans, Judas Iscariot, and yes, the devil himself would be used, but the plan of salvation was God's design. *God spared not his own Son, but delivered him up for us all.* (**Romans 8:32**)

> **John 13:33-35** - *Little children, yet a little while I am with you. Ye shall seek me: and as I said unto the Jews, Whither I go, ye cannot come; so now I say to you. A new commandment I give unto you, That ye love one another; as I have loved you, that ye also love one another. By this shall all men*

know that ye are my disciples, if ye have love one
to another.

Jesus calls His disciples, "little children." The apostle John
would use that term over fifty years later when writing to
believers in **I John 2:12.** Where is Jesus going that they
cannot follow Him? The cross? The grave? The Father?
Following him had been their life for over three years.
He was going to suffer and die on a cross. They could not
understand at this moment why Jesus had to die and why He
would have to die alone. But little did they know that they
would see Him resurrected and ascending back to heaven.

Did not the Torah tell them to love their neighbors?
(**Lev.19:18**) What did Jesus mean when He said, "A new
commandment I give unto you"? The law had said to love
your neighbor as yourself, but here the disciples are *to love*
one another as Jesus has loved them. The distinguishing mark
on a true disciple of Jesus is love, just like they had seen in
the ministry of Jesus: not just emotions, but love put into
action. This is how Christianity conquered the known
world. The people saw something in the lives of these
disciples that they wanted. It was more than knowing the
truth, it was Jesus living inside of them. This was promised
back in **Jeremiah 31:32-33** :

> *Not according to the covenant that I made with their*
> *fathers in the day that I took them by the hand*
> *to bring them out of the land of Egypt; which my*
> *covenant they brake, although I was an husband*

unto them, saith the LORD: *But this shall be the covenant that I will make with the house of Israel; After those days, saith the* LORD, *I will put my law in their inward parts, and write it in their hearts; and will be their God, and they shall be my people.*

It is no wonder that the apostle John wrote so much about love in his epistles. (**I John 4:7-21**) He was called the apostle whom Jesus loved and he lived out this new commandment that Jesus gave Him.

John 13:36-38 – *Simon Peter said unto him, Lord, whither goest thou? Jesus answered him, Whither I go, thou canst not follow me now; but thou shalt follow me afterwards. Peter said unto him, Lord, why cannot I follow thee now? I will lay down my life for thy sake. Jesus answered him, Wilt thou lay down thy life for my sake? Verily, verily, I say unto thee, The cock shall not crow, till thou hast denied me thrice.*

Going back to the statement that Jesus made back in **vs.33**, where he is going the disciples cannot come, but they will follow afterwards. Jesus is going to the tomb and He is going to rise from the tomb. The disciples could not follow Jesus through His death and resurrection now. They would one day lay down their lives for Jesus and then they would go to be with the Lord forever. Jesus told Peter that he would deny Him three times. Jesus knew when He called Peter on the shores of Galilee that he would deny Him in Jerusalem. But through the bad and through the good, Jesus had a plan for Peter's life. So Peter would deny the Lord and Judas would betray the Lord. What was the difference? Peter repented and found restoration. Judas did not. Peter would go on to become one of the world's greatest preachers and lay down his life for Jesus. Peter would be one of the pillars of the first church on Mt. Zion in Jerusalem and later write two epistles. Most scholars even believe that Peter is the real author of the gospel of Mark. However, Judas would go to his doom. (**Acts 1:18-19**)

CHAPTER FOURTEEN

JESUS COMFORTS HIS DISCIPLES

> **John 14:1-3** - *Let not your heart be troubled: ye believe in God, believe also in me. In my Father's house are many mansions: if it were not so, I would have told you. I go to prepare a place for you. And if I go and prepare a place for you, I will come again, and receive you unto myself; that where I am, there ye may be also.*

Jesus had told the disciples that He was going away and where He was going they could not come at this time. Now He begins to comfort them and He gives His last major teaching before His arrest. If you have a red-letter edition of the Bible, you can see that most of the words within the next three chapters are the words of our Lord. The first few verses in **John 14** are some of the most precious words in the sacred scriptures. If I had to choose a favorite passage, this would probably be the one. There is more than one way to look at these tremendous words of Jesus our Lord.

Context

The disciples had been following Jesus for over three years. Now He tells them that they will be separated. But Jesus was worried about them and He spent extra time comforting them. Try to imagine the expressions on their faces. At this moment, they did not understand the Messiah of Israel having to leave them. Jesus takes them back to the very heart of their faith: "ye believe in God, believe also in me." *Do you believe in the God of Israel - the one, true God? If so, then believe in me because I came forth from God.* Jesus is telling them that all of the things that He had told them are true. *All of the miracles that you have witnessed are proof that I am God in the flesh. Don't be troubled, because everything is on schedule!*

Historical Background

In the days when Jesus walked this earth, families did not live separately like we do in the western world. The sons would bring their brides home after they had added a room onto the father's house. Within a few years, the house was filled with courtyards and dwelling places for all of the family. Through children being born and marriages, it became one big family living in one big house. So it was a large house with many rooms and the Romans called it an *insula*. So like the Jewish bridegroom preparing a place for his bride, Jesus, the *Bridegroom*, is preparing a place for *His* bride, the church. The bridegroom would promise the bride that he will return when the room is completed *(normally about one year).* Jesus is promising His disciples that He will come back to receive them once He has prepared a place.

Spiritual Application

Just like the disciples, we can trust in what Jesus has told us. He is God in the flesh. There really is a Father's house, or *beit Av,* where all of God's children will dwell together. There will be plenty of rooms, or dwelling places, for all of those who know Jesus as their Savior. This is the only time that the English word *mansions* is in the Bible. It was translated from the Greek word, *mone* (monay), which means *abode or dwelling place.* The only other time this Greek word is used is in **John 14:23**, where it was translated *abode.* Jesus only used the term *Father's house* one other time, in **John 2:16**. So in the original meaning is that there will be plenty of *dwelling places* in the Father's house. Another way of looking at this passage is that Jesus was also preparing a place for us by going to the cross. His victory over the grave assures us that, once we leave this world, we will be ushered into His presence faster than sound! The ultimate plan of Almighty God, through the Lord Jesus Christ, is that "where I am, there ye may be also." Adam and Eve were driven out of the garden (**Gen. 3:24**) after they were tempted and fell into sin. But through the finished work of Christ, the *last Adam,* giving Himself as a perfect sacrifice for all sin, God's children will never have to worry about leaving the garden anymore. Much time and effort has been given over the centuries trying to describe what heaven is going to be like. But the most important thing is that God will be *dwelling with His people.* Our Lord will be *with us* throughout all of eternity! What a thought!

> **John 14:4-6** – *And whither I go ye know, and the way ye know. Thomas saith unto him, Lord, we know not whither thou goest; and how can we know the way? Jesus saith unto him, I am the way, the truth, and the life: no man cometh unto the Father, but by me.*

The disciples were now conscious of the fact that they were in the presence of the One who was the *true way* to the Father's house, unlike the Judean leadership who had rejected their Messiah. It helps us again to see the contrast between the disciples of Jesus and the unbelieving Jewish authorities. Thomas wanted to know how they could be where Jesus is going. If you recall, Thomas is the one who was willing to go to Jerusalem and die with Jesus. (**John 11:16**) He just wants to be where Jesus is! One of the most powerful and comforting "I am" statements of Jesus is three fold: "I am the way, the truth, and the life." In the Hebrew language of Jesus: *Anee ha derech ha emet ve ha chayim.* The Hebrew word for *way* is *derech,* the word for *truth* is *emet,* and the word for *life* is *chay.* Why is it important to know these words? *Derech* means *a trodden way* and Jesus has already walked the road before us. *Emet* means *absolute certainty* and trusting in Jesus is not wishful thinking; it is a sure thing.

Chay means that the *living Christ* gives us His life. Jesus is not just a̱ way, or a̱ truth, or a̱ life; He personifies all three.

So how do we as believers today find our way past the cross, past the tomb, and to the throne in heaven? Jesus is saying that He is the only way! There are thousands of different religions, thousands of churches that have different names, and ALL people are invited. But there is <u>only one way to heaven</u>: THE LORD JESUS CHRIST! Gentiles do not stop being Gentiles and Jews do not stop being Jews. We all come through the same person, Jesus! There is not one path for some and a different path for others. This is why the first name for the early Jewish believers in Jesus was *the people of the Way.* (**Acts 9:2**)

> **John 14:7-11-** *If ye had known me, ye should have known my Father also: and from henceforth ye know him, and have seen him. Philip saith unto him, Lord, show us the Father, and it sufficeth us. Jesus saith unto him, Have I been so long time with you, and yet hast thou not known me, Philip? he that hath seen me hath seen the Father; and how sayest thou then, Show us the Father? Believest thou not that I am in the Father, and the Father in me? the words that I speak unto you I speak not of myself: but the Father that dwelleth in me, he doeth the works. Believe me that I am in the Father, and the Father in me: or else believe me for the very works' sake.*

Just like the words of Jesus in **John 10:30**, Jesus is telling His disciples that when they *see* Him, they are *seeing* the Father. We need to connect this back to **John 1:18**: "No man hath seen the God at any time; the only begotten Son, which is in the bosom of the Father, he hath declared him." Through the incarnation, God could be *seen* and *heard*. Jesus was not saying that the Father looks like Him, but that He was God in the flesh. Jesus represented the Father's person, His character, His personality, His behavior, His passion, and His words. But since the incarnation, the way we perceive the Father has forever changed. When this same apostle John saw the glorified Christ in **Revelation 1:12–18**, He was still in the *form* of a man. When Jesus walked this earth, He was a dark-skinned Galilean Jew. But when we see him face to face, He will be the Almighty God who reigns over the universe. This thought is deep and mysterious and the Jewish way was to wrestle or struggle with the concept. We shouldn't accept it casually, because it is something that is outside of our human understanding.

"*...or else believe me for the very works' sake.*" Incredible claims like Jesus just made require credible evidence. When Jesus said, "he that hath seen me hath seen the Father," He knew that this would cause the disciples to question at first, but he knew that they would later understand. So Jesus tells them to examine His *works*. The *works* of the Messiah were the very *works* of the Father. Who can turn the water into wine? Who can heal a man from twenty miles away? Who can speak the word and cause a lame man to walk? Who can take a few loaves and fishes and feed thousands?

Who can walk on the water? Who can give a man back his sight that was born blind? Who can raise a man who had been dead for four days? This is what Jesus is saying. Once again, we need to list the seven major *sign* miracles in the gospel of John:

- *Water into wine* – **John 2:1-11**
- *Healing the nobleman's son in Cana* – **John 4:43-54**
- *Healing at the Pool of Bethesda* – **John 5:1-15**
- *Feeding the Multitude* – **John 6:1-15**
- *Healing the man born blind* – **John 9:1-12**
- *The raising of Lazarus* – **John 11:1-44**
- *The resurrection of the Messiah* – **John 20**

> **John 14:12-14** – *Verily, verily, I say unto you, He that believeth on me, the works that I do shall he do also; and greater works than these shall he do; because I go unto my Father. And whatsoever ye shall ask in my name, that will I do, that the Father may be glorified in the Son. If ye shall ask any thing in my name, I will do it.*

Just as Jesus had the authority that was given from the Father, now He is giving His authority to the disciples. This verse has caused a lot of confusion in the body of Christ. So to clarify the point, the disciples had walked with the very Son of God. They would be able to perform miracles in order to show the world that they had been with Jesus. The sign miracles ended when the apostles died. God still performs miracles today but not in the same way as when Jesus and His disciples walked this earth. For example: Do you know anyone who can walk on water? Do you know anyone who can go into a funeral home and raise a dead person? No one can repeat the miracles that Jesus did! They were to vindicate His messianic claims. So what did Jesus mean when He said, "greater works than these shall ye do"? Jesus only traveled a little over one hundred miles in His earthly ministry. His earthly ministry only lasted for a little over three years. But the disciples would travel far and wide taking the message to the uttermost parts of the known world. Multitudes of people would see their miracles and they would live several more years on the earth. Think of the apostle John who lived to be ninety-eight before he died. Their works were _greater_ in *quantity* not *quality*.

"And whatsoever ye shall ask in my name, that will I do." We do not need to explain away the promise and the power of what Jesus said. But what did it really mean? He was not talking about ending their prayers by saying, "in Jesus' name, Amen." It wasn't a magic formula for getting their prayers answered, like many Christians have taught. They would be asking in His name if they pray according to God's will and if their prayers are motivated by promoting God's kingdom and bringing honor and glory to Jesus. Listen to what the apostle John said in **I John 5:14**:

> *And this is the confidence that we have in him, that, if we ask any thing according to his will, he heareth us:*

Because of *who* Jesus is, we can ask *in His name* and *the Father is glorified in the Son*. We all need a stronger faith, and a deeper prayer life, but we must understand that praying to our Father *in Jesus name* means that we sincerely desire for Jesus to be glorified. Is what we are asking for going to bring a smile on the face of Jesus? Our prayers will not be answered if we just want our needs met or if we are just trying to boss the Lord around.

> *Ye ask, and receive not, because ye ask amiss, that ye may consume it upon your lusts.*
>
> **—James 4:3**

John 14:15 – *If ye love me, keep my commandments.*

What commandments do we obey? It has been said that there are over 1,000 commandments in the New Testament. The laws that were given to Moses in the Old Testament are not all null and void. Jesus fulfilled the sacrificial system by offering Himself on the cross, but many of the ethical laws are still to be obeyed. The New Testament clearly says that no one can be saved by obeying the commandments. That is why He had to die for us. (**Gal. 2:21**)

JESUS PROMISES THE HOLY SPIRIT

> **John 14:16-18 –** *And I will pray the Father, and he shall give you another Comforter, that he may abide with you for ever; Even the Spirit of truth;*

whom the world cannot receive, because it seeth him
not, neither knoweth him: but ye know him; for he
dwelleth with you, and shall be in you. I will not
leave you comfortless: I will come to you.

Remember that Jesus had just said that *when they had seen*
Him, they had seen the Father. Now, by sending the *Comforter,*
Jesus is saying, "I will come to you." The Hebrew word for
Comforter is *nacham*. From this word, many Jews are today
named *Menachem*. One of the meanings of this word is
console. So Jesus is saying that He will not leave the disciples
as orphans, He will come to them in the form of the Holy
Spirit, or the Hebrew *Ruach ha Qodesh*. He is leaving their
presence physically, but He is going to come back to them
spiritually. Please notice the oneness of the *Father,* the *Son,*
and the *Holy Spirit.* All three Persons are mentioned in this
chapter. (**John 14:1, 6, 9, 16, 23, 26**) It was believed in
Jesus' time by many of the Jewish Sages that the days of
the Messiah would be a time of *consolation.* You may recall
that, when Mary and Joseph brought the baby Jesus to the
Temple, Simeon was looking for the *consolation of Israel.*
(**Luke 2:25**) When the prophet Isaiah begins his servant
songs, he begins with **Isaiah 40:1** :

Comfort ye, comfort ye my people, saith your God.

John 14:19-24 – *Yet a little while, and the world*
seeth me no more; but ye see me: because I live, ye
shall live also. At that day ye shall know that I am

in my Father, and ye in me, and I in you. He that hath my commandments, and keepeth them, he it is that loveth me: and he that loveth me shall be loved of my Father, and I will love him, and will manifest myself to him. Judas saith unto him, not Iscariot, Lord, how is it that thou wilt manifest thyself unto us, and not unto the world? Jesus answered and said unto him, If a man love me, he will keep my words: and my Father will love him, and we will come unto him, and make our abode with him. He that loveth me not keepeth not my sayings: and the word which ye hear is not mine, but the Father's which sent me.

Again, we see that Jesus is in the Father, His disciples are in Him, and He is in them. In the Old Testament, the only two people who had the Holy spirit living inside of them were *Joseph* (**Gen. 41:38**) and *Bezaleel* (**Exodus 31:3**). The Old Testament prophets were anointed by the Holy Spirit, but now Jesus is saying that His followers will be *filled* with the Holy Spirit. This *Judas* is identified with the name *Thaddaeus*, in **Matthew 10:3**. Judas is saying: *We know that you are going away Lord, and no one will be able to see you. How are you going to manifest yourself to us, while at the same time, the world will not be able see you?* Looking at things from the natural perspective, that is a good question. Jesus gives a good answer: *It all will depend on you disciples keeping my words.* Notice that Jesus promises: <u>we</u> *will come unto you.* The Father, the Son, and the Holy Spirit are all three at work! This *love and obedience* theme is continued on through the

New Testament. Since we are focusing here on the work of John the apostle, listen to his later words:

And hereby we do know that we know him, if we keep his commandments.

—I John 2:3

And he that keepeth his commandments dwelleth in him, and he in him. And hereby we know that he abideth in us, by the Spirit which he hath given us.

—I John 3:24

By this we know that we love the children of God, when we love God, and keep his commandments. For this is the love of God, that we keep his commandments: and his commandments are not grievous.

—I John 5:2-3

John 14:25-26 - *These things have I spoken unto you, being yet present with you. But the Comforter, which is the Holy Ghost, whom the Father will send in my name, he shall teach you all things, and bring all things to your remembrance, whatsoever I have said unto you.*

One of the wonderful functions of the blessed Holy Spirit will be to *teach* the disciples and bring back to *remembrance* the things that Jesus has said. We would not have the gospel of John, or the other three gospels, if it were not for the Holy Spirit bringing to their minds and hearts what to write down. Dear reader, have you ever contemplated this thought? Without the Holy Spirit there would be no scriptures. Without the Holy Spirit there would be no way for us to understand the scriptures. We have never seen Jesus face to face, but we know Him, we love Him, we can understand His words, because of the Holy Spirit! Hallelujah!

> **John 14:27-31** - *Peace I leave with you, my peace I give unto you: not as the world giveth, give I unto you. Let not your heart be troubled, neither let it be afraid. Ye have heard how I said unto you, I go away, and come again unto you. If ye loved me, ye would rejoice, because I said, I go unto the Father: for my Father is greater than I. And now I have told you before it come to pass, that, when it is come to pass, ye might believe. Hereafter I will not talk much with you: for the prince of this world cometh, and hath nothing in me. But that the world may know that I love the Father; and as the Father gave me commandment, even so I do. Arise, let us go hence.*

The Jewish Passover meal is almost over, and Jesus assures them that he is leaving His *peace*, or *shalom*, with them. In the Hebrew language, shalom is used for greeting or farewell and it means *peace, health, wholeness, and integrity* that can only from God Himself. Jesus is not promising them that they will not suffer, He is promising them that

He will never leave them, and they will have His peace even in the darkest moments of their lives. There is a false peace that we can receive from the world, but Jesus is talking about a heavenly peace that the world cannot give or take away.

"...for my Father is greater than I." Jesus is speaking of Himself in his limited capacity as a human being. In essence, He is equal with the Father, but while He walked this earth as a man, He humbled Himself. Listen to what the apostle Paul would later write in **Philippians 2:6-8**:

> *Who, being in the form of God, thought it not robbery to be equal with God: But made himself of no reputation, and took upon him the form of a servant, and was made in the likeness of men: And being found in fashion as a man, he humbled himself, and became obedient unto death, even the death of the cross.*

The adversary, *the prince of the world* is coming, but he will not prevent Jesus the Son from finishing the Father's work. Jesus and His disciples are leaving and now walking east from Jerusalem, down the Kidron Valley, toward the Garden of Gethsemane. His conversation with His disciples continues with the next chapter.

CHAPTER FIFTEEEN

> **John 15:1-3 -** *I am the true vine, and my Father is the husbandman. Every branch in me that beareth not fruit he taketh away: and every branch that beareth fruit, he purgeth it, that it may bring forth more fruit. Now ye are clean through the word which I have spoken unto you.*

I find it interesting that the very last prayer that Jesus would have prayed during the Passover meal was before they drank the wine: *Blessed are you, O Lord our God, King of the Universe, Creator of the fruit of the vine.* With the words of Jesus fresh on the minds of the disciples, they were probably crossing the Kidron Valley where many vineyards could be seen. Jesus is saying that He is the *true vine*, and the nation of Israel is the *untrue vine*. This echoes back to the *vineyard* prophecies that are found in Isaiah, Jeremiah, Ezekiel, Joel, and Hosea. One is found in **Isaiah 5:1-16,** where Israel is God's vineyard:

Now will I sing to my wellbeloved a song of my beloved touching his vineyard. My wellbeloved hath a vineyard in a very fruitful hill: And he fenced it, and gathered out the stones thereof, and planted it with the choicest vine, and built a tower in the midst of it, and also made a winepress therein: and he looked that it should bring forth grapes, and it brought forth wild grapes. And now, O inhabitants of Jerusalem, and men of Judah, judge, I pray you, betwixt me and my vineyard. What could have been done more to my vineyard, that I have not done in it? wherefore, when I looked that it should bring forth grapes, brought it forth wild grapes? And now go to; I will tell you what I will do to my vineyard: I will take away the hedge thereof, and it shall be eaten up; and break down the wall thereof, and it shall be trodden down: And I will lay it waste: it shall not be pruned, nor digged; but there shall come up briers and thorns: I will also command the clouds that they rain no rain upon it. For the vineyard of the LORD of hosts is the house of Israel, and the men of Judah his pleasant plant: and he looked for judgment, but behold oppression; for righteousness, but behold a cry. Woe unto them that join house to house, that lay field to field, till there be no place, that they may be placed alone in the midst of the earth! In mine ears said the LORD of hosts, Of a truth many houses shall be desolate, even great and fair, without inhabitant. Yea, ten acres of vineyard shall yield one bath, and the seed of an homer shall yield an ephah. Woe unto them that rise up early in the morning, that they may follow strong drink; that continue until night, till wine inflame them! And the harp, and the viol, the tabret, and pipe, and wine, are in their feasts: but they regard not the work of the LORD, *neither consider the operation of his hands. Therefore my people are gone into captivity, because they have no knowledge: and their honourable men are famished, and their multitude dried up with thirst. Therefore hell hath enlarged herself, and opened her mouth without measure: and their glory, and their multitude, and their pomp, and he that rejoiceth, shall descend into it. And the mean man shall be brought down, and the mighty man shall be humbled, and the eyes of the lofty shall be humbled: But the* LORD *of hosts shall be exalted in judgment, and God that is holy shall be sanctified in righteousness.*

Listen to **Jeremiah 12:10** :

Many pastors have destroyed my vineyard, they have trodden my portion under foot, they have made my pleasant portion a desolate wilderness.

Jesus the Messiah is the *greater* Israel! The Judean rulers in Jerusalem were repeating the evil deeds of their ancestors over seven hundred years earlier. The fact that Jesus calls

Himself the *true vine* reinforces the close identification that He has with Israel.

"Every branch in me that beareth not fruit he taketh away." This verse disturbed me for years, because Jesus said every branch *in me*, will be cast away if it does not bear fruit. Until I did a word study and found the word for *taketh away* in this verse is the Greek word *airo,* pronounced "ah-ee-ro." The word means *to lift up, or to take away.* I looked at other places where this Greek word was used: places like **John 5:9** where the man that had been lame at the Pool of Bethesda *took up* his bed, or he *lifted up* his bed. In **John 8:59**, the Jews took up, or *lifted up*, stones to cast at Jesus. Without being dogmatic, there is a good probability here that Jesus was saying: *Every branch in me that beareth not fruit he will lift up.* The 1611 translators did not understand Mesopotamian agriculture. When a branch grows too far from the vine, the farmers will lift up the branches with rocks to keep the branch from growing into the ground and therefore killing the entire vine. By *lifting up* the branches, they will bear more fruit.

*Since I have opened up a can of worms to some of you about the English translation, let me just say that I learned years ago that God has preserved the embodiment of truth of the scriptures down through the centuries of time. I have used the KJV for all of my years of ministry. I love it dearly and do not choose to use other translations. However, translations cannot be perfect and do not supersede the original language of Jesus. Our faith is not in a particular translation of the Bible, but our faith is in the Christ of

the Bible. The preface of the KJV has been removed since about 1804. In the preface, it is stated that it is not a perfect translation. It was removed by those who wanted to convince others that there was only one translation that had the truth: the KJV.

"...and every branch that beareth fruit, he purgeth it, that it may bring forth more fruit. Now ye are clean through the word which I have spoken unto you." When we look at the whole *periscope* of this lesson that Jesus gave, it is clear that the way to bring forth spiritual fruit is by:

- *Being cleansed by the word of God*
- *Abiding in Jesus*
- *Obeying Jesus' commandments*

What are the spiritual fruits that we as followers of Christ should bear? Listen to these familiar words and connect them to what Jesus said:

> *But the fruit of the Spirit is love, joy, peace, longsuffering, gentleness, goodness, faith, Meekness, temperance: against such there is no law.*
>
> **—Galatians 5:22-23**

Jesus came looking for spiritual fruit among His Judean people, but all He found was religious leaves. (**Matt. 21:18-20**) Dear reader, is your life yielding the spiritual fruit that brings glory to God? Many times we get caught up the outward ceremonialism, like Israel of old, and do not walk in the Spirit.

John 15:4-8 - *Abide in me, and I in you. As the branch cannot bear fruit of itself, except it abide in the vine; no more can ye, except ye abide in me. I am the vine, ye are the branches: He that abideth in me, and I in him, the same bringeth forth much fruit: for without me ye can do nothing. If a man abide not in me, he is cast forth as a branch, and is withered; and men gather them, and cast them into the fire, and they are burned. If ye abide in me, and my words abide in you, ye shall ask what ye will, and it shall be done unto you. Herein is my Father glorified, that ye bear much fruit; so shall ye be my disciples.*

The disciples had the responsibility of *abiding in Jesus,* but this teaching also took the burden off of them by revealing that only Jesus can do the real work. There would be a lot of good things that the disciples could produce in the flesh, but there would be nothing accomplished in the Spirit unless they *abide* in Christ. Those who *do not abide in the vine will be cast forth as a branch.* Jesus is not saying that anything they ask for will be given, as it seems to sound. He is saying that the real principle of being His disciple is *abiding* in Him. If they do, then they will ask how they can imitate Him in their daily walk. For three years the disciples had been walking with Jesus, now it was time for them to bring forth spiritual fruit.

We prove our discipleship by bearing fruit for the Master. Notice this lesson begins with bearing *fruit* and then goes to bearing *much fruit*. Christ is in us and we are in Christ! We stay in His word so His word will be in us! This brings glory to the Father!

> **John 15:9-12** - *As the Father hath loved me, so have I loved you: continue ye in my love. If ye keep my commandments, ye shall abide in my love; even as I have kept my Father's commandments, and abide in his love. These things have I spoken unto you, that my joy might remain in you, and that your joy might be full. This is my commandment, That ye love one another, as I have loved you.*

The Father has loved the Son, the Son expresses that love to His disciples, and they reproduce *His love* for one another. The key is loving others in the way Jesus loved them. That love is nourished and kept alive by keeping the commandments of Jesus. Jesus embodied the Torah and His disciples are to still keep the Torah, but they are also to keep His commandments. The kingdom life that Jesus calls His followers to live is the Old Testament law taken to a higher level. **(Matt.5-7)** If the disciples stayed in the love of Jesus, then *His joy* would remain in them. When someone does not stay close to Jesus, they are incapable of bearing spiritual fruit. This causes a lack of joy and a fake spirituality.

> **John 15:13-17** - *Greater love hath no man than this, that a man lay down his life for his friends. Ye*

are my friends, if ye do whatsoever I command you. Henceforth I call you not servants; for the servant knoweth not what his lord doeth: but I have called you friends; for all things that I have heard of my Father I have made known unto you. Ye have not chosen me, but I have chosen you, and ordained you, that ye should go and bring forth fruit, and that your fruit should remain: that whatsoever ye shall ask of the Father in my name, he may give it you. These things I command you, that ye love one another.

Here Jesus is calling His disciples *friends*. This invokes much more than just being a close companion to Jesus. Abraham was called *God's friend* in **2 Chron. 20:7** and **Isa. 41:8**. It is a Semitic term for being a partner with God. In other words, Abraham kept the blood-covenant and the disciples are to keep the covenant that Jesus will sign with His own blood. Wow! Abraham did not know where the Lord was taking him, but he obeyed. Jesus had walked with the disciples for over three years and had made the Father's will known to them. Just like Abraham did not choose God, but God chose him, Jesus chooses His disciples. Jesus reiterates that they are to *love one another*. This sounds easy when reading it now, but it was different for Simon Peter to love Matthew, the tax collector. It was different for Matthew to love Simon the Zealot, who came from a line of rebel fighters. But through Jesus they could find common ground and a unity of Spirit.

"*...and that your fruit should remain.*" Little did these

disciples know that Jesus was preparing them to change the course of the world. Their fruit did *remain* and we can still study their works even to this very day.

> **John 15:18-25 -** *If the world hate you, ye know that it hated me before it hated you. If ye were of the world, the world would love his own: but because ye are not of the world, but I have chosen you out of the world, therefore the world hateth you. Remember the word that I said unto you, The servant is not greater than his lord. If they have persecuted me, they will also persecute you; if they have kept my saying, they will keep yours also. But all these things will they do unto you for my name's sake, because they know not him that sent me. If I had not come and spoken unto them, they had not had sin: but now they have no cloak for their sin. He that hateth me hateth my Father also. If I had not done among them the works which none other man did, they had not had sin: but now have they both seen and hated both me and my Father. But this cometh to pass, that the word might be fulfilled that is written in their law, They hated me without a cause.*

From this moment on, Jesus uses the contrast of *this world* to the *world to come*. *This world* is used for the temporary state of disorder compared to *the world to come* being the Messianic Age when everything will be redeemed and restored. This world is the fallen world and, because of the sin in the world, they hate the perfect Son of God. This fallen world will hate the followers of Jesus just like they hated Him. In a narrow sense, this passage is talking about the Judean leadership once again. Not only will they deliver the precious Son of God over to the Romans in order to execute Him, but they will also try to root out the Jesus movement from Judaism in the book of Acts. The *sin* of the leadership in Jerusalem was so great because Jesus had walked in their midst and His works proved that He was from God. But Jesus came into the world when He knew these things were going to happen to Him. Why? So the scriptures would be fulfilled. What scriptures?

> *They that hate me without a cause* are more than the hairs of mine head: they that would destroy me, being mine enemies wrongfully, are mighty: then I restored that which I took not away.
> **—Psalm 69:4**

John 15:26-27 - *But when the Comforter is come, whom I will send unto you from the Father, even the Spirit of truth, which proceedeth from the Father, he shall testify of me: And ye also shall bear witness, because ye have been with me from the beginning.*

The third Person of the Triune Godhead, the blessed Holy Spirit, is coming! Here Jesus calls Him the *Comforter* and the *Spirit of truth*. What is His job? *To testify* of Jesus! The Holy

Spirit does not exalt Himself, He exalts the Son of God. There is a huge movement around the world that began about one hundred years ago that focuses on the gifts of the Spirit and everything they say exalts the Holy Ghost. This is biblically wrong! The purpose of the coming of the Holy Spirit was to lift up Jesus to the people. Always beware of any religious movement that focuses on anything or anyone more than they focus on the Lord Jesus the Christ!

"And ye also shall bear witness, because ye have been with me from the beginning." The disciples are qualified because they have been with Jesus. This is repeated in Peter's sermon in **Acts 1:21-22**:

> *Wherefore of these men which have companied with us all the time that the Lord Jesus went in and out among us, Beginning from the baptism of John, unto that same day that he was taken up from us, must one be ordained to be a witness with us of his resurrection.*

CHAPTER SIXTEEN

JESUS WARNS HIS DISCIPLES

John 16:1-6 - *These things have I spoken unto you, that ye should not be offended. They shall put you out of the synagogues: yea, the time cometh, that whosoever killeth you will think that he doeth God service. And these things will they do unto you, because they have not known the Father, nor me. But these things have I told you, that when the time shall come, ye may remember that I told you of them. And these things I said not unto you at the beginning, because I was with you. But now I go my way to him that sent me; and none of you asketh me, Whither goest thou? But because I have said these things unto you, sorrow hath filled your heart.*

Because the Jewish establishment did not know the God of Israel, whom they pretended to know, they would persecute the followers of the Son of God. This passage could have two possible meanings:

1. *The disciples of Jesus would be put out of the Temple Assembly.*
2. *The disciples of John the apostle in Ephesus would be excommunicated from the Jewish synagogues there.*

After the destruction of the Temple in Jerusalem in 70 AD, there was a great watershed that separated Jewish believers in Jesus and unbelievers. During the period from 70-135 AD, there was the *Council of Yavneh* that excluded Jewish Christians from worshipping in the synagogues. The decree was so much in the minds of Judaism that they thought they were doing the God of Israel a favor by excommunicating these Jewish Christians. When Jesus told the disciples that He was going back to the Father who sent Him into the world, he proved the *pre-existence* of the Messiah. The *truth* that Jesus was telling His disciples made them feel *sorrow*. A sincere disciple of Jesus today needs to understand that not all things will be peaches and ice cream. We should not expect all people to love us and treat us fairly. There is this *duality* in the world: the forces of good and the forces of evil. Many times, evil will come in the form of false religion.

FOUR TRUTHS ABOUT THE HOLY SPIRIT

John 16:7-11 - *Nevertheless I tell you the truth; It is expedient for you that I go away: for if I go not away, the Comforter will not come unto you; but if I depart, I will send him unto you. And when he is come, he will reprove the world of sin, and of* *righteousness, and of judgment: Of sin, because they believe not on me; Of righteousness, because I go to my Father, and ye see me no more; Of judgment, because the prince of this world is judged.*

1. *Jesus must go away before the Holy Spirit will come.* (**vs.7**)
2. *He will expose the world of sin, primarily the rejection of Jesus as the Messiah.* (**vs.8–9**)
3. *He will reveal the righteousness of God by establishing the commandments of Jesus in their hearts.* (**vs.10**)
4. *He will show judgment to the adversary, the devil, as the kingdom of God is advanced in the lives of others.* (**vs.11**)

As the disciples of Jesus take the gospel of the risen Messiah into the world for the very first time, they will realize that the world has the wrong concept of what sin is. They will see that many people will not place their trust in Jesus. The world will rather choose to believe men's theories and men's philosophy about life. As the Holy Spirit empowers the disciples, they will have the power and conviction to preach to the people that the only way to be righteous in God's eyes is through the finished work of Jesus the Son of God.

John 16:12-15 - *I have yet many things to say unto you, but ye cannot bear them now. Howbeit when he, the Spirit of truth, is come, he will guide you into all truth: for he shall not speak of himself; but whatsoever he shall hear, that shall he speak:*

and he will shew you things to come. He shall glorify me: for he shall receive of mine, and shall shew it unto you. All things that the Father hath are mine: therefore said I, that he shall take of mine, and shall shew it unto you.

The Holy Spirit will not only *guide* the disciples into all *truth,* but also the transfer of authority is going to be given to the disciples by Him. Jesus is investing His power and His *truth* by the coming of the Holy Spirit in these men. Wow! We find a parallel to Jesus transferring His authority to His disciples in the 70 elders and the ordination of Joshua in the Old Testament:

And the LORD came down in a cloud, and spake unto him, and took of the spirit that was upon him, and gave it unto the seventy elders: and it came to pass, that, when the spirit rested upon them, they prophesied, and did not cease.

—Numbers 11:25

And the LORD said unto Moses, Take thee Joshua the son of Nun, a man in whom is the spirit, and lay thine hand upon him; And set him before Eleazar the priest, and before all the congregation; and give him a charge in their sight. And thou shalt put some of thine honour upon him, that all the congregation of the children of Israel may be obedient.

—Numbers 27:18–20

John 16:16-22 - *A little while, and ye shall not see me: and again, a little while, and ye shall see me, because I go to the Father. Then said some of his disciples among themselves, What is this that he saith unto us, A little while, and ye shall not see me: and again, a little while, and ye shall see me: and, Because I go to the Father? They said therefore, What is this that he saith, A little while? we cannot tell what he saith. Now Jesus knew that they were desirous to ask him, and said unto them, Do ye enquire among yourselves of that I said, A little while, and ye shall not see me: and again, a little while, and ye shall see me? Verily, verily, I say unto you, That ye shall weep and lament, but the world shall rejoice: and ye shall be sorrowful, but your sorrow shall be turned into joy. A woman when she is in travail hath sorrow, because her hour is come: but as soon as she is delivered of the child, she remembereth no more the anguish, for joy that a man is born into the world. And ye now therefore have sorrow: but I will see you again, and your heart shall rejoice, and your joy no man taketh from you.*

We find several times here where the two little words, *little while*, are mentioned. It will be only a *little while* before Jesus will go the cross. But the good news to the disciples is that it will only be another *little while* until they will see Jesus again. When Jesus tells them that they will *weep and lament, but the world shall rejoice*, He is referring to the cross.

But when He tells them that their *sorrow will be turned into joy*, He is referring to His resurrection. But then Jesus seems to cast an eschatological shadow over the passage. He starts talking about *Birth Pains*, and this was a Jewish term for the Advent of the Messiah of Israel. So there seems to be a double meaning to the entire *periscope* of what Jesus is saying. The absence of Jesus for a *little while* is the cross, but *the joy that no man can take away from them* seems to refer both to the resurrection *and* His *Second Coming*.

> **John 16:23–27** – *And in that day ye shall ask me nothing. Verily, verily, I say unto you, Whatsoever ye shall ask the Father in my name, he will give it you. Hitherto have ye asked nothing in my name: ask, and ye shall receive, that your joy may be full. These things have I spoken unto you in proverbs: but the time cometh, when I shall no more speak unto you in proverbs, but I shall shew you plainly of the Father. At that day ye shall ask in my name: and I say not unto you, that I will pray the Father for you: For the Father himself loveth you, because ye have loved me, and have believed that I came out from God.*

Because the disciples loved Jesus (and to anyone in the future who will love Jesus), they are to pray to the Heavenly Father in the name of His Son, Jesus. Jesus will be the mediator but, through His blood that will be shed on the cross, believers can pray *directly* to the Father. There is no model in the New Testament for us to pray directly to Jesus or directly to the Holy Spirit. We are to pray, "Our Father which art in heaven." As long as we pray through the power and the authority of the Son Jesus, we can expect our prayers to be answered. I am reminded of the book of Hebrews that was written to Jewish Christians who were thinking about going back into Judaism because of their persecution:

> *Having therefore, brethren, boldness to enter into the holiest by the blood of Jesus, By a new and living way, which he hath consecrated for us, through the veil, that is to say, his flesh;*
>
> **—Hebrews 10:19–20**

John 16:28–33 - *I came forth from the Father, and am come into the world: again, I leave the world, and go to the Father. His disciples said unto him, Lo, now speakest thou plainly, and speakest no proverb. Now are we sure that thou knowest all things, and needest not that any man should ask thee: by this we believe that thou camest forth from God. Jesus answered them, Do ye now believe? Behold, the hour cometh, yea, is now come, that ye shall be scattered, every man to his own, and shall leave me alone: and yet I am not alone, because the Father is with me. These things I have spoken unto you, that in me ye might have peace. In the world ye* *shall have tribulation: but be of good cheer; I have overcome the world.*

The disciples seem to understand what Jesus is saying here. "I came forth from the Father, and am come into the world: again, I leave the world, and go to the Father." What a verse! Even though this powerful teaching of Jesus begins to sink into the ears of the disciples, they do not know that they are about to be *scattered* and that the fear from the Roman authorities and the Jewish Sanhedrin will cause them to *leave Jesus alone.* But *He will not be alone,* for *the Father will be there.* Jesus goes a step further to tell them that they will be scattered into the world and will experience *tribulations in the world,* but they need to have cheer because Jesus *has overcome the world.* What assurance this gives to all of us who are trying to serve our Lord. The world will always be against the work of the Kingdom of God and we can expect trials and even persecutions. But we must never forget that while Jesus came into this world, lived as man, and suffered at the hands of His own people, He overcame the world. The apostle John would later write these words:

For whatsoever is born of God overcometh the world: and this is the victory that overcometh the world, even our faith. Who is he that overcometh the world, but he that believeth that Jesus is the Son of God?
—I John 5:4–5

CHAPTER SEVENTEEN

John 17:1-5 – *These words spake Jesus, and lifted up his eyes to heaven, and said, Father, the hour is come; glorify thy Son, that thy Son also may glorify thee: As thou hast given him power over all flesh, that he should give eternal life to as many as thou hast given him. And this is life eternal, that they might know thee the only true God, and Jesus Christ, whom thou hast sent. I have glorified thee on the earth: I have finished the work which thou gavest me to do. And now, O Father, glorify thou me with thine own self with the glory which I had with thee before the world was.*

Just before crossing the Kidron Valley into the Garden of Gethsemane on the east side of Jerusalem, Jesus gives one of the most profound prayers ever uttered on planet earth. We cannot know the exact location of the prayer, but it was possibly on the Temple mount or somewhere just outside the city walls. This is one of the most underestimated chapters in the Bible and yet, it is one of the most powerful. This is where Jesus the Messiah, the Son of God, prays to the Father on behalf of His disciples and all believers in the future. What a thought! We can see deeply into the heart of our Lord, the intimacy between the Son and the Father, and the intimacy between the Son and His disciples. The entire prayer presupposes that Jesus is the second Person of the Triune Godhead.

"Father, the hour is come; glorify thy Son, that thy Son also may glorify thee." Jesus, while *lifting up His eyes to heaven*, is praying to the Father to *reveal* the Son so that the Son may accurately *reveal* the Father. Jesus represented the Father while on earth and He is about to finish the Father's work (**vs.4**), thus revealing the Father. In turn, Jesus is praying that the Father will reveal the Son and return Him back to the glory that He had before creation. (**vs.5**)

"And this is life eternal, that they might know thee the only true God, and Jesus Christ, whom thou hast sent." Eternal life is neither a theology nor the giving of mental agreement to a creed or a certain church doctrine. Eternal life is to *know the Father <u>and</u> Jesus Christ.* Eternal life is not just something that believers enjoy after they depart from this earthly life. They can enjoy it now by knowing God through Jesus. This takes us back to verses like **John 1:1-3, 10, 18; 10:30; 14:6** and **14:9.** Jesus is God and while He was on this earth He was God in the flesh! As the Father and the Son will live forever, so will every person who *knows* them. This connection between God <u>and</u> Jesus is used in other places

in the New Testament. I'm reminded of what the apostle Paul wrote in **Titus 2:13**:

> *Looking for that blessed hope, and the glorious appearing of the great God <u>and</u> our Saviour Jesus Christ;*

Also, the apostle John would later write that Jesus is the Almighty God in the book of the **Revelation 1:8** :

> *I am Alpha and Omega, the beginning and the ending, saith the Lord, which is, and which was, and which is to come, the Almighty.*

This thought of *knowing* God can only be made possible through *knowing* the Son of God. This connects us back to the prophecies of the New Covenant in **Jeremiah 31:33-34**:

> *But this shall be the covenant that I will make with the house of Israel; After those days, saith the LORD, I will put my law in their inward parts, and write it in their hearts; and will be their God, and they shall be my people. And they shall teach no more every man his neighbour, and every man his brother, saying, Know the LORD: for they shall all know me, from the least of them unto the greatest of them, saith the LORD: for I will forgive their iniquity, and I will remember their sin no more.*

John 17:6 – *I have manifested thy name unto the men which thou gavest me out of the world: thine they were, and thou gavest them me; and they have kept thy word.*

What did Jesus mean in His prayer by saying, "I have manifested thy name"? Did He pronounce a certain Hebrew name of the Father? Religious Jews are very strict on *pronouncing the Name of God, *YHVH*, which is found in one form in **Exodus 6:3** and another form in **Psalm 68:4**. They go around it by saying *HaShem* (The Name) or *Adonai* (The Lord). There must be a deeper meaning here. In Bible times, pronouncing someone's name was more than just a way to address a person; it conveyed his or her *character*. When God, through Moses, placed the plaques on Egypt, it was to show Egypt who the one true God was. Jesus demonstrated the character of God during His three-year ministry on earth through His works, signs, and teachings. The men that had been given to Jesus were so blessed and highly favored to be able to witness God at work on earth. They saw the *Name of God* manifested.

Pronouncing names is very important to the Jewish people. Unbelieving Jews today call Jesus "Yeshu" instead of His Hebrew name, "Yeshua." Yeshu means, "may his name be blotted out," while Yeshua means "Yahweh saves."

John 17:7–10– *"Now they have known that all things whatsoever thou hast given me are of thee.*

For I have given unto them the words which thou gavest me; and they have received them, and have known surely that I came out from thee, and they have believed that thou didst send me. I pray for them: I pray not for the world, but for them which thou hast given me; for they are thine. And all mine are thine, and thine are mine; and I am glorified in them."

Jesus is praying to the Father and giving credit to the disciples for their faith and their works. Jesus is being *glorified* through His disciples. Just like Jesus revealed the character of the Father to the world, the disciples will accurately reveal Jesus to the world. Wow! Jesus is not praying for the lost world, but He is praying for the ones who had followed Him during His ministry. What a lesson for everyone who professes the name of Christ! We will either *reveal* Jesus to those around us or our lives can *conceal* Jesus from those around us.

John 17:11-13 - *And now I am no more in the world, but these are in the world, and I come to thee. Holy Father, keep through thine own name those whom thou hast given me, that they may be one, as we are. While I was with them in the world, I kept them in thy name: those that thou gavest me I have kept, and none of them is lost, but the son of perdition; that the scripture might be fulfilled. And now come I to thee; and these things I speak*

> *in the world, that they might have my joy fulfilled*
> *in themselves.*

Jesus is praying as though He has already left the world. The work of the cross and the empty tomb is already a finished work in the mind of God. He is praying for those who will be left in the world, mainly His disciples. The Hebrew name *Yah*, was in the *name of *Yahshua*. Jesus *kept* the disciples through the power and the authority of God's name. This authority of Jesus became the theme of one of the early apostolic hymns:

> *Wherefore God also hath highly exalted him, and*
> *given him a name which is above every name: That*
> *at the name of Jesus every knee should bow, of things*
> *in heaven, and things in earth, and things under the*
> *earth; And that every tongue should confess that*
> *Jesus Christ is Lord, to the glory of God the Father.*
> **—Philippians 2:9-11**

Many religious groups have a superstition that the name of Jesus is like a magic word. They believe they can get anything from God just by pronouncing the name of Jesus over and over again. Not understanding what is in the true name of Yahshua causes religious ignorance.

The disciples are secure for all of eternity because of Jesus' prayer. Jesus is the seal of the King and the authority of the throne. Jesus is praying for the *joy to be fulfilled.* The only one that will be lost is the *son of perdition*. The scripture being fulfilled that Jesus is referring to is **Psalm 41:9** :

> *Yea, mine own familiar friend, in whom I trusted, which did eat of my bread, hath lifted up his heel against me.*

There seems to be a double meaning here. David was referring to his friend, *Ahithophel,* who conspired with Absalom to overthrow King David. But this friend of David seems to be a type of Judas, the son of perdition. So, when studying the Old Testament scriptures many times, we will often find the historical context and then a future prophecy woven within the same passage.

> **John 17:14–16 –** *I have given them thy word; and the world hath hated them, because they are not of the world, even as I am not of the world. I pray not that thou shouldest take them out of the world, but that thou shouldest keep them from the evil. They are not of the world, even as I am not of the world.*

Jesus offers a tremendous prayer to the Father on the behalf of His disciples. He tells the Father that *they are not of the world, and that is why they are hated.* Just like Jesus was not of this world, he rescues His children from the world system. However, He goes on to pray that they will stay in the world. Why? Because in Jewish thought the followers of the Messiah are supposed to make the world a better place. They are to be salt and light in this dark world. So the work of Jesus will continue on through His disciples. He prays for the Father to protect them from evil. Even before the disciples leave Israel, they will see evil at its worst through false religious leaders. As they go into the Roman world they will see evil from the heathen, pagan mind. They will one day die for the gospel of Christ, but they will be protected until their work is completed.

> **John 17:17-19** - *Sanctify them through thy truth: thy word is truth. As thou hast sent me into the world, even so have I also sent them into the world. And for their sakes I sanctify myself, that they also might be sanctified through the truth.*

Jesus is praying that His disciples will be made separate from the world to be holy vessels of honor. They are not to be removed from being around people, but they are to be sanctified through the word of truth and placed in a spiritual dimension while they are ministering. In His humanity, Jesus is *sanctifying Himself* for His death on the cross that will not only provide salvation for whosoever will believe, but will also sanctify the disciples when they see His sacrifice. They are being *sent into the world* and they will be in the world but not of the world. The words of Jesus and the cross of Jesus have the supernatural power to sanctify His people so they can be effective in His kingdom.

> **John 17:20 –** *Neither pray I for these alone, but for them also which shall believe on me through their word;*

All believers in Jesus are really descendants of the apostles of Jesus. Just think of their witness and the scriptures they were inspired to write down for us by the Holy Ghost. What a powerful verse this is! Jesus is praying for all of those who will believe in Him through the words of His disciples. We can also connect this thought back to **John 10:16**, where Jesus said that He must bring *other sheep* into the fold.

> **John 17:21-23 –** *That they all may be one; as thou, Father, art in me, and I in thee, that they also may be one in us: that the world may believe that thou hast sent me. And the glory which thou gavest me I have given them; that they may be one, even as we are one: I in them, and thou in me, that they may be made perfect in one; and that the world may know that thou hast sent me, and hast loved them, as thou hast loved me.*

What kind of oneness is Jesus referring to? How can all of the denominations, with their different doctrines, be one? With all of the divisions within the body of Christ today, did the prayer of Jesus go unanswered? We need to examine this oneness at a different level. Jesus was not praying that all of His followers would have the same theology, the same traditions, the same music, or the same prayers. The unity that he had with the Father is the pattern to go by here. The Messiah is in the Father, the Father is in the Messiah, and all believers in Jesus are joined together with a common bond with God. Even though there are some beliefs in the body of Christ today that would make the eyes of the disciples pop out, everyone who truly believes in Jesus as the Son of God is one, whether we know it or not. There is only one God. There is only one Messiah. There is only one salvation. There is only one true, universal church. There are more people around the world who believe in Jesus than we might think. Our identity is in Jesus, not in the names over our church doors.

"...that the world may believe that thou hast sent me." This is the motive of Jesus prayer. When God's people can join hands together, it brings forth a powerful message that the lost world needs to hear. We may not all agree on every little detail but, if we believe that Jesus died and rose again, we can have fellowship with each other. Just imagine all that could be accomplished if every believing Jew and Gentile would understand this prayer of Jesus. We are one, but we act like separated people.

"...and hast loved them, as thou hast loved me." What a thought! The Lord Jesus Christ loves us the same way the Father loved Him. This is how the false gods of Rome were toppled to the ground. This is how the message of Jesus has permeated the entire world over the centuries. People from almost every language have heard the word of the Lord. The reason why Christianity survived is because of the great love that Jesus has for His children and that great love is shown to others as we are filled with the Holy Spirit. What a thought!

> **John 17:24-26** – *Father, I will that they also, whom thou hast given me, be with me where I am; that they may behold my glory, which thou hast given me: for thou lovedst me before the foundation of the world. O righteous Father, the world hath not known thee: but I have known thee, and these have known that thou hast sent me. And I have declared unto them thy name, and will declare it: that the love wherewith thou hast loved me may be in them, and I in them.*

This is one of the most precious parts of the high priestly prayer of our Lord. He prays for His disciples and all who believe in Him *to be where He is*. Why? So we can *behold His glory!* I think it is needful for us to reflect on being *with the Lord*, and seeing *His glory* once again. Let these words be established in your heart:

> *And if I go and prepare a place for you, I will come again, and receive you unto myself; that where I am, there ye may be also.*
>
> **—John 14:3**

> *Then we which are alive and remain shall be caught up together with them in the clouds, to meet the Lord in the air: and so shall we ever be with the Lord.*
>
> **—I Thess. 4:17**

And was transfigured before them: and his face did shine as the sun, and his raiment was white as the light.

—Matthew 17:2

And I turned to see the voice that spake with me. And being turned, I saw seven golden candlesticks; And in the midst of the seven candlesticks one like unto the Son of man, clothed with a garment down to the foot, and girt about the paps with a golden girdle. His head and his hairs were white like wool, as white as snow; and his eyes were as a flame of fire; And his feet like unto fine brass, as if they burned in a furnace; and his voice as the sound of many waters. And he had in his right hand seven stars: and out of his mouth went a sharp twoedged sword: and his countenance was as the sun shineth in his strength.

—Revelation 1:12-16

Jesus closes His prayer to the heavenly Father by stating that *he has declared unto them the Father's name, and will declare it.* We have already discussed that declaring, or revealing, the name of God is to show forth His character. The work of the Messiah was to make the Father known. When Jesus prayed these words, the God of Israel was only known as the God of the Jews. This faith in the God of Israel was confined to the Temple in Jerusalem and the synagogues throughout the Diaspora. But since that time, the name of God has been made known throughout the entire world.

Jesus continued to declare God's name through the disciples as they carried the gospel into the known world. Just think what all has been accomplished through the work of Jesus the Messiah. He has turned the hearts of multitudes over the centuries to the God of Israel. Many reject Jesus, many despise Him, most of Christendom misunderstands Him, and the majority of His followers misinterpret His words. Nevertheless, He has accomplished the Father's mission. Every time someone places his or her trust in Jesus as the Son of God, God's name is being declared again. It all started with the God the Father loving His Son, Jesus, *before the foundation of the world.* That same love dwells within the hearts of every true believer.

CHAPTER EIGHTEEN

John 18:1-9 - *When Jesus had spoken these words, he went forth with his disciples over the brook Cedron, where was a garden, into the which he entered, and his disciples. And Judas also, which betrayed him, knew the place: for Jesus ofttimes resorted thither with his disciples. Judas then, having received a band of men and officers from the chief priests and Pharisees, cometh thither with lanterns and torches and weapons. Jesus therefore, knowing all things that should come upon him, went forth, and said unto them, Whom seek ye? They answered him, Jesus of Nazareth. Jesus saith unto them, I am he. And Judas also, which betrayed him, stood with them. As soon then as he had said unto them, I am he, they went backward, and fell to the ground. Then asked he them again, Whom seek ye? And they said, Jesus of Nazareth. Jesus answered, I have told you that I am he: if therefore ye seek me,*

308

let these go their way: That the saying might be fulfilled, which he spake, Of them which thou gavest me have I lost none.

The Garden of Gethsemane, or the *Garden of the olive press,* was just across the brook *Cedron (transliteration from the Hebrew Kidron to Greek)* and it was a place where Jesus went often with His disciples. Notice that John said there "<u>was</u> a garden." The Romans destroyed all of the olive trees on the Mt. of Olives during the destruction of Jerusalem in 70 AD, but the garden was still in the mind and heart of the apostle John as he was writing this gospel. On this spring night, with possibly a full moon shining through the olive trees, *soldiers and chief priests' officers* came to arrest the Lord Jesus carrying *lanterns, torches, and weapons.* The lead man during the arrest of Jesus was *Judas Iscariot,* so *the scriptures might be fulfilled.* (**John 17:12, 18:9, Acts 1:16**) They came with weapons to arrest the sinless Son of God. They didn't need their weapons. Jesus knew everything that was about to happen and he walked right into it.

There is a strange, evil, geographical connection to the *Kidron Valley* that is overlooked by many scholars. It is a conjecture, but it does hold some intriguing thoughts. The *Kidron Valley* lies on the east of Jerusalem and the *Valley of Hinnom* lies just to the south of Jerusalem. The *Valley of Hinnom (which is a biblical metaphor for hell, where children were burned in the fire to the god Moloch)* runs into the *Kidron Valley* and creates a long-running gorge that descends some twenty miles down to the Dead Sea, which is the lowest point on planet earth (*over 1300 ft. below sea level*). The salty Dead Sea receives its water from the fresh water of the Jordan River. The Jordan originates from the melting snow that falls on the top of Mt. Hermon in the north (*over 9200 ft. above sea level*) and runs into the Sea of Galilee. From there, the river meanders some 70 miles down into the Dead Sea. What is the connection? According to the apocryphal book of Enoch (*mentioned in* **Jude 14**) there was a group of fallen angels who descended to the top of Mt. Hermon and married earthly women from the region that would later be occupied by the tribe of Dan. This was an attempt to destroy God's creation in **Genesis 6:1-5** and this angelic-human relationship brought giants into the world: the *Nephillim* (**Genesis 6:4, Num. 13:33**) and their descendants, the *Rephaim* (**Num. 13:33, Deut. 2:11, 2:20, 3:11, 3:13, Josh. 12:4, 13:12, 15:8, 17:15, 18:16**). Many Hebrew scholars believe that the place of the Dead Sea was once *the garden of the Lord* (**Genesis 13:10**), but after the fire and brimstone that destroyed Sodom and Gomorrah, the garden changed into the salty Dead Sea, where there is no life. Some believe that this evil presence followed along these geographical bodies of water: through the valleys that ran from Mt. Hermon all the way down to the Dead Sea and up to Jerusalem. Could this be the reason why Jesus went into the *Kidron Valley*, in order to confront evil and ultimately be victorious? What a place for the Son of God to be betrayed by one of His own disciples, who was the devil! So there may be a two-fold meaning why Jesus went into this place:

1. *To fulfill the sacred, Hebrew scriptures*
2. *To do battle with Satan*

"As soon then as he had said unto them, I am he, they went backward, and fell to the ground." This should be understood as the final "I am" statement of Jesus. It demonstrated the power of God's name as they all, including Judas, fell backward to the ground. I think we need to review the "I am" statements of Jesus because they reveal His person and His mission. They are unique to John's gospel:

1. *I am He (the Messiah)* – **John 4:26**
2. *I am the Bread of Life* – **John 6:35, 41, 48, 51**
3. *Before Abraham was, I am* – **John 8:58**
4. *I am the Light of the world* – **John 8:12, 9:5**
5. *I am the Gate* – **John 10:7, 9**
6. *I am the Good Shepherd* – **John 10:11, 14**
7. *I am the Way, the Truth, and the Life* – **John 14:6**
8. *I am the True Vine* – **John 15:1**
9. *I am He (Yeshua of Nazareth)* – **John 18:5**

> **John 18:10-11** - *Then Simon Peter having a sword drew it, and smote the high priest's servant, and cut off his right ear. The servant's name was Malchus. Then said Jesus unto Peter, Put up thy sword into the sheath: the cup which my Father hath given me, shall I not drink it?*

The days of comfort and favor that the disciples had enjoyed for over three years with their Master was over. A time of darkness, danger, and certain persecution lay ahead. *Simon Peter* was no doubt a tough, hard-working man from Galilee and he was taking up for Jesus. Try to imagine Simon Peter swinging his sword wildly in the dark, aiming for the head of *Malchus*, a servant of the high priest. After Peter *cut off the right ear of Malchus*, the gospel of Luke tells us that Jesus healed his ear. (**Luke 22:51**) Peter cutting off *Malchus'* ear is mentioned again in **John 18:26**. But Peter did not understand that Jesus deliberately walked into the garden in order to be arrested. He came to this earth to *drink the cup*, which meant to take all of the sins of the world upon Himself.

RELIGIOUS TRIAL AND PETER'S DENIAL

> **John 18:12-14 -** *Then the band and the captain and officers of the Jews took Jesus, and bound him, And led him away to Annas first; for he was father in law to Caiaphas, which was the high priest that same year. Now Caiaphas was he, which gave counsel to the Jews, that it was expedient that one man should die for the people.*

What paradoxical words: "And led him away to Annas first." The eternal Son of God could have killed the entire band of soldiers and officers, but they *led him away*. Annas had been the high priest in Jerusalem from 6-15 AD and he had five sons to follow after him in that position. But he also had a son-in-law who followed after him: *Caiaphas, or

Kayafa, who was high priest from 18–36 AD. The corrupt *Annas* was apparently still giving orders to *Caiaphas* and that is why they brought Jesus to *Annas* first. The high priest in Jerusalem was a position that was bought and sold annually. Several men could carry the title, but there was only one high priest that could serve in that station. It's interesting that John quotes his own gospel regarding *Caiaphas* making the prophecy back in **John 11:49–50**.

In November of 1990, an ornately carved ossuary was found in Jerusalem with the bones of a man inside. The name on the side of the ossuary was Joseph son of Caiaphas, which was the full name of Caiaphas in the trial of Jesus. While it cannot be certain that this is the same person, ossuaries were only used for about one hundred years, which include the time that Jesus of Nazareth walked the earth. Many other ossuaries were found with some of the names depicted in the gospels as well.

> **John 18:15–18 -** *And Simon Peter followed Jesus, and so did another disciple: that disciple was known unto the high priest, and went in with Jesus into the palace of the high priest. But Peter stood at the door without. Then went out that other disciple, which was known unto the high priest, and spake unto her that kept the door, and brought in Peter. Then saith the damsel that kept the door unto Peter, Art not thou also one of this man's disciples? He saith, I am not. And the servants and officers stood there, who had made a fire of coals; for it was cold: and*

they warmed themselves: and Peter stood with them, and warmed himself.

Two disciples followed Jesus back up the Kidron Valley into the courtyard of Caiaphas. One was *Peter*, and one was that *other disciple*. The *other disciple* that was *known by the high priest* is of course believed to have been John. Some Hebrew scholars think that John's mother, *Salome*, or *Shulamit*, was related to the high priest. If so, then this would explain why the high priest knew John and didn't know Peter. John helped Peter to enter into the courtyard. Peter warmed himself by a *fire of coals*. This same kind of fire would be the setting that was later used by Jesus on the shores of Galilee to help restore Peter. (**John 21:9**)

> **John 18:19-27** - *The high priest then asked Jesus of his disciples, and of his doctrine. Jesus answered him, I spake openly to the world; I ever taught in the synagogue, and in the temple, whither the Jews always resort; and in secret have I said nothing. Why askest thou me? ask them which heard me, what I have said unto them: behold, they know what I said. And when he had thus spoken, one of the officers which stood by struck Jesus with the palm of his hand, saying, Answerest thou the high priest so? Jesus answered him, If I have spoken evil, bear witness of the evil: but if well, why smitest thou me? Now Annas had sent him bound unto Caiaphas the high priest. And Simon Peter stood and warmed*

> *himself. They said therefore unto him, Art not thou*
> *also one of his disciples? He denied it, and said, I*
> *am not. One of the servants of the high priest, being*
> *his kinsman whose ear Peter cut off, saith, Did not*
> *I see thee in the garden with him? Peter then denied*
> *again: and immediately the cock crew."*

Jesus is being questioned by *Annas*. Even though he was not the actual high priest at that time, he still retained the title. Before he was deposed by Rome at the age of thirty-six, he had extreme influence and political power in Jerusalem. *Annas* was probably hoping that they would arrest Jesus *and* His disciples. He started asking Jesus about His *doctrine* and about His followers. This new movement of Jesus had brought hope to so many but it was a threat to the religious establishment. Jesus was not being disrespectful. He was just telling *Annas* that His ministry had been public *in the synagogue* and *in the Temple*. He was not trying to hide anything. In response to Jesus' answer, *one of the officers struck Jesus with the palm of his hand*. It causes me to shutter to think that someone could be so lost and so evil as to strike the precious face of the Lord Jesus Christ.

Simon Peter denied his Lord three times: **vs.17, 25,** and **27**. It has been preached many times over the years, but there seems to be a direct correlation with Peter denying Jesus *three times* and Jesus later asking him *three times* if he loved him. (**John 21:15-19**) Peter was the leader of the disciples and, even though he failed, he would be restored and lead the new Jesus community that was far greater than the corrupt religious establishment in Jerusalem.

JESUS BEFORE PONTIUS PILATE

> **John 18:28–32** – *Then led they Jesus from Caiaphas unto the hall of judgment: and it was early; and they themselves went not into the judgment hall, lest they should be defiled; but that they might eat the passover. Pilate then went out unto them, and said, What accusation bring ye against this man? They answered and said unto him, If he were not a malefactor, we would not have delivered him up unto thee. Then said Pilate unto them, Take ye him, and judge him according to your law. The Jews therefore said unto him, It is not lawful for us to put any man to death: That the saying of Jesus might be fulfilled, which he spake, signifying what death he should die.*

The religious Jews would not go into the *Hall of Hewn Stone*, as it was called, because it was the place of the Gentiles. (**Acts 10:28**) Because they were so close to the proximity of the Temple, they did not want to be *defiled* (this was not in the Torah, it was a rabbinic tradition). Jesus had already eaten the Passover meal with His disciples back in **John 13**, but there was other food eaten during the feast, on the day following the Passover.

Jesus was brought before the *Governor of Judea, *Pontius*

Pilate, who ruled from 26-36 AD. He usually resided in the beautiful seaport city of Caesarea, but during Jewish feasts he would come to Jerusalem in order to keep down insurrectionists. If one could not rule his territory well, then Rome would depose them to some isolated island or small country. Pilate would be deposed in 36 AD.

*After the deposing of Herod Archelaus in 6 AD, (**Matt.2:22**) Rome thought it was best to send Governors, or Procurators from Rome to rule the religious territory of Judea. The first Procurator was Coponius and the last one was Gessius Florus in 66 AD. Hebrew scholars are not sure when capital punishment was taken out of the hands of Israel, but there are two good possibilities: either in 6 AD when Coponius began to rule or in 30 AD.*

"*It is not lawful for us to put any man to death; That the saying of Jesus might be fulfilled, which he spake, signifying what death he should die.*" I find this verse to be very profound and it deserves our consideration. Jesus, the Son of God, came into the world when the power of capital punishment had been taken out of the hands of the Jews and placed into the hands of Rome because the scriptures had to be fulfilled concerning *how* the Messiah would die. Crucifixion was not a Jewish method of execution; it was a Roman method. The Almighty was using Rome and they didn't even know it. When God does not rule a nation, He overrules in order to fulfill His plan. Jesus had already stated in three other occasions that He must be lifted up. (**John 3:14, 8:28, 12:32**)

> **John 18:33-38** - *Then Pilate entered into the judgment hall again, and called Jesus, and said unto him, Art thou the King of the Jews? Jesus answered him, Sayest thou this thing of thyself, or did others tell it thee of me? Pilate answered, Am I a Jew? Thine own nation and the chief priests have delivered thee unto me: what hast thou done? Jesus answered, My kingdom is not of this world: if my kingdom were of this world, then would my servants fight, that I should not be delivered to the Jews: but now is my kingdom not from hence. Pilate therefore said unto him, Art thou a king then? Jesus answered, Thou sayest that I am a king. To this end was I born, and for this cause came I into the world, that I should bear witness unto the truth. Every one that is of the truth heareth my voice. Pilate saith unto him, What is truth? And when he had said this, he went out again unto the Jews, and saith unto them, I find in him no fault at all.*

Because Jesus had been preaching, "The Kingdom of Heaven is now," and because large crowds with Messianic enthusiasm were following Him, Pilate asked: "Art thou King of the Jews?" Pilate is looking for a pretense to try and convict Jesus as a criminal of Rome. Jesus lets Pilate know that He is a *King*, but He didn't come to start a revolution. He was not a Zealot who came to Jerusalem to fight the Romans.

When Jesus said, "My kingdom of not of this world,"

He was not saying that God's kingdom is only a spiritual kingdom and does not come into contact with the earth. God lives in His people on the earth, but His kingdom is from heaven. Jesus did not come into the world to change the politics of the world, but to change the hearts of men. One day the kingdom of God will come to the earth in a powerful, beautiful way, when all of the kingdoms of the world will vanish away.

Jesus lets Pilate know that His kingdom is the kingdom of *truth* and that He came to be a witness of that *truth*. Pilate cynically disregards what Jesus said and replied, "What is truth?" The pagan Roman culture did not believe in *truth*, they only lived for pleasure and power. But in the ancient Jewish writings, they believed that God is truth and that He is the only living God and King Eternal!

As pagan as Pilate was, he said for the <u>first time</u>, "I find no fault in him." Here we are reminded again that our Lord was blameless and without sin. What a thought! We can read about the holiness of the Messiah in places like **Isa. 53:9, 2 Cor. 5:21,** and **I Peter 2:22.** Think of all the sin of mankind since Adam being placed on the sinless Christ!

> **John 18:39-40** - *But ye have a custom, that I should release unto you one at the passover: will ye therefore that I release unto you the King of the Jews? Then cried they all again, saying, Not this man, but Barabbas. Now Barabbas was a robber.*

The Jewish custom of *Paschal Pardon* is not found in any other historical writings, only in the gospel accounts. It's interesting that the *bandit*, whose name is written *Barabbas*, was really *Yeshua bar-abba*, or *Yeshua the son of the father.* His name was shortened by some of the early scribes because they thought it was dishonoring to Jesus. But here we have the two sons: *Yeshua bar-abba*, the son of an earthly father, and *Yeshua Ha Noztri* (Jesus of Nazareth), the Son of the Heavenly Father. Barabbas represents all of the sinners in the history of the world, whose sins were paid for by the sinless Savior, Jesus Christ! Hallelujah!

CHAPTER NINETEEN

John 19:1-6 – *Then Pilate therefore took Jesus, and scourged him. And the soldiers platted a crown of thorns, and put it on his head, and they put on him a purple robe, And said, Hail, King of the Jews! and they smote him with their hands. Pilate therefore went forth again, and saith unto them, Behold, I bring him forth to you, that ye may know that I find no fault in him. Then came Jesus forth, wearing the crown of thorns, and the purple robe. And Pilate saith unto them, Behold the man! When the chief priests therefore and officers saw him, they cried out, saying, Crucify him, crucify him. Pilate saith unto them, Take ye him, and crucify him: for I find no fault in him.*

The *scourging* that the Romans usually handed out was very severe, even a tearing away of the flesh. Jesus, the Son of God, is being humiliated by Gentile soldiers under

Rome's authority all because of the corrupt, religious, Jewish leaders. The *crown of thorns* that was platted on the head of the Messiah could be a symbol of the result of sin coming into the world back in **Genesis 3:17-18** :

> *And unto Adam he said, Because thou hast hearkened unto the voice of thy wife, and hast eaten of the tree, of which I commanded thee, saying, Thou shalt not eat of it: cursed is the ground for thy sake; in sorrow shalt thou eat of it all the days of thy life; Thorns also and thistles shall it bring forth to thee; and thou shalt eat the herb of the field;*

It was common in the Roman world for a flogging to be followed by a mock-coronation. So with Jesus wearing a *purple robe*, a sign of royalty, with a *crown of thorns*, they said, "Hail, King of the Jews!" As if this was not enough, Pilate said unto the people, "Behold the man!" *Pilate took the opportunity to poke fun at the Jewish leadership and the entire Zealot movement. I find it interesting here to compare this to first chapter of John's gospel, where John the Baptist proclaims, "Behold the Lamb of God." (**John 1:29**) In order to pay for the redemption price for all mankind, God had to provide His perfect *Lamb* and that perfect *Lamb* had to become a perfect *man*! So "Behold the Lamb" and "Behold the man!"

There is a place in old city Jerusalem, where the Via Dolorosa begins, called Ecce Homo. These are the words in Latin that Pilate spoke when he said, "Behold the man?"

For the <u>second time</u> Pilate says, "I find no fault in him." Then, to reveal the evil that was in the hearts of the Judean rulers who felt no sympathy for Jesus, they yelled: "Crucify him, crucify him." Pilate knew that the Jews did not have the authority to crucify anyone, but he wanted to antagonize the Jewish leaders even more by saying, "Take ye him, and crucify him." The <u>third time</u> Pilate said, "I find no fault in him."

> **John 19:7-13** – *The Jews answered him, We have a law, and by our law he ought to die, because he made himself the Son of God. When Pilate therefore heard that saying, he was the more afraid; And went again into the judgment hall, and saith unto Jesus, Whence art thou? But Jesus gave him no answer. Then saith Pilate unto him, Speakest thou not unto me? knowest thou not that I have power to crucify thee, and have power to release thee? Jesus answered, Thou couldest have no power at all against me, except it were given thee from above: therefore he that delivered me unto thee hath the greater sin. And from thenceforth Pilate sought to release him: but the Jews cried out, saying, If thou let this man go, thou art not Caesar's friend: whosoever maketh himself a king speaketh against*

> *Caesar. When Pilate therefore heard that saying, he brought Jesus forth, and sat down in the judgment seat in a place that is called the Pavement, but in the Hebrew, Gabbatha.*

The Jews brought up the passage in the Torah where it says that a blasphemer should be killed.

> *And he that blasphemeth the name of the LORD, he shall surely be put to death, and all the congregation shall certainly stone him: as well the stranger, as he that is born in the land, when he blasphemeth the name of the Lord, shall be put to death.*
>
> **—Leviticus 24:16**

When the corrupt leaders said that Jesus *made himself the Son of God,* they were provoking Pilate. The only one in the entire world who could hold that title was Caesar himself, the Emperor of Rome. So this made Pilate *more afraid* and caused him to stop and rethink his position. Maybe now Pilate is thinking that his wife's dream was more than just a dream. (**Matt. 27:19**) Pilate went back into the judgment hall and asked Jesus, "Whence art thou?" When Jesus *gave him no answer,* Pilate began to tell Jesus about the power that he had to *crucify* Him or to *release* Him. Jesus then told Pilate that his power was only temporary and he was only in that position to fulfill the plan of God. Jesus says that Pilate not releasing Him was a *sin,* but the *greater sin* was committed by either the corrupt Jewish establishment, or, as possibly indicated by the pronoun *he,* Judas Iscariot.

"If thou let this man go, thou art not Caesar's friend." Many high-ranking Roman officials had been deposed, executed, or they had simply disappeared for allegedly not being a *friend* to Caesar. So Jesus was brought forth to where Pilate was seated on the elevated platform called *Gabbatha* (pronounced *Gab Baitha*), which meant *the ridge of the house,* which was part of the Antonia Fortress in Jerusalem.

> **John 19:14-16** – *And it was the preparation of the passover, and about the sixth hour: and he saith unto the Jews, Behold your King! But they cried out, Away with him, away with him, crucify him. Pilate saith unto them, Shall I crucify your King? The chief priests answered, We have no king but Caesar. Then delivered he him therefore unto them to be crucified. And they took Jesus, and led him away..*

It is the day before the festival of Passover, at about the *sixth hour,* which was the *Roman* calculation of time. Mark's gospel gives the Hebrew calculation of time, the *third hour,* which would have been about nine o'clock in the morning. (**Mark 15:25**) From the extreme pressure that was placed on him by the Jewish leaders, and for the sake of his political career, Pilate angrily says, "Behold your King!" The Jews are so filled with hatred toward Jesus that they again subscribe to the Roman method of execution by crying out, "Away with him, crucify him." Not only that, the chief priests told Pilate, "We have no king but Ceasar." What seems to us as a ridiculous trial by the corrupt Jewish leaders, and the Son of God being brought before a pagan Roman Governor, was all in the divine plan. Listen to these words and see how God used the different people of Israel at the right time:

> *The kings of the earth stood up, and the rulers were gathered together against the Lord, and against his Christ. For of a truth against thy holy child Jesus, whom thou hast anointed, both Herod, and Pontius Pilate, with the Gentiles, and the people of Israel, were gathered together, For to do whatsoever thy hand and thy counsel determined before to be done.*
> *- **Acts 4:26-28** quoting **Psalm 2:2***

Pilate delivered Jesus to the Roman soldiers and they *led him away.*

JESUS IS CRUCIFIED

> **John 19:17-20 -** *And he bearing his cross went forth into a place called the place of a skull, which is called in the Hebrew Golgotha: Where they crucified him, and two other with him, on either side one, and Jesus in the midst. And Pilate wrote a title, and put it on the cross. And the writing was JESUS OF NAZARETH THE KING OF THE JEWS. This title then read many of the Jews: for the place*

> *where Jesus was crucified was nigh to the city: and*
> *it was written in Hebrew, and Greek, and Latin.*

John does not mention that Simon of Cyrene carried the cross for Jesus. (**Luke 23:26**) There are several things that we need to consider. Jesus was believed to have been of medium stature, not a very large man in the flesh. He had just gone through being arrested in the Garden of Gethsemane, betrayal by one of His own, standing before Annas and Caiaphas, being brought before Pilate, scourging, being crowned with thorns, and being hit in the face and mocked before His own people. So a 125 lb. crossbar, or *patibulum*, would have been too much for Jesus to carry. We do not know where or when Simon took the cross but it was somewhere along the first part of the way to *Golgotha.* *

There are two possible places for Golgotha in Jerusalem. One is the Holy Sepulchre, which would have been outside the walls on the west side in Jesus' time. The other is Gordon's Calvary, just outside the walls on the north side. There are good arguments for both places. But the location should not be our focus; the focus should be on our precious Lord Jesus who died in order to conquer death for His people. It's not pleasing to our Lord to romanticize or to worship a place.

So the precious, sinless Lamb of God was crucified with two transgressors, fulfilling **Isaiah 53:12**. The scriptures do not go into detail about the crucifixion, but it was a very crude, primitive-looking scene that day. Almost all of the religious pictures depict Jesus dying on a big, hewn timber and being raised on the top of large hill. But according to Roman history, it was the custom to crucify their victims along the roadside, where the crowds could walk by and think twice of ever starting a revolt against Rome. According to archaeological finds, we believe that Jesus was nailed to the crossbar that was then possibly nailed to a stump of an old olive tree, close to the ground. As we will see, He was so close to the ground that He could talk to His mother.

"And Pilate wrote a title, and put it on the cross. And the writing was JESUS OF NAZARETH THE KING OF THE JEWS. *This title then read many of the Jews: for the place where Jesus was crucified was nigh to the city: and it was written in Hebrew, and Greek, and Latin."* As a final way of mocking Jesus, Pilate wrote an inscription and put it above the cross of Jesus. Although Pilate meant it to be a form of mockery, it announced to the entire world the eternal truth of who Jesus really was. There are some Hebrew scholars who believe that it read, JESUS OF NAZARETH <u>and</u> THE KING OF THE JEWS. If this is true, then the acrostic of those words would spell the Hebrew name of God, YHVH. This would say that the God of the Old Testament had come in human form in order to die for the sins of His people. The title was written in three languages, *Hebrew, Greek, and Latin.* Why? Contrary to what many Bible colleges teach, *Hebrew* was still the language of the religious Jews. It was <u>not</u> a dead language. Many of the common people in the Galilee spoke Aramaic, which was a dialect of Hebrew.

Greek was the language of the majority of the populace of the Hellenized world and *Latin* was the language of the Romans. Jesus was the *King of Israel* and one day all of Israel and the whole world will acknowledge Him as the *King*. One of His names would have been *Yeshua Ha Melech*, or *Jesus the King*. We can see Jesus being the *King* in many places in the New Testament:

- *His Birth* – **Matthew 2:2**
- *His Ministry* – **John 1:49**
- *His City*- **Matthew 5:35**
- *His Triumphal Entry* – **Matthew 21:5, John 12:13**
- *His Judgments* – **Matthew 25:34**
- *His Enemies* – **Matthew 27:42, John 19:14**
- *His Cross* – **John 19:19**
- *His Return* – **Revelation 19:16**

> **John 19:21-22** - *Then said the chief priests of the Jews to Pilate, Write not, The King of the Jews; but that he said, I am King of the Jews. Pilate answered, What I have written I have written.*

While the *chief priests* did not like the title *THE KING OF THE JEWS*, Pilate refused to take it down. Again, it was the Sovereign Lord using Pontius Pilate to fulfill the scriptures and to tell the world that Jesus of Nazareth was the real King!

> **John 19:23-24** - *Then the soldiers, when they had crucified Jesus, took his garments, and made*

four parts, to every soldier a part; and also his coat: now the coat was without seam, woven from the top throughout. They said therefore among themselves, Let us not rend it, but cast lots for it, whose it shall be: that the scripture might be fulfilled, which saith, They parted my raiment among them, and for my vesture they did cast lots. These things therefore the soldiers did.

It seems as though there were *four* Roman soldiers who actually carried out the crucifixion. They parted the garment of Jesus into *four parts* but they did not rend His *coat*, or the outer garment, which was *without seam*. The gambling over His *vesture*, or cloak, and *parting His garments* was a fulfillment of **Psalm 22:18**:

They part my garments among them, and cast lots upon my vesture.

Psalm 22 is quoted more than any other chapter of the Old Testament during the crucifixion of Christ. It is such a powerful chapter that it is also quoted in ten books of the New Testament.

John 19:25-27 - *Now there stood by the cross of Jesus his mother, and his mother's sister, Mary the wife of Cleophas, and Mary Magdalene. When Jesus therefore saw his mother, and the disciple standing by, whom he loved, he saith unto his mother, Woman, behold thy son! Then saith he to*

the disciple, Behold thy mother! And from that hour
that disciple took her unto his own home.

What a moving scene this is! *The mother of Jesus* was at the cross, along with *Mary the wife of Cleophas,* (**Luke 24:18**) and *Mary Magdalene.* It was written in the Torah that they were to honor their father and mother. (**Ex.19:12**) Honoring their father and mother meant to provide for their physical needs. Jesus, being the firstborn, was to take care of Mary His mother after the assumed death of Joseph. What Jesus said to Mary and to John the apostle, *the disciple standing by, whom he loved,* had the language of adoption: "Woman, behold thy son!" "Behold thy mother!" This was much more than just a commendation or a suggestion. This adds a deeper meaning to John's gospel when we consider that Jesus loved John so much that He asked him to take care of His mother while He was hanging on the cross. Jesus didn't tell Peter or any other disciple, but He left Mary* into the hands of John!

*Hippolytus of Thebes, a Byzantine author from the 7th or 8th century, says that Mary died eleven years after Jesus' ascension. There is a strong tradition that says that Mary followed John to Ephesus where she died around 45 AD.

John 19:28-30 - *After this, Jesus knowing that all things were now accomplished, that the scripture might be fulfilled, saith, I thirst. Now there was set a vessel full of vinegar: and they filled a spunge*

with vinegar, and put it upon hyssop, and put it to
his mouth. When Jesus therefore had received the
vinegar, he said, It is finished: and he bowed his
head, and gave up the ghost.

The last time it is recorded where Jesus needed something to drink was at the well in Samaria. (**John 4:7**) The one who gives living water now says, "I thirst." The one who created the rivers that never run dry, said, "I thirst." This all would be a part of the scriptures being fulfilled. Listen to the second half of **Psalm 69:21**:

…and in my thirst they gave me vinegar to drink.

The mention of them *putting the vinegar upon the hyssop* evokes Passover imagery. Jesus is the Passover Lamb and His blood is our protection from judgment. Listen to **Exodus 12:22**:

And ye shall take a bunch of hyssop, and dip it in
the blood that is in the bason, and strike the lintel
and the two side posts with the blood that is in the
bason; and none of you shall go out at the door of
his house until the morning.

Jesus, who knew everything that was taking place and that the scriptures were being fulfilled, said, "It is finished." The Almighty God had defeated the powers of hell. The primary reason of the incarnation was for the Messiah to die for His people. It was going to take more than performing miracles and preaching sermons to save a lost world. It was going to take the cross. Let these words be established in your hearts:

> *Blotting out the handwriting of ordinances that was against us, which was contrary to us, and took it out of the way, nailing it to his cross; And having spoiled principalities and powers, he made a shew of them openly, triumphing over them in it.*
> **—Colossians 2:14-15**

> *For this purpose the Son of God was manifested, that he might destroy the works of the devil.*
> **—I John 3:8**

Jesus saw His cross as the finished work that would defeat the seed of the serpent, prophesied in **Genesis 3:15**:

> *And I will put enmity between thee and the woman, and between thy seed and her seed; it shall bruise thy head, and thou shalt bruise his heel.*

"*...and he bowed his head, and gave up the ghost.*" Jesus deposited His life into the hands of the Father. No one took His life; He *gave* it! This connects us back to what Jesus said during His discourse about the Good Shepherd:

> *No man taketh it from me, but I lay it down of myself. I have power to lay it down, and I have*

power to take it again. This commandment have I received of my Father.

—John 10:18

John 19:31 - *The Jews therefore, because it was the preparation, that the bodies should not remain upon the cross on the sabbath day, (for that sabbath day was an high day,) besought Pilate that their legs might be broken, and that they might be taken away."*

Jesus died on the day before the *High Sabbath* of that Passover week, *not* the weekly Sabbath. Without confusing anyone, after in-depth Hebrew studies, I have come to believe that Jesus was crucified on Thursday, the day before Friday (*the High Sabbath*) and two days before the weekly Sabbath on Saturday. Why did the Jews desire for the body of Jesus to not remain on the cross on the High Sabbath?

> *And if a man have committed a sin worthy of death, and he be to be put to death, and thou hang him on a tree: His body shall not remain all night upon the tree, but thou shalt in any wise bury him that day; (for he that is hanged is accursed of God;) that thy land be not defiled, which the LORD thy God giveth thee for an inheritance.*
>
> **—Deut.21:22-23**

We know that this prophecy in the Torah, written centuries before the Messiah came into the world, was referring to His death on the cross because it is quoted in **Galatians**

3:13. Think of Jesus dying on a *tree*, and then think of the land of Israel being *defiled* if he stayed on the tree until the High Sabbath. This is what was on the minds of the Jewish leaders. They wanted the soldiers to *break the legs* of Jesus so He could not push Himself up with His nailed feet on the tree in order to breathe.

> **John 19:32-37** – *Then came the soldiers, and brake the legs of the first, and of the other which was crucified with him. But when they came to Jesus, and saw that he was dead already, they brake not his legs: But one of the soldiers with a spear pierced his side, and forthwith came there out blood and water. And he that saw it bare record, and his record is true: and he knoweth that he saith true, that ye might believe. For these things were done, that the scripture should be fulfilled, A bone of him shall not be broken. And again another scripture saith, They shall look on him whom they pierced.*

Jesus died on the tree before the two transgressors died. They broke their legs in order to finish killing them but, when they came to Jesus, they did not break His legs. He was already dead. There are two scriptures that were fulfilled:

> *In one house shall it be eaten; thou shalt not carry forth ought of the flesh abroad out of the house; neither shall ye break a bone thereof.*
>
> **—Exodus 12:46**

He keepeth all his bones: not one of them is broken.
—Psalm 34:20

But just to make sure He was dead, one of the soldiers*
pierced the side of Jesus. This fulfilled another passage of
scripture:

> *And I will pour upon the house of David, and upon*
> *the inhabitants of Jerusalem, the spirit of grace and of*
> *supplications: and they shall look upon me whom they*
> *have pierced, and they shall mourn for him, as one*
> *mourneth for his only son, and shall be in bitterness*
> *for him, as one that is in bitterness for his firstborn.*
> **—Zechariah 12:10**

Notice the words "the house of David," and "they shall
look upon me." This tells us that the Messiah would be
pierced by His own people and that Jesus is the same person
as the pronoun "me." The apostle John would later mention
the pierced Messiah in **Revelation 1:7**.

*The soldier who pierced the side of Jesus was identified as Longinus.
History records that he became a convert to Christianity and won
many souls to Christ. He was later martyred.

"...*and forthwith came there out blood and water.*" If we just
look at the context of these words, it just simply tells us that
Jesus, the Son of God, was fully man and that He really
died. John was writing his gospel to protect his readers
from the false doctrine of *Docetism*, which said that a holy

God would not allow Himself to take on flesh and blood. John would later mention this again in **I John 5:6:**

> *This is he that came by water and blood, even Jesus Christ; not by water only, but by water and blood. And it is the Spirit that beareth witness, because the Spirit is truth.*

THE BURIAL OF JESUS

> **John 19:38-42** - *And after this Joseph of Arimathaea, being a disciple of Jesus, but secretly for fear of the Jews, besought Pilate that he might take away the body of Jesus: and Pilate gave him leave. He came therefore, and took the body of Jesus. And there came also Nicodemus, which at the first came to Jesus by night, and brought a mixture of myrrh and aloes, about an hundred pound weight. Then took they the body of Jesus, and wound it in linen clothes with the spices, as the manner of the Jews is to bury. Now in the place where he was crucified there was a garden; and in the garden a new sepulchre, wherein was never man yet laid. There laid they Jesus therefore because of the Jews' preparation day; for the sepulchre was nigh at hand.*

Within the corrupt Sanhedrin, there were two godly men, *Joseph of Arimathea* and *Nicodemus.* We cannot over-emphasize the devotion that *Joseph of Arimathea* had for

Jesus. He went and begged Pilate for the body of his Lord. He did not send his servants but he went to Pilate himself. It was *Joseph of Arimathea* who pulled the cruel nails out of the precious hands and feet of dear Lord.

We find here once again the very wealthy Nicodemus that met Jesus by night back in **John 3:1-2, 7:50**. He brings about a *hundred pounds* of spices to anoint the dead body of Jesus. He must have known that the bloody, mangled body of Jesus would need plenty of spices. Not only was the *myrrh and aloes* very expensive, it would have been a huge amount to bring. Joseph and Nicodemus wanted Jesus to have a Jewish burial and this also would have publicly announced their faith in Jesus. So *they took the body of Jesus and wound it in linen clothes with the spices, as the manner of the Jews is to bury.* In the minds of a religious Jew, both of these men were considered unclean, after touching a dead body. So this would prevent them from partaking of the Passover. But there was a clause in the Jewish custom that allowed someone to celebrate the Passover at a later date.

Joseph of Arimathea had paid for his own tomb that had been hewn out in a rock. It was prophesied that the Messiah would be buried with the rich in **Isaiah 53:9**. The tomb was also *in a garden*, and *no man had ever been laid in it before.* These two men, *Joseph and Nicodemus*, gave very expensive gifts for the Master's burial. Sometimes we think about the death and resurrection of our Lord but forget about His *burial.* He had to be buried! Jesus had to not only die for our sins, but he also had to go through the process of being buried so he could rise again. We don't have to be afraid.

Jesus our Lord has already conquered every part of death. This is part of the gospel! Listen to **I Corinthians 15:3-4** :

> *For I delivered unto you first of all that which I also received, how that Christ died for our sins according to the scriptures; And that he was buried, and that he rose again the third day according to the scriptures:*

CHAPTER TWENTY

John 20:1-9 – *The first day of the week cometh Mary Magdalene early, when it was yet dark, unto the sepulchre, and seeth the stone taken away from the sepulchre. Then she runneth, and cometh to Simon Peter, and to the other disciple, whom Jesus loved, and saith unto them, They have taken away the* LORD *out of the sepulchre, and we know not where they have laid him. Peter therefore went forth, and that other disciple, and came to the sepulchre. So they ran both together: and the other disciple did outrun Peter, and came first to the sepulchre. And he stooping down, and looking in, saw the linen clothes lying; yet went he not in. Then cometh Simon Peter following him, and went into the sepulchre, and seeth the linen clothes lie, And the napkin, that was about his head, not lying with the linen clothes, but wrapped together in a place by itself. Then went in also that other disciple, which came first to the*

> *sepulchre, and he saw, and believed. For as yet they knew not the scripture, that he must rise again from the dead.*

It was still dark, very early on the **first day of the week* (Sunday). The fact that a woman, **Mary Magdalene*, was the first to be mentioned at the tomb of Jesus goes against the Jewish culture of the day. This also testifies of the truthfulness of the gospel account. This woman, who had been set free from seven demons (**Mark 16:9**), was so thankful and such a devoted follower of our Lord that she would be given the life-changing privilege to be the first one to see the risen Christ that changed all of history. Jesus did not rise from the grave on the Jewish Sabbath, but on the first day of the week, bringing about a new order. The Sabbath was a *shadow of things to come.* (**Colossians 2:16-17**)

*This was the Jewish Yom Rishon (the first day of the week), between Saturday sunset and Sunday sunset. This is the reason why Gentile believers worship on the first day of the week and not on the Jewish Sabbath. There was a reason why Jesus the Messiah arose the day after the Sabbath. He was bringing about a new community that would not be empowered by their Jewish traditions, but by the finished work of their Messiah.

Mary Magdalene has been depicted throughout much of church history as being a former prostitute. This is the result of believing that Mary Magdalene was the sinful woman in **Luke 7:36-50. But there is no biblical evidence that Mary Magdalene was ever*

*a prostitute. The seven demons that Jesus cast out of her (***Mark 16:9***) could have been demons of sickness or of a spiritual nature. I believe that Mary was a prominent woman who lived in Magdala, on the northern shore of the Galilee. When she met Jesus she found the true meaning of life. She had such a thankful heart and such a strong faith; that is why she was allowed to see the risen Messiah first.*

Mary ran to tell *Simon Peter and the other disciple, whom Jesus loved* (John) that they had taken the body of Jesus out of the tomb. Try to imagine Mary banging on their door and, when they open the door, they see Mary out of breath from running. While everyone was still asleep in Jerusalem, and while the streets were empty, Peter and John began to run through the city, outside the walls, into the garden where Jesus had been buried. John, being the younger, outran Peter. John looked in the tomb first but did not go in. Could it be that John, being known by the high priest in some way (**John 18:16**), felt a sense of being *unclean* by going into the tomb?* But after Peter, who was not connected to the high priest, went inside and saw the grave clothes, then John may have felt that he would not be *unclean* sinse the body of Jesus was gone. The tomb was no longer about death. It was about life! When John went inside *he saw and believed.*

This is just a conjecture, but we need to remember the Jewish worldview in the early first century concerning clean and unclean.

As we mentioned back in **John 11:44**, the fact that the grave clothes of Jesus were lying in the sepulcher shows the contrast between the raising of Lazarus and the resurrection of Jesus the Messiah. Lazarus came forth with his grave clothes on, but Jesus left His grave clothes in the tomb. Lazarus would have to die again but Jesus only had to die once. (**Heb.9:28, 10:14**) Lazarus's body saw corruption (*four days*, **John 11:39**) while the body of Jesus did not see corruption (*three days*, **Psalm 16:10, John 2:19, Acts 2:31**).

Even though Jesus had told them on more than one occasion that He would die and rise again, *they knew not the scriptures* that were in the Old Testament about the resurrected Messiah. During the forty days between the resurrection and the ascension of Jesus, He would open their understanding about His first and second coming.

John 20:10–16 – *Then the disciples went away again unto their own home. But Mary stood without at the sepulchre weeping: and as she wept, she stooped down, and looked into the sepulchre, And seeth two angels in white sitting, the one at the head, and the other at the feet, where the body of Jesus had lain. And they say unto her, Woman, why weepest thou? She saith unto them, Because they have taken away my LORD, and I know not where they have laid him. And when she had thus said, she turned herself back, and saw Jesus standing, and knew not that it was Jesus. Jesus saith unto her, Woman, why weepest thou? whom seekest thou? She, supposing*

him to be the gardener, saith unto him, Sir, if thou
have borne him hence, tell me where thou hast laid
him, and I will take him away. Jesus saith unto
her, Mary. She turned herself, and saith unto him,
Rabboni; which is to say, Master.

When Peter and John went back to where they were staying in Jerusalem, Mary Magdalene remained at the tomb, *weeping*. Through tear-filled eyes *she looked into the sepulcher.* She saw *two angels in white, sitting at the head and at the foot* of the place where Jesus' body had been laid. Why didn't Peter and John see the angels? Strange thing! Mary began to even talk back to the angels and tell them that they had taken away the body of her Lord. Mary then turns around and walks out of the tomb and there *she saw Jesus standing,* but *she knew not that it was Jesus.* The Messiah was hidden from her at this moment like He was hidden from the two men on the road to Emmaus. (**Luke 24:16**)

"Woman, why weepest thou?" Jesus repeats the very same words that the angels had spoken to Mary. Except Jesus adds, "whom seekest thou?" Mary thought that Jesus was the *gardener*, and surely he would know where they had laid the body of her Lord. Gardening is the oldest profession in the world. The *first* Adam was a gardener (**Gen.2:15**) and so was the *last* Adam. Death came into the world by Satan in a garden, and Jesus the Son of God would overcome death in a garden.

"Jesus saith unto her, Mary. She turned herself, and saith unto him, Rabboni; which is to say, Master." When Mary heard

Jesus speak her name, she knew who He was! Oh, the compassion of our Lord! There is no evidence that Jesus was ever ordained as a rabbi, but it is implied. His disciples and the women who followed Him regarded Him as the *Master Rabbi!*

> **John 20:17-18** - *Jesus saith unto her, Touch me not; for I am not yet ascended to my Father: but go to my brethren, and say unto them, I ascend unto my Father, and your Father; and to my God, and your God. Mary Magdalene came and told the disciples that she had seen the* LORD, *and that he had spoken these things unto her.*

There are two conjectures concerning why Jesus told Mary to "Touch me not." One is that the work that Jesus had to do in the days ahead required urgency and He did not need Mary to cling to Him. The other theory is of a deeper, spiritual nature: That Jesus was about to *ascend to the Father* as the *great High Priest* before He could appear to the disciples in His glorified state. Jesus mentions this *ascension* twice in this verse. So were there two *ascensions* of the Messiah? Or was Jesus referring to His *ascension* that would occur some forty days later?

JESUS BREATHES ON HIS DISCIPLES

> **John 20:19-23** - *Then the same day at evening, being the first day of the week, when the doors were*

> *shut where the disciples were assembled for fear of the Jews, came Jesus and stood in the midst, and saith unto them, Peace be unto you. And when he had so said, he shewed unto them his hands and his side. Then were the disciples glad, when they saw the* LORD. *Then said Jesus to them again, Peace be unto you: as my Father hath sent me, even so send I you. And when he had said this, he breathed on them, and saith unto them, Receive ye the Holy Ghost: Whose soever sins ye remit, they are remitted unto them; and whose soever sins ye retain, they are retained.*

The same Judean leadership that had crucified the Messiah of Israel might be interested in killing His followers as well. So the disciples of Jesus were hidden in a place where *the doors were shut.* The Hebrew words that Jesus spoke to them were *Shalom Aleichem.* Jesus did not want to see His disciples afraid (**John 6:20**) so the first words He said were to give them His eternal peace. Jesus showed them *His hands and His side,* proving that the same Jesus who was nailed to a tree had risen from the grave. Hallelujah! Jesus was *sent* by the Heavenly Father into the world, and now Jesus is about to *send* His disciples out into the world. The disciples will become *apostles!*

"*Receive ye the Holy Ghost.*" The sinless, holy, crucified and risen Messiah *breathed the Holy Ghost* on His eleven disciples. The *breath* that came out of the mouth of Jesus the Messiah was the Holy *breath* of God! The ultimate fulfillment would occur on the day of Pentecost in **Acts 2**, but Jesus wanted to show His disciples that the *Holy Ghost* would come upon them only because He had completed the work of redemption. *Breathing* on them was the anticipation of what was to come.

This also connects us back to God breathing the world into existence in Genesis and when God breathed life into the nostrils of man:

> *By the word of the* Lord *were the heavens made; and all the host of them by the breath of his mouth.*
> **—Psalm 33:6**

> *And the* Lord *God formed man of the dust of the ground, and breathed into his nostrils the breath of life; and man became a living soul.*
> **—Genesis 2:7**

"*Whose soever sins ye remit, they are remitted unto them; and whose soever sins ye retain, they are retained.*" The time had come for Jesus to transfer His authority to His disciples. Their authority would go beyond just keeping their Jewish traditions and being leaders in the new community. They would have the power to proclaim forgiveness of sin in the name of the Messiah. If the people that heard their message about Jesus did not repent and believe, they had to power and authority to tell them that their sins were not forgiven. This is a major transition in the life of the disciples!

John 20:24-29 - *But Thomas, one of the twelve, called Didymus, was not with them when Jesus* *came. The other disciples therefore said unto him, We have seen the LORD. But he said unto them, Except I shall see in his hands the print of the nails, and put my finger into the print of the nails, and thrust my hand into his side, I will not believe. And after eight days again his disciples were within, and Thomas with them: then came Jesus, the doors being shut, and stood in the midst, and said, Peace be unto you. Then saith he to Thomas, Reach hither thy finger, and behold my hands; and reach hither thy hand, and thrust it into my side: and be not faithless, but believing. And Thomas answered and said unto him, My LORD and my God. Jesus saith unto him, Thomas, because thou hast seen me, thou hast believed: blessed are they that have not seen, and yet have believed.*

Thomas probably believed that the other disciples saw something but, being the honest person that he was, he wanted to see the proof himself. Church history says that Thomas was a stonemason and a regular, blue-collar guy. The word *Didymus* means *twin* and may relate to the closeness that Jesus was with Thomas. Jesus gives a special resurrection appearance for Thomas. It was *eight days later* when Jesus appeared and said the same words that he said to the other disciples: *Shalom Aleichem*. The timing seems to indicate a connection with the Jewish *brit milah*, or the eighth-day circumcision of the Jews. We could say that when Jesus breathed on the disciples; that was their new birth; and the eighth-day resurrection appearance could be their ultimate sign.

"My Lord and my God." This was not just a series of words that Thomas uttered. The new community would know that Jesus of Nazareth was none other than the Lord God! Notice the two words together: *Adoneinu Eloheinu.* Instead of rebuking Thomas, Jesus took away his skepticism. Before anyone can be truly born again they must believe that Jesus is the Lord:

> *That if thou shalt confess with thy mouth the Lord*
> *Jesus, and shalt believe in thine heart that God hath*
> *raised him from the dead, thou shalt be saved.*
>
> **—Romans 10:9**

"Jesus saith unto him, Thomas, because thou hast seen me, thou hast believed: blessed are they that have not seen, and yet have believed." This anticipates all of the people who will believe in Jesus as the Lord, like you and I. We did not have the privilege to see what the apostles saw, but Jesus pronounces an even greater blessing upon those who will believe without seeing Him. I am reminded of what the apostle Peter would later write:

> *Whom having not seen, ye love; in whom, though*
> *now ye see him not, yet believing, ye rejoice with*
> *joy unspeakable and full of glory:*
>
> **—I Peter 1:8**

THE PURPOSE OF JOHN'S GOSPEL

> **John 20:30-31 –** *And many other signs truly did Jesus in the presence of his disciples, which are not written in this book: But these are written, that ye might believe that Jesus is the Christ, the Son of God; and that believing ye might have life through his name.*

The Holy Spirit inspired the apostle John to record certain miracles of the Messiah. His gospel has been selective, but not comprehensive. John's purpose of writing was so that his readers would believe that Jesus was not only the Messiah of Israel, but that He was also the Son of God! Sometimes we forget about believing in the two: both Messiah *(Christ)* and Son of God. When we say "Jesus Christ," we are really saying, "Jesus the Messiah." When we say, "Lord Jesus Christ," we are really saying that *Jesus* is the *Lord* and the *Messiah.* Jesus was the long-awaited Messiah that Moses and the prophets wrote about, but He was also the Creator: the God of the Old Testament in human form. John wanted his readers to experience *life through his name.* John, through the inspiration of the Holy Spirit, realized that time was short, and there was no need for him to write more. The miracles that John recorded should be enough to cause any reader to believe in Jesus.

CHAPTER TWENTY-ONE

John 21:1-3 - *After these things Jesus shewed himself again to the disciples at the sea of Tiberias; and on this wise shewed he himself. There were together Simon Peter, and Thomas called Didymus, and Nathanael of Cana in Galilee, and the sons of Zebedee, and two other of his disciples. Simon Peter saith unto them, I go a fishing. They say unto him, We also go with thee. They went forth, and entered into a ship immediately; and that night they caught nothing.*

The scene jumps about eighty miles north of Jerusalem, back to the *Sea of Tiberias*, or the Sea of Galilee. This occurred sometime during the forty days that the risen Jesus was with His disciples. (**Acts 1:3**) Jesus had told them that He would meet them back in Galilee:

351

> *But after that I am risen, I will go before you into*
> *Galilee.*
>
> **—Mark 14:28**

The angels at the garden tomb also told Mary to tell the disciples *and Peter* to meet Him back at Galilee:

> *But go your way, tell his disciples and Peter that he*
> *goeth before you into Galilee: there shall ye see him,*
> *as he said unto you.*
>
> **—Mark 16:7**

It is believed that Jesus appearing on the shore of Galilee to His disciples occurred sometime before His appearance on the mountain in **Matthew 28:16–20**. There was something very special about Jesus appearing to His disciples back where He had called them at the very beginning of His ministry. The familiar ground of their everyday occupations would become a spiritual place where they would experience the risen Savior. Here, he would give them very important lessons before they went into the Roman world for the very first time. We should never think that our jobs, careers, and daily responsibilities are a hindrance to serving the Lord. He wants to meet us there and help us to prioritize our lives.

"*Simon Peter saith unto them, I go a fishing. They say unto him, We also go with thee. They went forth, and entered into a ship immediately; and that night they caught nothing.*" I have always heard that the reason why Peter went fishing was because he felt so bad about his denial in Jerusalem that he just decided he better go back to fishing. But, after much consideration, I would like to present you with a different theory. The disciples were filled with so much joy after seeing the risen Jesus back down in Jerusalem. They had touched the resurrected Lord! They had heard Him speak and even felt Him breathe on them the Holy Ghost! They had eaten with Him and their faith was secure. But they were still ordinary men who had family responsibilities. Their pockets were empty and so were the stomachs of their families. They were trying to support themselves and catch something to sell and something to eat. But Jesus is about to teach them a lesson on how to act on His bidding and have faith that He would provide for them in the future. Just like at the beginning of Jesus' earthly ministry in the Galilee, they went fishing one night and *caught nothing.*

And Simon answering said unto him, Master, we have toiled all the night, and have taken nothing: nevertheless at thy word I will let down the net.

—Luke 5:5

John 21:4-6 - *But when the morning was now come, Jesus stood on the shore: but the disciples knew not that it was Jesus. Then Jesus saith unto them, Children, have ye any meat? They answered him, No. And he said unto them, Cast the net on the right side of the ship, and ye shall find. They*

> *cast therefore, and now they were not able to draw*
> *it for the multitude of fishes.*

Imagine the disciples pulling in their last dropped net and, as they were pulling, the sun came up over the Sea of Galilee. They caught sight of a stranger on the shore, but *they knew not that it was Jesus.* Mary, at the tomb, thought Jesus was the gardener; maybe the disciples thought Jesus was just another fisherman. Somehow Jesus, in His mysterious power, was hidden from them for a moment, like He was to the two men on the road to Emmaus. (**Luke 24:16**) But this stranger called them *Children.* This stranger also told them to "cast the net on the right side of the ship." This was not a simple job; the huge dragnets required the help of all of the apostles to move it to the other side of the little boat. After casting the net like the stranger told them to, the net was filled with so many fish that they couldn't even pull it in.

> **John 21:7 –** *Therefore that disciple whom Jesus loved saith unto Peter, It is the Lord. Now when Simon Peter heard that it was the Lord, he girt his fisher's coat unto him, (for he was naked,) and did cast himself into the sea.*

The apostle John realizes that the stranger is none other than the *Lord.* He tells Peter, "It is the Lord." It was the custom in those days to fish without your outer robe and to gird up your loins by tucking the bottom of their tunic into their belt, in order to have free movement. We also believe this because the Greek word for *coat* here is *ependutes*, which means *the outer garment*. Peter, in his excitement, jumps into the Sea of Galilee.

> **John 21:8-10** - *And the other disciples came in a little ship; (for they were not far from land, but as it were two hundred cubits,) dragging the net with fishes. As soon then as they were come to land, they saw a fire of coals there, and fish laid thereon, and bread. Jesus saith unto them, Bring of the fish which ye have now caught.*

John had outrun Peter to the tomb, but Peter wanted to be the first to get to the shore. They were about 300 ft., or *two hundred cubits*, from the shore. The fishing boats in Jesus' time were about twenty-eight ft. long, so try to imagine pulling a huge dragnet to the shore full of fish. The net was too heavy to lift it into the little boat, so they were *dragging the net*. As soon as they came to the shore*, *they saw a fire of coals there, and fish laid thereon, and bread*. Where did Jesus get the fish? Where did He get the bread? The same Lord who had fed the multitudes twice with fish and bread just three years earlier was the same Lord who had prepared breakfast for His disciples with more fish and bread. Jesus tells them however to *bring the fish which they had caught*. What emotions must have been running through the minds of the disciples; especially Peter, when he saw *the fire of coals*. (**John 18:18**) That was all Peter needed to remind him of his denial back in Jerusalem. But Jesus wasn't trying to make Peter feel bad. He wanted to restore Peter and bring him to the place where he could be effective in the kingdom.

This shore has been identified as the modern place called in the Arabic language as Tabgha. The Hebrew place is Ein Sheva, or the springs of seven. Fishermen of long ago would wash their nets under the seven springs that gush out of the mountain there. Stones have been found that lead archaeologists to believe that this was the place where Jesus called His disciples and the place where He appeared to them after the resurrection. The first documented history of this being the place was in 381 AD, by Egeria, where she saw rock steps leading up out of the water. A fourth-century church was built there. This led to the erecting of the little, Franciscan church called Peter's Primacy that was built in 1933 and stands on the shore today. Tabgha happens to be one of my personal favorite locations to visit in Israel.

> **John 21:1 1-** *Simon Peter went up, and drew the net to land full of great fishes, an hundred and fifty and three: and for all there were so many, yet was not the net broken.*

I find something very interesting here. The Greek word for fish, in **vs.9**, is *opsarion*, or *little broiled fish*. The words for *great fishes*, in this verse are, *megas ichthus*, or *large fish*. The same type of fish that Jesus had prepared for breakfast was the same type of fish that He used to feed the multitude in **John 6:9**. But the fish that He creates to be caught in the net for His disciples are *large fish*. The risen Jesus is the same Jesus who fed the multitude some three years before and He is the same Lord of the Old Testament that blesses His children. By showing them fish already on the shore, Jesus was telling His disciples that He didn't have to have them to catch people for His kingdom, but He would give them the opportunity to be a vital part. The Lord doesn't have to have us, but He graciously gives us the opportunity to share His glorious gospel.

"…an hundred and fifty three: and for all there were so many, yet was not the net broken." There have been many theories over the centuries about the 153 fish. One Jewish scholar said that it represented all the nations of the world, but there are close to 200 nations in the world at this time. Another Jewish scholar said that 153 is the numerical value, (Hebrew *gematria*) of the complete unity of gospel of John, but this seems to be a stretch to me, or the true *gematria* has been lost. I think the reason the 153 fish were counted is to show that it was a genuine miracle. The disciples were used to counting the fish in order to pay taxes on what they had caught. It also shows that, some sixty years later, John remembered the exact number of the fish that they caught on that morning on the shore of Galilee. Sometimes we are guilty of trying to over-spiritualize every number in the Bible. Sometimes we need to just explain things from the simple context.

But I believe there is a direct correlation between this miracle of the fish in **John 21:1-11** and the miraculous catch in **Luke 5:1-11**. We would be wise to read them in comparison:

> And it came to pass, that, as the people pressed upon him to hear the word of God, he stood by the lake of Gennesaret, And saw two ships standing by the lake: but the fishermen were gone out of them, and were washing their nets. And he entered into one of the ships, which was Simon's, and prayed him that he would thrust out a little from the land. And he sat down, and taught the people out of the ship. Now when he had left speaking, he said unto Simon, Launch out into the deep, and let down your nets for a draught. And Simon answering said unto him, Master, we have toiled all the night, and have taken nothing: nevertheless at thy word I will let down the net. And when they had this done, they inclosed a great multitude of fishes: and their net brake. And they beckoned unto their partners, which were in the other ship, that they should come and help them. And they came, and filled both the ships, so that they began to sink. When Simon Peter saw it, he fell down at Jesus' knees, saying, Depart from me; for I am a sinful man, O Lord. For he was astonished, and all that were with him, at the draught of the fishes which they had taken: And so was also James, and John, the sons of Zebedee, which were partners with Simon. And Jesus said unto Simon, Fear not; from henceforth thou shalt

catch men. And when they had brought their ships to land, they forsook all, and followed him.

—Luke 5:1-11

A little over three years earlier, Jesus had called His disciples to be fishers of men. Up until now, they had not caught one person in the gospel net. In the first miracle their *nets broke*, but here they *did not break*. Because of the death, burial, and resurrection of the Messiah, the disciples would be able to *catch*, or *zogreo – make alive*, countless people for the kingdom. This connects it all back together full-circle and was a sign of things to come. The disciples would truly become fishers of men!

> **John 21:12-14** – *Jesus saith unto them, Come and dine. And none of the disciples durst ask him, Who art thou? knowing that it was the Lord. Jesus then cometh, and taketh bread, and giveth them, and fish likewise. This is now the third time that Jesus shewed himself to his disciples, after that he was risen from the dead.*

I find it very interesting that in **John 1:39**, that Jesus told some of His disciples to "Come and see." In **John 7:37**, Jesus said, "If any man thirst, let him come unto me and drink." Here, in the last chapter of John, Jesus says to His disciples, "Come and dine." They had seen the place where Jesus lived. They had tasted of the living water. They now could rest and have fellowship with the Master. The mission of the Messiah was complete! Hallelujah!

The only sounds were the sound of the waves washing on the rocks and the popping of the coals of fire. The disciples ate quietly, keeping their eyes on Jesus, knowing that they were eating with the Son of God! Just like Jesus had distributed bread and fish to the disciples in order to feed the multitude, back in **John 6:11,** He is now distributing the bread and fish to His disciples again; reassuring them that He is the one who had called them three years earlier at this very place to become fishers of men.

RESTORATION OF SIMON PETER

John 21:15-17 - *So when they had dined, Jesus saith to Simon Peter, Simon, son of Jonas, lovest thou me more than these? He saith unto him, Yea, Lord; thou knowest that I love thee. He saith unto him, Feed my lambs. He saith to him again the second time, Simon, son of Jonas, lovest thou me? He saith unto him, Yea, Lord; thou knowest that I love thee. He saith unto him, Feed my sheep. He saith unto him the third time, Simon, son of Jonas, lovest thou me? Peter was grieved because he said unto him the third time, Lovest thou me? And he said unto him, Lord, thou knowest all things; thou knowest that I love thee. Jesus saith unto him, Feed my sheep.*

So, after breakfast had ended, Jesus calls Peter three times: "Simon, son of Jonas." This was the name that Jesus called him when they first met at Galilee. in **John 1:42**. Jesus asked Peter if he loved Him *more* than the other disciples because Peter had said that he would lay down his life for Jesus back in **John 13:37**. So three times Jesus asked Peter, "lovest thou me?" It has been preached for centuries that the two Greek words for love, *agapao* and *phileo*, are how we are to interpret the questions of Jesus and the answers of Peter. Many Greek scholars say that Jesus asked in the stronger language of *agapao* while Peter answered Him in the weaker language of *phileo*. But I do not agree with this and I will tell you why. Jesus did not speak Greek. He spoke Hebrew and Aramaic. Jesus would have used either the Hebrew word, *ahava,* or the Aramaic, *rakhma*. Simon Peter would have not answered Jesus in Greek because the Galileans spoke Aramaic most of the time. The real problem I have with the Greek wording is that the two words, *agapeo* and *phileo,* are interchangeable throughout the rest of the Bible. As I mentioned at the beginning of this work, John was writing to a Greek-speaking audience, but the thoughts and context were from the Jewish mind. Studying the Greek wording can be helpful in some cases, as we have seen, but not when we are studying the language of Jesus. The true meaning of the passage is that Jesus is *restoring* Peter by asking him if he really loved him. Think of the look in Jesus' eyes, the sound of His voice, and the grieving that was going on within the heart of Peter. Jesus told him that if he really loved him that he would prove it by *feeding His sheep*. As we read the epistles of Peter, we find that Peter did *feed the sheep* like Jesus told him to do.

No doubt these three questions and three answers are meant to correspond to Simon Peter's three denials back in Jerusalem. Jesus is sifting Peter of his pride and arrogance. We need to remember that Jesus told Peter that He would give him the keys of the kingdom of heaven, back in **Matthew 16:19**. Jesus knew that Peter would need some sifting, but Jesus saw what Peter would become even before He called him. The purpose that Jesus had for Simon Peter would not be in vain. Peter would become one of the greatest leaders and preachers that the world has ever known. This should bring encouragement to all of us. Just because we fail does not mean that we do not love our Lord. God's purpose for our life is not forfeited because we stumble along the journey. Just like Jesus restored Simon Peter, He restores us! Aren't you thankful that He does?

PETER'S CROSS

> **John 21:18-19** - *Verily, verily, I say unto thee, When thou wast young, thou girdest thyself, and walkedst whither thou wouldest: but when thou shalt be old, thou shalt stretch forth thy hands, and another shall gird thee, and carry thee whither thou wouldest not. This spake he, signifying by what death he should glorify God. And when he had spoken this, he saith unto him, Follow me.*

The apostle John was writing in retrospect after the death of Simon Peter. John knew that what Jesus told Peter came true just like He said. Jesus is giving Peter the final test of his faith. Will Peter follow Jesus knowing that suffering is coming? We must first look at the words of Peter shortly before he was martyred for the cause of Christ. Read the words of **2 Peter 1:12-14**:

> *Wherefore I will not be negligent to put you always in remembrance of these things, though ye know them, and be established in the present truth. Yea, I think it meet, as long as I am in this tabernacle, to stir you up by putting you in remembrance; Knowing that shortly I must put off this my tabernacle, even as our Lord Jesus Christ hath shewed me.*

History records that Peter was feeding the Lord's sheep in Rome when Nero ordered his arrest. The brothers and sisters urged him to leave the city. While Peter was passing through the gates he saw Jesus. Peter asked Jesus, "Master, where are you going?" Jesus told him, "To Rome to be crucified." When Peter heard this, he understood what the Lord meant. He returned to the believers and was arrested by Nero the Emperor. The Romans stretched out his hands and dressed him with a cross. They nailed him upside down, at Peter's request, because he had said that he was not worthy to die in the same way that his Lord had died. This all took place in the year 64 AD, three months after the fire of Rome. Peter died *loving* Jesus and *feeding* His sheep. He obeyed the Lord's voice, "Follow me."

There are three major lessons that we can gather from the miracle of the multitude of fish and the conversation that Jesus had with Peter:

- *We need to love our Lord supremely.*
- *We need to obey our Lord.*
- *We need to follow our Lord until the very end.*

> **John 21:20-23** - *Then Peter, turning about, seeth the disciple whom Jesus loved following; which also leaned on his breast at supper, and said, Lord, which is he that betrayeth thee? Peter seeing him saith to Jesus, Lord, and what shall this man do? Jesus saith unto him, If I will that he tarry till I come, what is that to thee? follow thou me. Then went this saying abroad among the brethren, that that disciple should not die: yet Jesus said not unto him, He shall not die; but, If I will that he tarry till I come, what is that to thee?*

The beloved John was there when this conversation took place between Jesus and Peter. If he had not been there, we would not have these words recorded. So, when Peter sees John walking behind them, he quickly asks, "Lord, and what shall this man do?" In other words, Peter was asking if John would die before the kingdom is restored to Israel. It's all a question of death and the timing of death. But

Jesus does not answer Peter's question the way Peter wants Him to. Jesus tells Peter that it is none of His business. He is to follow Jesus, do his job, and quit worrying about what is going to happen to John. Jesus was saying that, if John lives until He returns, or if he dies, it should not be Peter's concern.

The kingdom of God is much too important to have jealous competition between the brethren. We should never compare our God-given gifts and services to those of others. God has given us a purpose and all we are required to do is to fulfill God's will for <u>our</u> lives. It matters not how long we may *live* on this earth or the manner in which we may *leave* this earth.

The apostle John lived until the time of the Roman Emperor Trajan. He died in Ephesus, at the age of 99, in the year 104 AD. He didn't live until Jesus returned, but he was the only disciple to die a natural death. The followers of John thought that John might live until Jesus returned. That is the reason for the clarification in **vs.23**.

> **John 21:24 –** *This is the disciple which testifieth of these things, and wrote these things: and we know that his testimony is true.*

Who is the "we," in this verse? It is believed that John wrote his gospel while he was in Ephesus, sometime between 90-104 AD.* In order to preserve his writings, the Johannine Community compiled his works and it is they who are telling us in this epilogue that everything in John's gospel is true. The gospel is in reality the words of John.

The beloved John was exiled on the Isle of Patmos by Domitian in 95 AD and, after the assassination of Domitian in 96 AD, the Emperor Nerva had John released.

JOHN'S CLOSING

> **John 21:25** – *And there are also many other things which Jesus did, the which, if they should be written every one, I suppose that even the world itself could not contain the books that should be written. Amen.*

Only heaven knows all the miracles that the sinless Jesus performed while walking this sinful earth. This world is not worthy to even read the gospel of John. But God, in His mercy and grace toward us, has preserved these words of John. A full biography of Jesus would only give skeptics a reason to scoff and to cast doubt on the things that do not pertain to eternal life. The apostle John, who leaned on the bosom of the Son of God (**John 13:23**) was loved by Jesus so much that He blessed John to be the writer of this fourth gospel. And we are so blessed to be able to read it almost two thousand years later!

A NOTE FROM THE EDITOR

Editing *John - The Jewish Gospel* has been a joy, an honor, and a personal blessing for me. Carroll Roberson is a dear friend to my family and a mighty servant of our Lord, Jesus Christ. He is the mentor and father in the faith who directed me down the path to seeking the knowledge and wisdom of Messiah several years ago and I thank God for him. His ministry of word and song has enriched the faith of many and led many more to finding salvation in Yeshua. I'm grateful for the opportunity to have a small part in bringing the message to you. It is my prayer that this volume will become a powerful tool for you in your study of the Bible. Please dog-ear pages, highlight, and make notes as you read and re-read this exposition of the Gospel as told by the beloved apostle, John. Most importantly, keep your Bible open and pray for the Holy Spirit to bless your heart and mind as you read. It is my prayer that it helps to guide you to a deeper relationship with Jesus the Messiah. Brother Carroll Roberson has dedicated his life to serving Messiah, the study of God's Word, proclaiming the truth to the lost, and to edifying the Church through music, preaching, television, conferences, and Christ-centered tours of Israel. This book reflects Carroll's passion for the Lord and understanding the Jewish roots of the Christian faith apart from Gentile and man-made tradition. He has a powerful and unique voice that is down-to-earth and meaningful to people of all walks of life. The words and thoughts of this commentary are a genuine and sincere invitation for all to seek and find the Messiah of Israel as He was, is, and ever shall be: The Living Word of God.

Nathan Wood
Editor

Printed in the United States
By Bookmasters